Keras Reinforcement Learning Projects

9 projects exploring popular reinforcement learning techniques to build self-learning agents

Giuseppe Ciaburro

BIRMINGHAM - MUMBAI

Keras Reinforcement Learning Projects

Commissioning Editor: Pravin Dhandre
Acquisition Editor: Dayne Castelino
Content Development Editor: Karan Thakkar
Technical Editor: Nilesh Sawakhande
Copy Editor: Safis Editing
Project Coordinator: Nidhi Joshi
Proofreader: Safis Editing
Indexer: Mariammal Chettiyar
Graphics: Jisha Chirayil
Production Coordinator: Jyoti Chauhan

First published: September 2018

Production reference: 2091018

Published by Packt Publishing Ltd.
Livery Place
35 Livery Street
Birmingham
B3 2PB, UK.

ISBN 978-1-78934-209-3

www.packtpub.com

`mapt.io`

Mapt is an online digital library that gives you full access to over 5,000 books and videos, as well as industry leading tools to help you plan your personal development and advance your career. For more information, please visit our website.

Why subscribe?

- Spend less time learning and more time coding with practical eBooks and Videos from over 4,000 industry professionals

- Improve your learning with Skill Plans built especially for you

- Get a free eBook or video every month

- Mapt is fully searchable

- Copy and paste, print, and bookmark content

Packt.com

Did you know that Packt offers eBook versions of every book published, with PDF and ePub files available? You can upgrade to the eBook version at `www.packt.com` and as a print book customer, you are entitled to a discount on the eBook copy. Get in touch with us at `customercare@packtpub.com` for more details.

At `www.packt.com`, you can also read a collection of free technical articles, sign up for a range of free newsletters, and receive exclusive discounts and offers on Packt books and eBooks.

Contributors

About the author

Giuseppe Ciaburro holds a PhD in environmental technical physics and two master's degrees. His research focuses on machine learning applications in the study of urban sound environments. He works at Built Environment Control Laboratory – Università degli Studi della Campania Luigi Vanvitelli (Italy). He has over 15 years of work experience in programming (in Python, R, and MATLAB), first in the field of combustion and then in acoustics and noise control. He has several publications to his credit.

About the reviewer

Sudharsan Ravichandiran is a data scientist, researcher, artificial intelligence enthusiast, and YouTuber (search for Sudharsan reinforcement learning). He completed his bachelors in information technology at Anna University. His area of research focuses on practical implementations of deep learning and reinforcement learning, which includes natural language processing and computer vision. He is an open source contributor and loves answering questions on Stack Overflow. He also authored a best seller *Hands on Reinforcement Learning with Python* published by Packt.

Packt is searching for authors like you

If you're interested in becoming an author for Packt, please visit `authors.packtpub.com` and apply today. We have worked with thousands of developers and tech professionals, just like you, to help them share their insight with the global tech community. You can make a general application, apply for a specific hot topic that we are recruiting an author for, or submit your own idea.

Table of Contents

Preface

This book brings human-level performance into your applications using the algorithms and techniques of reinforcement learning coupled with Keras, the fast experimental library. Some of the projects that are covered are a delivery vehicle routing application, forecasting stock market prices, a robot control system, a optimal portfolio selection, and the dynamic modeling of a Segway. Throughout this book, you will get your hands dirty with the most popular algorithms, such as the Markov Decision Process, the Monte Carlo method, and Q-learning, so that you can be equipped with complex statistics to get better results.

Who this book is for

This book suits data scientists, machine learning engineers, and AI engineers who want to understand reinforcement learning by developing practical projects.

A sound knowledge of machine learning and a basic familiarity with Keras is all you need to get started with this book.

What this book covers

Chapter 1, *Overview of Keras Reinforcement Learning*, will get you ready to enjoy reinforcement learning using Keras, looking at topics ranging from the basic concepts right to the building of models. By the end of this chapter, you will be ready to dive into working on real-world projects.

Chapter 2, *Simulating Random Walks*, will have you simulate a random walk using Markov chains through a Python code implementation.

Chapter 3, *Optimal Portfolio Selection*, explores how to select the optimal portfolio using dynamic programming through a Python code implementation.

Chapter 4, *Forecasting Stock Market Prices*, guides you in using the Monte Carlo methods to forecast stock market prices.

Chapter 5, *Delivery Vehicle Routing Application*, shows how to use **Temporal Difference (TD)** learning algorithms to manage warehouse operations through Python and the Keras library.

Chapter 6, *Continuous Balancing of a Rotating Mechanical System*, helps you to use deep reinforcement learning methods to balance a rotating mechanical system.

Chapter 7, *Dynamic Modeling of a Segway as an Inverted Pendulum System*, teaches you the basic concepts of Q-learning and how to use this technique to control a mechanical system.

Chapter 8, A *Robot Control System Using Deep Reinforcement Learning*, will confront you with the problem of robot navigation in simple maze-like environments where the robot has to rely on its on-board sensors to perform navigation tasks.

Chapter 9, *Handwritten Digit Recognizer*, shows how to set up a handwritten digit recognition model in Python using an image dataset.

Chapter 10, *Playing the Board Game Go*, explores how reinforcement learning algorithms were used to address a problem in game theory.

Chapter 11, *What's Next?*, gives a good understanding of the real-life challenges in building and deploying machine learning models, and explores additional resources and technologies that will help sharpen your machine learning skills.

To get the most out of this book

In this book, reinforcement learning algorithms are implemented in Python. To reproduce the many examples in this book, you need to possess a good knowledge of the Python environment. We have used Python 3.6 and above to build various applications. In that spirit, we have tried to keep all of the code as friendly and readable as possible. We feel that this will enable you to easily understand the code and readily use it in different scenarios.

Download the example code files

You can download the example code files for this book from your account at www.packt.com. If you purchased this book elsewhere, you can visit www.packt.com/support and register to have the files emailed directly to you.

You can download the code files by following these steps:

1. Log in or register at www.packt.com.
2. Select the **SUPPORT** tab.
3. Click on **Code Downloads & Errata**.
4. Enter the name of the book in the **Search** box and follow the onscreen instructions.

Once the file is downloaded, please make sure that you unzip or extract the folder using the latest version of:

- WinRAR/7-Zip for Windows
- Zipeg/iZip/UnRarX for Mac
- 7-Zip/PeaZip for Linux

The code bundle for the book is also hosted on GitHub at **https://github.com/PacktPublishing/Keras-Reinforcement-Learning-Projects**. In case there's an update to the code, it will be updated on the existing GitHub repository.

We also have other code bundles from our rich catalog of books and videos available at https://github.com/PacktPublishing/. Check them out!

Download the color images

We also provide a PDF file that has color images of the screenshots/diagrams used in this book. You can download it here: https://www.packtpub.com/sites/default/files/downloads/9781789342093_ColorImages.pdf.

Conventions used

There are a number of text conventions used throughout this book.

CodeInText: Indicates code words in text, database table names, folder names, filenames, file extensions, pathnames, dummy URLs, user input, and Twitter handles. Here is an example: "To calculate the logarithm of returns, we will use the log() function from numpy."

A block of code is set as follows:

```
plt.figure(figsize=(10,5))
plt.plot(dataset)
plt.show()
```

Any command-line input or output is written as follows:

```
git clone https://github.com/openai/gym
cd gym
pip install -e .
```

Warnings or important notes appear like this.

 Tips and tricks appear like this.

Get in touch

Feedback from our readers is always welcome.

General feedback: If you have questions about any aspect of this book, mention the book title in the subject of your message and email us at `customercare@packtpub.com`.

Errata: Although we have taken every care to ensure the accuracy of our content, mistakes do happen. If you have found a mistake in this book, we would be grateful if you would report this to us. Please visit `www.packt.com/submit-errata`, selecting your book, clicking on the Errata Submission Form link, and entering the details.

Piracy: If you come across any illegal copies of our works in any form on the Internet, we would be grateful if you would provide us with the location address or website name. Please contact us at `copyright@packt.com` with a link to the material.

If you are interested in becoming an author: If there is a topic that you have expertise in and you are interested in either writing or contributing to a book, please visit `authors.packtpub.com`.

Reviews

Please leave a review. Once you have read and used this book, why not leave a review on the site that you purchased it from? Potential readers can then see and use your unbiased opinion to make purchase decisions, we at Packt can understand what you think about our products, and our authors can see your feedback on their book. Thank you!

For more information about Packt, please visit `packt.com`.

1
Overview of Keras Reinforcement Learning

Nowadays, most computers are based on a symbolic elaboration, that is, the problem is first encoded in a set of variables and then processed using an explicit algorithm that, for each possible input of the problem, offers an adequate output. However, there are problems in which resolution with an explicit algorithm is inefficient or even unnatural, for example with a speech recognizer; tackling this kind of problem with the classic approach is inefficient. This and other similar problems, such as autonomous navigation of a robot or voice assistance in performing an operation, are part of a very diverse set of problems that can be addressed directly through solutions based on reinforcement learning.

Reinforcement learning is a very exciting part of machine learning, used in applications ranging from autonomous cars to playing games. Reinforcement learning aims to create algorithms that can learn and adapt to environmental changes. To do this, we use external feedback signals (reward signals) generated by the environment according to the choices made by the algorithm. A correct choice will result in a reward, while an incorrect choice will lead to a penalization of the system. All of this is in order to achieve the best result obtainable.

The topics covered in this chapter are the following:

- An overview of machine learning
- Reinforcement learning
- **Markov Decision Process** (**MDP**)
- **Temporal difference** (**TD**) learning
- Q-learning
- Deep Q-learning networks

At the end of the chapter, you will be fully introduced to the power of reinforcement learning and will learn the different approaches to this technique. Several reinforcement learning methods will be covered.

Basic concepts of machine learning

Machine learning is a multidisciplinary field created at the intersection of, and by the synergy between, computer science, statistics, neurobiology, and control theory. Its emergence has played a key role in several fields and has fundamentally changed the vision of software programming. If the question before was, how to program a computer, now the question becomes is how computers will program themselves. Thus, it is clear that machine learning is a basic method that allows a computer to have its own intelligence.

As might be expected, machine learning interconnects and coexists with the study of, and research on, human learning. Like humans, whose brain and neurons are the foundation of insight, **Artificial Neural Networks (ANNs)** are the basis of any decision-making activity of the computer.

Machine learning refers to the ability to learn from experience without any outside help, which is what we humans do, in most cases. Why should it not be the same for machines?

From a set of data, we can find a model that approximates the set by the use of machine learning. For example, we can identify a correspondence between input variables and output variables for a given system. One way to do this is to postulate the existence of some kind of mechanism for the parametric generation of data, which, however, does not know the exact values of the parameters. This process typically makes reference to statistical techniques, such as the following:

- Induction
- Deduction
- Abduction

The extraction of general laws from a set of observed data is called induction; it is opposed to deduction, in which, starting from general laws, we want to predict the value of a set of variables. Induction is the fundamental mechanism underlying the scientific method in which we want to derive general laws, typically described in a mathematical language, starting from the observation of phenomena.

This observation includes the measurement of a set of variables and, therefore, the acquisition of data that describes the observed phenomena. Then, the resultant model can be used to make predictions on additional data. The overall process in which, starting from a set of observations, we want to make predictions for new situations, is called inference. Therefore, inductive learning starts from observations arising from the surrounding environment and generalizes obtaining knowledge that will be valid for not-yet-observed cases; at least we hope so.

Inductive learning is based on learning by example: knowledge gained by starting from a set of positive examples that are instances of the concept to be learned, and negative examples that are non-instances of the concept. In this regard, Galileo Galilei's (1564-1642) phrase is particularly clear:

> *"Knowledge forms part of the experience from which hypotheses are derived, based on quantitative data, which must be verified through experiments, also mentally, understood as artificial relationships between quantified variables, to arrive at the formulation of the law in the form of an equation."*

The following diagram consists of a flowchart showing inductive and deductive learning:

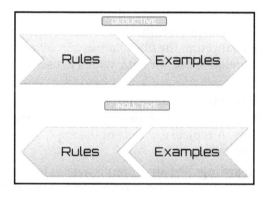

A question arises spontaneously: why do machine learning systems work where traditional algorithms fail? The reasons for the failure of traditional algorithms are numerous and typically include the following:

- **Difficulty in problem formalization**: For example, each of us can recognize our friends from their voices. But probably none can describe a sequence of computational steps enabling them to recognize the speaker from the recorded sound.
- **High number of variables at play**: When considering the problem of recognizing characters from a document, specifying all parameters that are thought to be involved can be particularly complex. In addition, the same formalization applied in the same context but on a different idiom could prove inadequate.
- **Lack of theory**: Imagine you have to predict exactly the performance of financial markets in the absence of specific mathematical laws.
- **Need for customization**: The distinction between interesting and uninteresting features depends significantly on the perception of the individual user.

A quick analysis of these issues highlights the lack of experience in all cases.

Discovering the different types of machine learning

The power of machine learning is due to the quality of its algorithms, which have been improved and updated over the years; these are divided into several main types depending on the nature of the signal used for learning or the type of feedback adopted by the system.

They are as follows:

- **Supervised learning**: The algorithm generates a function that links input values to a desired output through the observation of a set of examples in which each data input has its relative output data, which is used to construct predictive models.
- **Unsupervised learning**: The algorithm tries to derive knowledge from a general input without the help of a set of pre-classified examples that are used to build descriptive models. A typical example of the application of these algorithms is found in search engines.
- **Reinforcement learning**: The algorithm is able to learn depending on the changes that occur in the environment in which it is performed. In fact, since every action has some effect on the environment concerned, the algorithm is driven by the same feedback environment. Some of these algorithms are used in speech or text recognition.

The subdivision that we have just proposed does not prohibit the use of hybrid approaches between some or all of these different areas, which have often recorded good results.

Supervised learning

Supervised learning is a machine learning technique that aims to program a computer system so that it can resolve the relevant tasks automatically. To do this, the input data is included in a set I (typically vectors). Then, the set of output data is fixed as set O, and finally, it defines a function f that associates each input with the correct answer. Such information is called a training set. This workflow is presented in the following diagram:

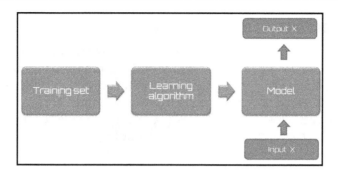

All supervised learning algorithms are based on the following thesis: if an algorithm provides an adequate number of examples, it will be able to create a derived function B that will approximate the desired function A.

If the approximation of the desired function is adequate, then when the input data is offered to the derived function, this function should be able to provide output responses similar to those provided by the desired function and then acceptable. These algorithms are based on the following concept: similar inputs correspond to similar outputs.

Generally, in the real world, this assumption is not valid; however, some situations exist in which it is acceptable. Clearly, the proper functioning of such algorithms depends significantly on the input data. If there are only a few training inputs, the algorithm might not have enough experience to provide a correct output. Conversely, many inputs may make it excessively slow, since the derivative function generated by a large number of inputs increases the training time. Hence the slowness.

Moreover, experience shows that this type of algorithm is very sensitive to noise; even a few pieces of incorrect data can make the entire system unreliable and lead to wrong decisions.

In supervised learning, it's possible to split problems based on the nature of the data. If the output value is categorical, such as membership/non-membership of a certain class, then it is a classification problem. If the output is a continuous real value in a certain range, then it is a regression problem.

Unsupervised learning

The aim of unsupervised learning is to automatically extract information from databases. This process occurs without a priori knowledge of the contents to be analyzed. Unlike supervised learning, there is no information on the membership classes of examples, or more generally on the output corresponding to a certain input. The goal is to get a model that is able to discover interesting properties: groups with similar characteristics (clustering), for instance. Search engines are an example of an application of these algorithms. Given one or more keywords, they are able to create a list of links related to our search.

The validity of these algorithms depends on the usefulness of the information they can extract from the databases. These algorithms work by comparing data and looking for similarities or differences. Available data concerns only the set of features that describe each example.

The following diagram shows supervised learning (on the left) and unsupervised learning examples (on the right):

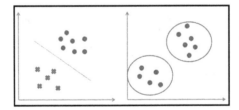

They show great efficiency with elements of numeric type, but are much less accurate with non-numeric data. Generally, they work properly in the presence of data that is clearly identifiable and contains an order or a clear grouping.

Reinforcement learning

Reinforcement learning aims to create algorithms that can learn and adapt to environmental changes. This programming technique is based on the concept of receiving external stimuli, the nature of which depends on the algorithm choices. A correct choice will involve a reward, while an incorrect choice will lead to a penalty. The goal of the system is to achieve the best possible result, of course.

In supervised learning, there is a teacher that tells the system the correct output (learning with a teacher). This is not always possible. Often, we have only qualitative information (sometimes binary, right/wrong, or success/failure).

The information available is called reinforcement signals. But the system does not give any information on how to update the agent's behavior (that is, weights). You cannot define a cost function or a gradient. The goal of the system is to create smart agents that have machinery able to learn from their experience.

Building machine learning models step by step

When developing an application that uses machine learning, we will follow a procedure characterized by the following steps:

- **Collecting the data**: Everything starts from the data, no doubt about it; but one might wonder from where so much data comes. In practice, it is collected through lengthy procedures that may, for example, derive from measurement campaigns or face-to-face interviews. In all cases, the data is collected in a database so that it can then be analyzed to derive knowledge.
- **Preparing the data**: We have collected the data; now, we have to prepare it for the next step. Once we have this data, we must make sure it is in a format usable by the algorithm we want to use. To do this, you may need to do some formatting. Recall that some algorithms need data in an integer format, whereas others require data in the form of strings, and finally others need it to be in a special format. We will get to this later, but the specific formatting is usually simple compared to the data collection.
- **Exploring the data**: At this point, we can look at data to verify that it is actually working and that we do not have a bunch of empty values. In this step, through the use of plots, we can recognize patterns and whether or not there are some data points that are vastly different from the rest of the set. Plotting data in one, two, or three dimensions can also help.
- **Training the algorithm**: Now, let's get serious. In this step, the machine learning algorithm works on the definition of the model and therefore deals with the training. The model starts to extract knowledge from the large amounts of data that we had available, and from which nothing has been explained so far. For unsupervised learning, there's no training step because you don't have a target value.
- **Testing the algorithm**: In this step, we use the information learned in the previous step to see if the model actually works. The evaluation of an algorithm is for seeing how well the model approximates the real system. In the case of supervised learning, we have some known values that we can use to evaluate the algorithm. In unsupervised learning, we may need to use some other metrics to evaluate success. In both cases, if we are not satisfied, we can return to the previous steps, change some things, and retry the test.

- **Evaluating the algorithm**: We have reached the point where we can apply what has been done so far. We can assess the approximation ability of the model by applying it to real data. The model, previously trained and tested, is then valued in this phase.
- **Improving algorithm performance**: Finally, we can focus on the finishing steps. We've verified that the model works, we have evaluated the performance, and now we are ready to analyze the whole process to identify any possible room for improvement.

 Before applying the machine learning algorithm to our data, it is appropriate to devote some time to the workflow setting.

Getting started with reinforcement learning

Reinforcement learning aims to create algorithms that can learn and adapt to environmental changes. This programming technique is based on the concept of receiving external stimuli that depend on the actions chosen by the agent. A correct choice will involve a reward, while an incorrect choice will lead to a penalty. The goal of the system is to achieve the best possible result, of course.

These mechanisms derive from the basic concepts of machine learning (learning from experience), in an attempt to simulate human behavior. In fact, in our mind, we activate brain mechanisms that lead us to chase and repeat what, in us, produces feelings of gratification and wellbeing. Whenever we experience moments of pleasure (food, sex, love, and so on), some substances are produced in our brains that work by reinforcing that same stimulus, emphasizing it.

Along with this mechanism of neurochemical reinforcement, an important role is represented by memory. In fact, the memory collects the experience of the subject in order to be able to repeat it in the future. Evolution has endowed us with this mechanism to push us to repeat gratifying experiences in the direction of the best solutions.

This is why we so powerfully remember the most important experiences of our life: experiences, especially those that are powerfully rewarding, are impressed in memories and condition our future explorations. Previously, we have seen that learning from experience can be simulated by a numerical algorithm in various ways, depending on the nature of the signal used for learning and the type of feedback adopted by the system.

The following diagram shows a flowchart that displays an agent's interaction with the environment in a reinforcement learning setting:

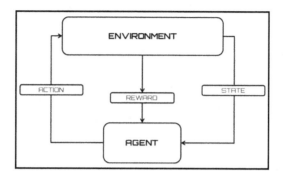

Scientific literature has taken an uncertain stance on the classification of learning by reinforcement as a paradigm. In fact, in the initial phase of the literature, it was considered a special case of supervised learning, after which it was fully promoted as the third paradigm of machine learning algorithms. It is applied in different contexts in which supervised learning is inefficient: the problems of interaction with the environment are a clear example.

The following list shows the steps to follow to correctly apply a reinforcement learning algorithm:

1. Preparation of the agent
2. Observation of the environment
3. Selection of the optimal strategy
4. Execution of actions
5. Calculation of the corresponding reward (or penalty)
6. Development of updating strategies (if necessary)
7. Repetition of steps 2 through 5 iteratively until the agent learns the optimal strategies

Reinforcement learning is based on a theory from psychology, elaborated following a series of experiments performed on animals. In particular, Edward Thorndike (American psychologist) noted that if a cat is given a reward immediately after the execution of a behavior considered correct, then this increases the probability that this behavior will repeat itself. On the other hand, in the face of unwanted behavior, the application of a punishment decreases the probability of a repetition of the error.

On the basis of this theory, after defining a goal to be achieved, reinforcement learning tries to maximize the rewards received for the execution of the action or set of actions that allows to reach the designated goal.

Agent-environment interface

Reinforcement learning can be seen as a special case of the interaction problem, in terms of achieving a goal. The entity that must reach the goal is called an agent. The entity with which the agent must interact is called the environment, which corresponds to everything that is external to the agent.

So far, we are more focused on the term *agent*, but what does it represent? The agent (software) is a software entity that performs services on behalf of another program, usually automatically and invisibly. These pieces of software are also called smart agents.

What follows is a list of the most important features of an agent:

- It can choose between a continuous and a discrete set for an action on the environment.
- The action depends on the situation. The situation is summarized in the system state.
- The agent continuously monitors the environment (input) and continuously changes the status
- The choice of the action is not trivial and requires a certain degree of intelligence.
- The agent has a smart memory.

The agent has a goal-directed behavior, but acts in an uncertain environment that is not known a priori or only partially known. An agent learns by interacting with the environment. Planning can be developed while learning about the environment through the measurements made by the agent itself. This strategy is close to trial-and-error theory.

 Trial and error is a fundamental method of problem solving. It is characterized by repeated, varied attempts that are continued until success, or until the agent stops trying.

The agent-environment interaction is continuous: the agent chooses an action to be taken, and in response, the environment changes state, presenting a new situation to be faced.

In the particular case of reinforcement learning, the environment provides the agent with a reward. It is essential that the source of the reward is the environment to avoid the formation, within the agent, of a personal reinforcement mechanism that would compromise learning.

The value of the reward is proportional to the influence that the action has in reaching the objective, so it is positive or high in the case of a correct action, or negative or low for an incorrect action.

In the following list are some examples of real life in which there is an interaction between agent and environment to solve a problem:

- A chess player, for each move, has information on the configurations of pieces that can be created, and on the possible countermoves of the opponent.
- A little giraffe, in just a few hours, learns to get up and run.
- A truly autonomous robot learns to move around a room to get out of it. For example: Roomba Robot Vacuum.
- The parameters of a refinery (oil pressure, flow, and so on) are set in real time, so as to obtain the maximum yield or maximum quality. For example, if particularly dense oil arrives, then the flow rate to the plant is modified to allow an adequate refining.

All the examples that we examined have the following characteristics in common:

- Interaction with the environment
- A specific goal that the agent wants to get
- Uncertainty or partial knowledge of the environment

From the analysis of these examples, it is possible to make the following observations:

- The agent learns from its own experience.
- The actions change the status (the situation), the possibilities of choice in the future change (delayed reward).
- The effect of an action cannot be completely predicted.
- The agent has a global assessment of its behavior.
- It must exploit this information to improve its choices. Choices improve with experience.
- Problems can have a finite or infinite time horizon.

Essentially, the agent receives sensations from the environment through its sensors. Depending on its feelings, the agent decides what actions to take in the environment. Based on the immediate result of its actions, the agent can be rewarded.

If you want to use an automatic learning method, you need to give a formal description of the environment. It is not important to know exactly how the environment is made; what is interesting is to make general assumptions about the properties that the environment has. In reinforcement learning, it is usually assumed that the environment can be described by a MDP.

Markov Decision Process

To avoid load problems and computational difficulties, the agent-environment interaction is considered an MDP. An MDP is a discrete-time stochastic control process.

Stochastic processes are mathematical models used to study the evolution of phenomena following random or probabilistic laws. It is known that in all natural phenomena, both by their very nature and by observational errors, a random or accidental component is present. This component causes the following: at every instance of t, the result of the observation on the phenomenon is a random number or random variable s_i. It is not possible to predict with certainty what the result will be; one can only state that it will take one of several possible values, each of which has a given probability.

A stochastic process is called Markovian when, having chosen a certain instance of t for observation, the evolution of the process, starting with t, depends only on t and does not depend in any way on the previous instances. Thus, a process is Markovian when, given the moment of observation, only this instance determines the future evolution of the process, while this evolution does not depend on the past.

In a Markov process, at each time step, the process is in a state $s \in S$, and the decision maker may choose any action $a \in A$ that is available in state s. The process responds at the next timestamp by randomly moving into a new state s', and giving the decision maker a corresponding reward $r(s,s')$.

The following diagram shows the agent-environment interaction in a MDP:

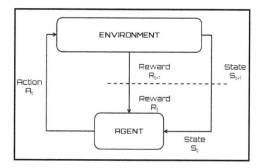

The agent-environment interaction shown in the preceding diagram can be schematized as follows:

- The agent and the environment interact at discrete intervals over time, $t = 0, 1, 2... n$.
- At each interval, the agent receives a representation of the state s_t of the environment.
- Each element $s_t \in S$, where S is the set of possible states.
- Once the state is recognized, the agent must take an action $a_t \in A(s_t)$, where $A(s_t)$ is the set of possible actions in the state s_t.
- The choice of the action to be taken depends on the objective to be achieved and is mapped through the policy indicated with the symbol π (discounted cumulative reward), which associates the action with $a_t \in A(s)$ for each state s. The term $\pi_t(s,a)$ represents the probability that action a is carried out in the state s.
- During the next time interval $t + 1$, as part of the consequence of the action a_t, the agent receives a numerical reward $r_{t+1} \in R$ corresponding to the action previously taken a_t.
- The consequence of the action represents, instead, the new state s_t. At this point the agent must again code the state and make the choice of the action.
- This iteration repeats itself until the achievement of the objective by the agent.

The definition of the status s_{t+1} depends on the previous state and the action taken (MDP), that is as follows:

$$s_{t+1} = \delta \ (s_t, a_t)$$

Here, δ represents the status function.

In summary:

- In an MDP, the agent can perceive the state $s \in S$ in which it is and has an A set of actions at its disposal
- At each discrete interval of time t, the agent detects the current status s_t and decides to implement an action $a_t \in A$
- The environment responds by providing a reward (a reinforcement) $r_t = r\ (st,\ at)$ and moving into the state $s_{t+1} = \delta\ (st,\ at)$
- The r and δ functions are part of the environment; they depend only on the current state and action (not the previous ones) and are not necessarily known to the agent
- The goal of reinforcement learning is to learn a policy that, for each state s in which the system is located, indicates to the agent an action to maximize the total reinforcement received during the entire action sequence

Let's go deeper into some of the terms used:

- A reward function defines the goal in a reinforcement learning problem. It maps the detected states of the environment into a single number, thereby defining a reward. As already mentioned, the only goal is to maximize the total reward it receives in the long term. The reward function then defines what the good and bad events are for the agent. The reward function has the need to be correct, and it can be used as a basis for changing the policy. For example, if an action selected by the policy is followed by a low reward, the policy can be changed to select other actions in that situation in the next step.
- A policy defines the behavior of the learning agent at a given time. It maps both the detected states of the environment and the actions to take when they are in those states. This corresponds to what, in psychology, would be called a set of rules or associations of stimulus response. The policy is the fundamental part of a reinforcing learning agent, in the sense that it alone is enough to determine behavior.
- A value function represents how good a state is for an agent. It is equal to the total reward expected for an agent from the status s. The value function depends on the policy with which the agent selects the actions to be performed.
- An action-value function returns the value, that is, the expected return (overall reward) for using action a in a certain state s, following a policy.

Discounted cumulative reward

In the previous section, we said that the goal of reinforcement learning is to learn a policy that, for each state s in which the system is located, indicates to the agent an action to maximize the total reward received during the entire action sequence. How can we maximize the total reinforcement received during the entire sequence of actions?

The total reinforcement derived from the policy is calculated as follows:

$$R_T = \sum_{i=0}^{T} r_{t+1} = r_t + r_{t+1} + \ldots + r_T$$

Here, r_T represents the reward of the action that drives the environment in the terminal state s_T.

A possible solution to the problem is to associate the action that provides the highest reward to each individual state; that is, we must determine an optimal policy such that the previous quantity is maximized.

For problems that do not reach the goal or terminal state in a finite number of steps (continuing tasks), R_t tends to infinity.

In these cases, the sum of the rewards that one wants to maximize diverges at the infinite, so this approach is not applicable. Then, it is necessary to develop an alternative reinforcement technique.

The technique that best suits the reinforcement learning paradigm turns out to be the discounted cumulative reward, which tries to maximize the following quantity:

$$R_T = \sum_{i=0}^{\infty} \gamma^i r_{t+1} = r_t + \gamma r_{t+1} + \gamma^2 r_{t+2} + \ldots$$

Here, γ is called a discount factor and represents the importance for future rewards. This parameter can take the values $0 \leq \gamma \leq 1$, with the following value:

- If $\gamma < 1$, the sequence r_t will converge to a finite value
- If $\gamma = 0$, the agent will have no interest in future rewards, but will try to maximize the reward only for the current state
- If $\gamma = 1$, the agent will try to increase future rewards even at the expense of the immediate ones

The discount factor can be modified during the learning process to highlight particular actions or states. An optimal policy can lead to the reinforcement obtained in performing a single action to be low (or even negative), provided that this leads to greater reinforcement overall.

Exploration versus exploitation

Ideally, the agent must associate with each action a_t the respective reward r, in order to then choose the most rewarding behavior for achieving the goal. This approach is therefore impracticable for complex problems in which the number of states is particularly high and, consequently, the possible associations increase exponentially.

This problem is called the exploration-exploitation dilemma. Ideally, the agent must explore all possible actions for each state, finding the one that is actually most rewarded for exploiting in achieving its goal.

Thus, decision-making involves a fundamental choice:

- **Exploitation**: Make the best decision, given current information
- **Exploration**: Collect more information

In this process, the best long-term strategy can lead to considerable sacrifices in the short term. Therefore, it is necessary to gather enough information to make the best decisions.

The exploration-exploitation dilemma makes itself known whenever we try to learn something new. Often, we have to decide whether to choose what we already know (exploitation), leaving our cultural baggage unaltered, or choosing something new and learning more in this way (exploration). The second choice puts us at the risk of making the wrong choices. This is an experience that we often face; think, for example, about the choices we make in a restaurant when we are asked to choose between the dishes on the menu:

- We can choose something that we already know and that, in the past, has given us back a known reward with gratification (exploitation), such as pizza (who does not know the goodness of a margherita pizza?)
- We can try something new that we have never tasted before and see what we get (exploration), such as lasagna (alas, not everyone knows the magic taste of a plate of lasagna)

The choice we will make will depend on many boundary conditions: the price of the dishes, the level of hunger, knowledge of the dishes, and so on. What is important is that the study of the best way to make these kinds of choices has demonstrated that optimal learning sometimes requires us to make bad choices. This means that, sometimes, you have to choose to avoid the action you deem most rewarding and take an action that you feel is less rewarding. The logic is that these actions are necessary to obtain a long-term benefit: sometimes, you need to get your hands dirty to learn more.

The following are more examples of adopting this technique for real-life cases:

- Selection of a store:
    - **Exploitation**: Go to your favorite store
    - **Exploration**: Try a new store
- Choice of a route:
    - **Exploitation**: Choose the best route so far
    - **Exploration**: Try a new route

In practice, in very complex problems, convergence to a very good strategy would be too slow.

A good solution to the problem is to find a balance between exploration and exploitation:

- An agent that limits itself to exploring will always act in a casual way in every state, and it is evident that the convergence to an optimal strategy is impossible
- If an agent explores little, it will always use the usual actions, which may not be optimal ones

Finally, we can say that at every step the agent has to choose between repeating what it has done so far, or trying out new movements that could achieve better results.

Reinforcement learning algorithms

As we have seen in the previous sections, reinforcement learning is a programming technique that aims to develop algorithms that can learn and adapt to changes in the environment. This programming technique is based on the assumption of the agent being able to receive stimuli from the outside and to change its actions according to these stimuli. So, a correct choice will result in a reward while an incorrect choice will lead to a penalization of the system.

The goal of the system is to achieve the highest possible reward and consequently the best possible result. This result can be obtained through two approaches:

- The first approach involves evaluating the choices of the algorithm and then rewarding or punishing the algorithm based on the result. These techniques can also adapt to substantial changes in the environment. An example is the image recognition programs that improve their performance with use. In this case we can say that learning takes place continuously.
- In the second approach, a first phase is applied in which the algorithm is previously trained, and when the system is considered reliable, it is crystallized and no longer modifiable. This derives from the observation that constantly evaluating the actions of the algorithm can be a process that cannot be automated or that is very expensive.

These are only implementation choices, so it may happen that an algorithm includes the newly analyzed approaches.

So far, we have introduced the basic concepts of reinforcement learning. Now, we can analyze the various ways in which these concepts have been transformed into algorithms. In this section, we will list them, providing an overview, and we will deepen them in the practical cases that we will address in the following chapters.

Dynamic Programming

Dynamic Programming (DP) represents a set of algorithms that can be used to calculate an optimal policy given a perfect model of the environment in the form of an MDP. The fundamental idea of DP, as well as reinforcement learning in general, is the use of state values and actions to look for good policies.

The DP methods approach the resolution of MDP processes through the iteration of two processes called policy evaluation and policy improvement:

- The policy evaluation algorithm consists of applying an iterative method to the resolution of the Bellman equation. Since convergence is guaranteed to us only for $k \to \infty$, we must be content to have good approximations by imposing a stopping condition.
- The policy improvement algorithm improves policy based on current values.

A Bellman equation, named after *Richard E. Bellman*, an American applied mathematician, is a necessary condition for the optimality associated with the DP method. It allows us to obtain the value of a decision problem at some point in time in terms of payoff from some initial choices and the value of the remaining decision problem resulting from those initial choices.

The iteration of the two aforementioned processes is shown in the following diagram:

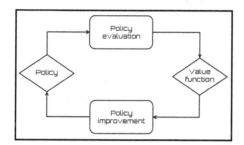

A disadvantage of the policy iteration algorithm is that we have to evaluate the policy at every step. This involves an iterative process in which we do not know a priori the time of convergence, which will depend, among other things, on how the starting policy was chosen.

One way to overcome this drawback is to cut off the evaluation of the policy at a specific step. This operation does not change the guarantee of convergence to the optimal value. A special case in which the assessment of the policy is blocked step by step (also called sweep) defines the value iteration algorithm. In the value iteration algorithm, a single iteration of calculation of the values is performed between each step of the policy improvement. In the following snippet, a pseudocode for a value-iteration algorithm is shown:

```
initialize value function V
repeat
    for all s
        for all a
            update Q function
            V = max Q function
until V converge
```

Thus, in the value iteration algorithm, the system was initiated by setting a random value function. Starting from this value, a new function is sought in an iterative process which, compared to the previous one, has been improved, until reaching the optimal value function.

As we said previously, the DP algorithms are therefore essentially based on two processes that take place in parallel: policy evaluation and policy improvement. The repeated execution of these two processes makes the general process converge toward the optimal solution. In the policy iteration algorithm, the two phases alternate and one ends before the other begins.

In policy iteration algorithms, we start by initializing the system with a random policy, so we first must find the value function of that policy. This phase is called the policy evaluation step. So, we find a new policy, also improved compared to the previous one, based on the previous value function, and so on. In this process, each policy presents an improvement over the previous one until the optimal policy is reached. In the following snippet, a pseudocode for a policy iteration algorithm is shown:

```
initialize value function V and policy π
repeat
    evaluate V using policy π
    improve π using V
until convergence
```

DP methods operate through the entire set of states that can be assumed by the environment, performing a complete backup for each state at each iteration. Each update operation performed by the backup updates the value of a state based on the values of all possible successor states, weighed for their probability of occurrence, induced by the policy of choice and by the dynamics of the environment. Full backups are closely related to the Bellman equation; they are nothing more than the transformation of the equation into assignment instructions.

When a complete backup iteration does not bring any change to the state values, convergence is obtained and, therefore, the final state values fully satisfy the Bellman equation. The DP methods are applicable only if there is a perfect model of the environment, which must be equivalent to an MDP.

Precisely for this reason, the DP algorithms are of little use in reinforcement learning, both for their assumption of a perfect model of the environment, and for the high and expensive computation, but it is still opportune to mention them, because they represent the theoretical basis of reinforcement learning. In fact, all the methods of reinforcement learning try to achieve the same goal as that of the DP methods, only with lower computational cost and without the assumption of a perfect model of the environment.

The DP methods converge to the optimal solution with a number of polynomial operations with respect to the number of states n and actions m, against the number of exponential operations $m*n$ required by methods based on direct search.

The DP methods update the estimates of the values of the states, based on the estimates of the values of the successor states, or update the estimates on the basis of past estimates. This represents a special property, which is called bootstrapping. Several methods of reinforcement learning perform bootstrapping, even methods that do not require a perfect model of the environment, as required by the DP methods.

Monte Carlo methods

The **Monte Carlo** (**MC**) methods for estimating the *value* function and discovering excellent policies do not require the presence of a model of the environment. They are able to learn through the use of the agent's experience alone or from samples of state sequences, actions, and rewards obtained from the interactions between agent and environment. The experience can be acquired by the agent in line with the learning process or emulated by a previously populated dataset. The possibility of gaining experience during learning (online learning) is interesting because it allows obtaining excellent behavior even in the absence of a priori knowledge of the dynamics of the environment. Even learning through an already populated experience dataset can be interesting, because, if combined with online learning, it makes automatic policy improvement induced by others' experiences possible.

In general, MC methods rely on repeated random sampling to obtain numerical results. To do this, they use randomness to solve deterministic problems. In our case, we will use random sampling of states and action-state pairs and we will look at the rewards and then we will review the policy in an iterative way. The iteration of the process will converge on optimal policy as we explore every possible action-state pair.

For example, we could take the following procedure:

- We will assign a reward of +1 to a right action, -1 to a wrong action, and 0 to a draw.
- We will establish a table in which each key corresponds to a particular state-action pair and each value is the value of that pair. This represents the average reward received for that action in that state.

To solve the reinforcement learning problems, MC methods estimate the value function on the basis of the total sum of rewards, obtained on average in the past episodes. This assumes that the experience is divided into episodes, and that all episodes are composed of a finite number of transitions. This is because, in MC methods, the estimation of new values, and the modification of policies, takes place at the end of each episode. MC methods iteratively estimate policy and value function. In this case, however, each iteration cycle is equivalent to completing an episode—the new estimates of policy and value function occur episode by episode.

The following is a pseudocode for MC policy evaluation:

```
Initialize
    arbitrary policy π
    arbitrary state-value function
Repeat
    generate episode using π
    for each state s in episode
        the received reinforcement R is added to the set of rewards obtained
so far
        estimate the value function on the basis on the average of the total
sum of rewards obtained
```

Usually, the term MC is used for estimation methods, the operations of which involve random components. In this case, the term MC refers to reinforcement learning methods based on total reward averages. Unlike the DP methods that calculate the values for each state, the MC methods calculate the values for each state-action pair, because, in the absence of a model, the only state values are not sufficient to decide which action is best performed in a certain state.

Temporal difference learning

TD learning algorithms are based on reducing the differences between estimates made by the agent at different times. TD algorithms try to predict a quantity that depends on the future values of a given signal. Its name derives from the differences used in predictions on successive time steps to guide the learning process. The prediction at any time is updated to bring it closer to the prediction of the same quantity at the next time step. In reinforcement learning, they are used to predict a measure of the total amount of reward expected in the future.

It is a combination of the ideas of the MC method and the DP.

 MC methods allow solving reinforcement learning problems based on the average of the results obtained. DP represents a set of algorithms that can be used to calculate an optimal policy given a perfect model of the environment in the form of a MDP.

TD algorithm can learn directly from raw data, without a model of the dynamics of the environment (such as MC). This algorithm updates the estimates based partly on previously learned estimates, without waiting for the final result (bootstrap, like DP). Converge (using a fixed policy) if the time step is sufficiently small, or if it reduces over time.

The consecutive predictions are often related to each other; the TD methods are based on this assumption. These methods try to minimize the error of consecutive time forecasts. To do this, calculate the value function update using the Bellman equation. As already mentioned, to improve the prediction, the bootstrap technique is used, thereby reducing the variance of the prediction in each update step.

The different types of algorithms based on time differences can be distinguished on the basis of the methodology of choosing an action adopted. There are methods of time differences on-policy, in which the update is made on the basis of the results of actions determined by the selected policy and off-policy methods, in which various policies can be assessed through hypothetical actions, not actually undertaken. Unlike on-policy methods, the latter can separate the problem of exploration from that of control, learning tactics not necessarily applied during the learning phase.

The most used TD learning algorithms are the following:

- SARSA
- Q-learning
- Deep Q-learning

In the following sections, we will analyze the main characteristics of the two algorithms and the substantial differences.

SARSA

The **State-action-reward-state-action (SARSA)** algorithm implements an on-policy time differences method, in which the update of the action-value function is performed based on the outcome of the transition from state s to state s' through action a, based on a selected policy π (s, a).

There are policies that always choose the action that provides the maximum reward and non-deterministic policies (ε-greedy, ε-soft, softmax), which ensure an element of exploration in the learning phase.

 Greedy is a term used to represent a family of algorithms trying to get a global solution, through excellent local choices.

In SARSA, it is necessary to estimate the action-value function $q\ (s, a)$, because the total value of a state $v\ (s)$ (value function) is not sufficient in the absence of an environment model to allow the policy to determine, given a state, which action is best performed. In this case, however, the values are estimated step by step following the Bellman equation with the update parameter $v\ (s)$, considering, however, in place of a state, the state-action pair.

Being of an on-policy nature, SARSA estimates the action-value function based on the behavior of the π policy, and at the same time modifies the greedy behavior of the policy with respect to the updated estimates from the action-value function. The convergence of SARSA, and more generally of all TD methods, depends on the nature of policies.

The following is a pseudocode for the SARSA algorithm:

```
Initialize
    arbitrary action-value function
Repeat (for each episode)
    Initialize s
    choose a from s using policy from action-value function
    Repeat (for each step in episode)
        take action a
        observe r, s'
        choose a' from s' using policy from action-value function
        update action-value function
        update s,a
```

The update rule of the action-value function uses all five elements $(s_t, a_t, r_{t+1}, s_{t+1}, a_{t+1})$; for this reason, it is called SARSA.

Q-learning

Q-learning is one of the most used reinforcement learning algorithms. This is due to its ability to compare the expected utility of the available actions without requiring an environment model. Thanks to this technique, it is possible to find an optimal action for every given state in a finished MDP.

A general solution to the reinforcement learning problem is to estimate, thanks to the learning process, an evaluation function. This function must be able to evaluate, through the sum of the rewards, the optimality/utility or otherwise of a particular policy. In fact, Q-learning tries to maximize the value of the Q function (action-value function), which represents the maximum discounted future reward when we perform actions a in the state s.

Q-learning, like SARSA, estimates the function value q (s, a) incrementally, updating the value of the state-action pair at each step of the environment, following the logic of updating the general formula for estimating the values for the TD methods. Q-learning, unlike SARSA, has off-policy characteristics, that is, while the policy is improved according to the values estimated by q (s, a), the value function updates the estimates following a strictly greedy secondary policy: given a state, the chosen action is always the one that maximizes the value max q (s, a). However, the π policy has an important role in estimating values because, through it, the state-action pairs to be visited and updated are determined.

The following is a pseudocode for a Q-learning algorithm:

```
Initialize
    arbitrary action-value function
Repeat (for each episode)
    Initialize s
    choose a from s using policy from action-value function
    Repeat (for each step in episode)
        take action a
        observe r, s'
        update action-value function
        update s
```

Q-learning uses a table to store each state-action pair. At each step, the agent observes the current state of the environment and, using the π policy, selects and executes the action. By executing the action, the agent obtains the reward R_{t+1} and the new state S_{t+1}. At this point the agent is able to calculate $Q(S_t, a_t)$, updating the estimate.

Deep Q-learning

Deep Q-learning represents an evolution of the basic Q-learning method the state-action is replaced by a neural network, with the aim of approximating the optimal value function.

Compared to the previous approaches, where it was used to structure the network in order to request both input and action and providing its expected return, Deep Q-learning revolutionizes the structure in order to request only the state of the environment and supply as many status-action values as there are actions that can be performed in the environment.

Summary

Reinforcement learning aims to create algorithms that can learn and adapt to environmental changes. This programming technique is based on the concept of receiving external stimuli depending on the algorithm choices. A correct choice will involve a reward, while an incorrect choice will lead to a penalty. The goal of the system is to achieve the best possible result, of course. In this chapter, we dealt with the basics of reinforcement learning.

To start, we explored the amazing world of machine learning and took a tour of the most popular machine learning algorithms to choose the right one for our needs. To understand what is most suitable for our needs, we learned to perform a preliminary analysis. Then we analyzed how to build machine learning models step by step.

In the central part of the chapter, we saw that the goal of learning with reinforcement is to create intelligent agents that are able to learn from their experience. So we analyzed the steps to follow to correctly apply a reinforcement learning algorithm. Later we explored the agent-environment interface. The entity that must achieve the goal is called an agent. The entity with which the agent must interact is called the environment, which corresponds to everything outside the agent.

To avoid load problems and computational difficulties, the agent-environment interaction is considered an MDP. An MDP is a stochastic control process. Then the discount factor concept was introduced. The discount factor is used during the learning process to highlight or not highlight particular actions or states. An optimal policy can cause the reinforcement obtained in performing a single action to be even low (or negative), provided that overall this leads to greater reinforcement.

Finally, we analyzed the most common reinforcement learning techniques. Q-learning, TD learning, and Deep Q-learning networks were covered.

In the next chapter, the reader will know the basic concepts of the Markov process, the basic concepts of random walks, understand how the random walk algorithms work, know how to use a Markov chain to forecast the weather, and learn how to simulate random walks using Markov chains.

Simulating Random Walks 2

Stochastic processes involve systems that evolve over time (but also more generally in space) according to probabilistic laws. Such systems or models describe the complex phenomena of the real world that have the possibility of being random. These phenomena are more frequent than we can believe. We encounter these phenomena when the quantities we are interested in are not predictable with absolute certainty. However, when such phenomena show a variability of possible outcomes that can be somehow explained or described, then we can introduce a probabilistic model of the phenomenon.

For example, say that we are examining the motion involved in a random walking movement. We study the motion of an object that is constrained to move along a straight line in the two directions allowed. At each movement, it moves randomly to the right or left, each step being of equal length and independent of the other steps. A Markov chain is a stochastic process whereby the evolution of a system depends only on its present state and not on its past state. A Markov chain is characterized by a set of states and by the probability of transition between states. Think of a point that can move randomly forward or backward along a line at discrete intervals of time, covering a certain distance at each interval. This is an example of a random walk. In this chapter, we will simulate a random walk using Markov chains through a Python code implementation.

In this chapter, we will cover the following topics:

- Random walk
- Random walk simulation
- Basic probability concepts
- Markov chain
- Forecasting using a Markov chain
- Markov chain text generator

At the end of the chapter, the reader will know the basic concepts of the Markov process, the basic concepts of random walks, how the random walk algorithms work, know how to use a Markov chain to forecast the weather, and how to simulate random walks using Markov chains.

Random walks

Random walks are a mathematical model that is used to describe a path that is given by a succession of random steps, which, depending on the system that we want to describe, may have a certain number of degrees of freedom or direction. The term *random walk* was introduced by Karl Pearson in 1905. In a random walk, each step has a random direction and possibly also a random dimension. It represents a theoretical model to describe any random process through the evolution of known quantities that follow a precise statistical distribution. Physically speaking, the path that we are going to draw over time will not necessarily describe a real motion, but rather indicate more generally the evolution of features over time. This means that random walks find applications in physics, chemistry, and biology, but also in other fields, such as computer science, economics, and sociology.

One-dimensional random walk

In a one-dimensional random walk, we study the motion of a point-like particle that is constrained to move along a straight line in one of only two directions (right and left). For each (random) movement, it can move one step to the right with a fixed probability p or to the left with a q probability. Each step is of equal length, and is independent of the others, as shown in the following diagram:

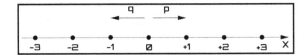

The position of the point after n steps—identified by its abscissa, $X(n)$—obviously contains a random term. We want to calculate the probability after n movements that the particle will return to the starting point (it should be noted that nothing assures us with any certainty that the point will actually return to that position). To do this, we will use the $X(n)$ variable, which gives the abscissa of the straight line after the particle has moved n steps to the left. Obviously, this is a discrete random variable with a binomial distribution.

This variable takes the following scheme: at every instant, n takes a step to the right or left according to the result of a random variable, $Z(n)$, which takes on +1 value with probability of $p > 0$ and a -1 value with a probability of q, with $p + q = 1$, as shown in the previous diagram. Suppose that the random Zn variable with $n = 1, 2,...$ are independent, and all have the same distribution. Then the position of the particle at the n instant is given by the following equation:

$$X_n = X_{n-1} + Z_n; \; for \; n = 1, 2, \ldots$$

The X_n variable represents a Markov chain because, to determine the probability that the particle is in a certain position in the next moment, we only need to know where it is at the current moment, even if we are aware of where it was in all moments prior to the current one.

Simulating 1D random walk

We have previously said that a random walk contains a random term. To simulate a random walk, it is not enough to generate a list of random numbers, because the next value in the sequence is a modification of the previous value. This dependency provides a certain coherence from one passage to the next that does not happen in the generation of independent random numbers, which instead shows great jumps from one number to the next.

A simple model of a casual walk can be simulated through the following pseudocode:

1. Start from position 0
2. Randomly select a number with a value of -1 or 1
3. Add it to the observation of the previous time step
4. Repeat these steps from step 2

To implement this algorithm in Python, just refer to the previous equation:

$$X_n = X_{n-1} + Z_n; \; for \; n = 1, 2, \ldots$$

In this formula, X_n is the next value in the walk, X_{n-1} is the observation at the previous time step, and Z_n is the random fluctuation at that time. In Python, it is obtained by looping over this process and building up a list of 1,000 time steps for the random walk. The following shows the Python code to generate a random walk:

```
from random import seed
from random import random
from matplotlib import pyplot
seed(4)
RandomWalk = list()
RandomWalk.append(-1 if random() < 0.5 else 1)
for i in range(1, 1000):
    Zn = -1 if random() < 0.5 else 1
    Xn = RandomWalk[i-1] + Zn
    RandomWalk.append(Xn)
pyplot.plot(RandomWalk)
pyplot.show()
```

We will analyze this code line by line. The first lines load the libraries:

```
from random import seed
from random import random
```

The `random` module in Python contains a number of random number generators for various distributions. For integers, we use a uniform selection from a range. For sequences, we use a uniform selection of a random element, a function to generate a random permutation of a list in place, and a function for random sampling without replacement.

Two functions are loaded from this module: `seed` and `random`. The `seed` function sets the seed of a random number generator, which is useful for creating simulations or random objects that can be reproduced. You have to use this function every time you want to get a reproducible random result. In this case, the random numbers are the same, and they will continue to be the same no matter how far out in the sequence we go. Each seed value will correspond to a sequence of values that is generated for a given random number generator. That is, if you supply the same seed twice, you get the same sequence of numbers twice.

The `random` function returns the next random floating point number in the range [0.0, 1.0]. Another important library is loaded. This is the `matplotlib` library, as shown in the following code:

```
from matplotlib import pyplot
```

Matplotlib is a Python 2D-plotting library that produces publication-quality figures in a variety of hardcopy formats and interactive environments across platforms. Matplotlib tries to make easy things easy and hard things possible. You can generate plots, histograms, power spectra, bar charts, error charts, scatter plots, and so on with just a few lines of code. It consists of a collection of command style functions that make Matplotlib work like MATLAB. Each `pyplot` function makes a change to a figure, such as creating a figure, creating a plotting area in a figure, plotting some lines in a plotting area, decorating the plot with labels, and so on.

After correctly importing the libraries, we pass a command to analyze the individual operations. Let's start with setting the `seed` using the following code:

```
seed(4)
```

Recall that if you supply the same seed twice then you get the same sequence of numbers twice. Let's move on to creating the main variable, as shown in the following code:

```
RandomWalk = list()
```

The `RandomWalk` variable will be the variable that will contain the sequence of values that are representative of the random walk. This variable will be of the `list` type. A list is an ordered collection of values, and can contain various types of values. A list is a mutable container. This means that we can add values, delete values, or modify existing values. A Python list represents a mathematical concept of a finite sequence. For our needs (a sequence of mutable values), the list represents the most suitable container. The `list()` method takes sequence types and converts them to lists. To start, it is necessary to initialize the first value of the list, as shown in the following code:

```
RandomWalk.append(-1 if random() < 0.5 else 1)
```

This value will serve us in the next calculation. We can move on to the iterative cycle, as shown in the following code:

```
for i in range(1, 1000):
```

At each step, we get the following random term:

```
Zn = -1 if random() < 0.5 else 1
```

Two values will be returned: -1 and 1. We get -1 if the `random` function (which, as you may recall, returns values in the [0.0, 1.0] interval) returns a value lower than 0.5; otherwise, we get 1. At this point, we can evaluate the value of the walk at the current step using the following code:

```
Xn = RandomWalk[i-1] + Zn
```

Then the value of the walk at the current pace will be given by the sum of the value of the walk at the previous step and the random term. Once calculated, this value must be added to the list, as follows:

```
RandomWalk.append(Xn)
```

This procedure will be repeated for the *n* programmed steps. At the end, we will have the entire sequence stored in the list. We just have to visualize it, as shown in the following code:

```
pyplot.plot(RandomWalk)
pyplot.show()
```

The `pyplot.plot` phrase plots `RandomWalk` on the *y* axis using an array *0 .... N-1* as the *x* axis. The `plot()` phrase is a versatile command, and will take an arbitrary number of arguments. Finally, `pyplot.show` displays the created diagram.

The following graph shows a random walk drawn with the previous code:

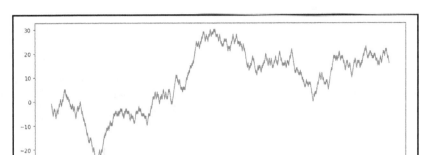

In the graph, we see a random process describing the trends of a specific function. In it, the next step is independent of the position of the previous step, depending only on the current step. The random walk is a natural model that can be used to simulate the **efficient market hypothesis** (**EMH**)—that is, the theory according to which the price varies given the arrival of new information, which, by definition, is independent of what we already know.

Markov chains

A Markov chain is a mathematical model of a random phenomenon that evolves over time in such a way that the past influences the future only through the present. The time can be discrete (a whole variable), continuous (a real variable), or, more generally, a totally ordered whole. In this discussion, only discrete chains are considered. Markov chains were introduced in 1906 by Andrei Andreyevich Markov (1856–1922), from whom the name derives.

The example of a one-dimensional random walk seen in the previous section is a Markov chain; the next value in the chain is a unit that is more or less than the current value with the same probability of occurrence, regardless of the way in which the current value was reached.

Stochastic process

In order to provide a formal definition of a Markov chain, it is first necessary to specify what is meant by a set of random variables having a temporal ordering. Such a set of random variables can best be represented by a stochastic process.

We define a stochastic process in discrete time and discrete states using the following sequence of random variables:

$$X_0, X_1, X_2, \ldots, X_n, \ldots$$

Here, each X_n is a discrete random variable with values in a $S = s_1, s_2, \ldots, s_n$ set, called the space of the states. Without losing generality, suppose that S is a subset of the relative integers, Z. We will use the index n of X_n to denote the time in which the states evolve; we will call states, the possible ones with the values of X_n. The process starts in one of these states and moves successively from one state to another. Each move is called a step.

As time passes, the process can jump from one state to another. If the system is in state i during time step n, and is in state $j \neq i$ during time step $n + 1$, then we say that there has been a transition.

Probability calculation

We are interested in calculating the probabilities associated with a stochastic process (X_n). Let's spend a few minutes talking about the basic concepts of probability. If you are already familiar with these concepts, you may want to skip this section; otherwise, it will be in your interest to deepen the basic knowledge needed to understand how probabilities are calculated.

The a priori probability that a given event (E) occurs is the ratio between the number (s) of favorable cases of the event itself and the total number (n) of the possible cases, provided all considered cases are equally probable. This can be summarized in the following formula:

$$P = P(E) = \frac{number\ of\ favorable\ cases}{total\ number\ of\ possible\ cases} = \frac{s}{n}$$

Let's look at a simple example.

What is the probability that a thrown die shows the number 3? The number of possible results is 6—{1, 2, 3, 4, 5, 6}—and the favorable cases are 1{3}. So P(3) =1/6 =0.166 =16.6 %.

The probability of an event $(P(E))$ is always a number between 0 and 1, as shown in the following formula:

$$0 \leq P(E) \leq 1$$

The extreme values are defined as follows:

- An event that has a probability of *0* is called an impossible event. Suppose we have six red balls in a bag. What is the probability of picking a black ball? The number of possible cases is 6 and the number of favorable cases is 0 because there are no black balls in the bag. We can summarize this as *P(E) = 0/6 = 0.*

- An event that has a probability of 1 is called a certain event. Suppose we have six red balls in a bag. What is the probability of picking a red ball? The number of possible cases is 6 and the number of favorable cases is 6 because there are only red balls in the bag. We can summarize this as *P(E) = 6/6 =1.*

So far, we've talked about the likelihood of an event, but what happens when the possible events are more than one? Two random events, *A* and *B*, are independent if the probability of the occurrence of event *A* is not dependent on whether event *B* has occurred, and vice versa. For example, say that we have two 52-card decks of French playing cards. When extracting a card from each deck, the following two events are independent:

- E_1: The card extracted from the first deck is an ace
- E_2: The card extracted from the second deck is a club

The two events are independent—each can happen with the same probability independently of the other's occurrence.

Conversely, a random event, *A*, is dependent on another event, *B*, if the probability of event *A* depends on whether event *B* has occurred or not. Suppose we have a deck of 52 cards. By extracting two cards in succession without putting the first card back in the deck, the following two events are dependent:

- E_1: The first extracted card is an ace
- E_2: The second extracted card is an ace

To be precise, the probability of E_2 depends on whether or not E_1 occurs. From this, we can extrapolate the following:

- The probability of E_1 is 4/52
- The probability of E_2 if the first card was an ace is 3/51
- The probability of E_2 if the first card was not an ace is 4/51

Let's now deal with the case of **joint probability**, both independent and dependent. If two events, *A* and *B*, are independent (meaning that the occurrence of one does not affect the probability of the other), then the joint probability of the event is equal to the product of the probabilities of *A* and *B*. This can be summarized as follows:

$$P(A \cap B) = P(A) \times P(B)$$

Let's take an example. We have two decks of 52 cards. By extracting a card from each deck, let's consider the two independent events:

- *A*: The card extracted from the first deck is an ace
- *B*: The card extracted from the second deck is a clubs card

What is the probability that both of them occur?

- *P(A) = 4/52*
- *P(B) = 13/52*
- *P(A ∩ B) = 4/52 * 13/52 = 52 /(52 * 52) = 1/52*

If the two events are dependent (that is, the occurrence of one affects the probability of the other), then the same rule may apply, provided that *P(B|A)* is the probability of event *B* given that event *A* has occurred. This condition introduces **conditional probability**, which we are going to dive into. This can be summarized as follows:

$$P(A \cap B) = P(A) \times P(B|A)$$

Say that a bag contains two white balls and three red balls. Two balls are pulled out from the bag in two successive extractions without reintroducing the first ball that was pulled out of the bag.

Calculate the probability that the two balls extracted are both white given the following facts:

- The probability that the first ball is white is 2/5
- The probability that the second ball is white, provided that the first ball is white, is 1/4

The probability of having two white balls is as follows:

- *P(two white) = 2/5 * 1/4 = 2/20 = 1/10*

As promised, it is now time to introduce the concept of conditional probability. The probability that event B occurs, calculated on the condition that event A occurred, is called **conditional probability**, and is indicated by $P(B \mid A)$. It is calculated using the following formula:

$$P(B|A) = \frac{P(A \cap B)}{P(A)}$$

Now that we are able to understand the different kinds of probabilities, let's apply them to the stochastic processes. Let's start from the simplest kind of probability, written as $P(X_n = i)$.

This represents the probability of observing at step n the system in state i. In addition to these simple probabilities, we can also be interested in the calculation of more complex probabilities, such as those involving multiple steps at the same time.

For example, it may be interesting to calculate the probability of being in state j at step $n + 1$ knowing that it is in state i at step n (as you may have noticed, this is the conditional probability defined previously). This can be summarized as follows:

$$P(X_{n+1} = j|Xn = i)$$

This calculates the transition probability from i to j at step n. Using the conditional probability definition, this rewrites itself to take the following form:

$$P(X_{n+1} = j|X_n = i) = \frac{P(X_n = i \cap X_{n+1} = j)}{P(X_n = i)}$$

Therefore, for this calculation, it is sufficient that we know the a priori probability and the joint probability. We know that to calculate more complex expressions, it is necessary to know the generic joint probabilities given by the following formula:

$$P(X_0 = i_0 \cap \ldots \cap X_n = i_n)$$

Where $i_0, \ldots, .i_n \in Z$. In a certain sense, these probabilities exhaust all possible information; the stochastic process is completely statistically determined when all the combined (discrete) densities are known—that is, the densities of all the multiple discrete variables $(X_1, \ldots, X_n)$ to the variation of all the $i_0, \ldots, .i_n \in Z$. The calculation of these joint probabilities is generally intractable.

Markov chain definition

As we said, a Markov chain is a mathematical model of a random phenomenon that evolves over time in such a way that the past influences the future only through the present. In other words, a stochastic model describes a sequence of possible events in which the probability of each event depends only on the state that was attained in the previous event. So, Markov chains have the property of memorylessness.

Let's consider a random process described by a sequence of random variables, $X = X_0, ..., X_n$, which can assume the values in a $j_0, j_1,..., j_n$ set. We will say that it has the Markov property if the evolution of the process depends on the past only through the present—that is, the state in which we found ourselves after n steps. This can be defined as follows:

$$P(X_{n+1} = j | X_0 = i_0, \ldots, X_n = i_n) = P(X_{n+1} = j | X_n = i_n)$$

This relation must apply to all the parameters if they are well-defined conditional probabilities. A discrete-time stochastic process X that has the Markov property is said to be a Markov chain. A Markov chain is said to be homogeneous if the following transition probabilities do not depend on n, but only on i and j:

$$P(X_{n+1} = j | X_n = i)$$

When this happens, the following changes are made to the formula:

$$P_{i,j} = P(X_{n+1} = j | X_n = i)$$

Given this, we can calculate all the joint probabilities by knowing the numbers p_{ij}, plus the following initial distribution:

$$P_i^0 = P(X_0 = i)$$

This probability is called a distribution of the process over time zero. The p_{ij} probabilities are called transition probabilities, and, to be specific, p_{ij} is the probability of transition from i to j in a time step.

Transition matrix

The study of time-homogeneous Markov chains (whose transition probabilities are independent of time) becomes particularly simple and effective using matrix representation. In particular, the formula expressed by the previous proposition becomes much more readable. The structure of a Markov chain is therefore completely represented by the following transition matrix:

$$P = \begin{bmatrix} p_{11} & p_{12} & \cdots & p_{1n} \\ p_{21} & p_{22} & \cdots & p_{2n} \\ & \cdots & \cdots & \\ p_{n1} & p_{n2} & \cdots & p_{nn} \end{bmatrix}$$

The properties of transition probability matrices derive directly from the nature of the elements that compose them. In fact, by observing that the elements of the matrix are probabilities, they must have a value between 0 and 1. So, this is a positive matrix in which the sum of the elements of each row is unitary. In fact, the elements of the *i*-th row are the probabilities that the chain, being in the S_i state at the t instant, transits in S_1 or in S_2,... or in S_n at the next step, and such transitions are mutually exclusive and exhaustive of all possibilities. Such a matrix (positive with unit sum rows) is called stochastic, and we will call each positive row vector stochastic, as follows:

$$x^T = \begin{bmatrix} x_1 x_2 \ldots x_n \end{bmatrix}$$

In this vector, the sum of the elements takes the unit value, as shown in the following formula:

$$\sum_{i=1}^{n} x_i = 1$$

Now we will see that this particular form assumes this matrix in the case of the one-dimensional random walk. As we said previously, in a one-dimensional random walk, we study the motion of a point-like particle that is constrained to move along a straight line in only two directions (right and left).

It can either move (randomly) one step to the right with a fixed probability of **p** or to the left with a probability of **q** with $p + q = 1$. Each step is of equal length and independent of the others, as shown in the following diagram:

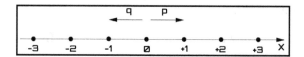

Suppose that the random variable of Z_n with $n = 1,2, ...$ are independent and all have the same distribution. Then the immediate position of the particle n is given by the following formula:

$$X_n = X_{n-1} + Z_n; \; for \; n = 1, 2, \ldots$$

Here, $X_0 = 0$ and the state space is $S = (0, \pm1, \pm2,...)$. The X_n process is a Markov chain because, to determine the probability that the particle in the next moment is in a certain position, we just need to know where it is at the current moment, even if we are aware of where it was in all the moments before the current one. This can be summarized as follows:

$$P(X_{n+1} = i + 1|X_0 = i_0, \ldots, X_n = i_n) = P(X_n + Z_{n+1} = i + 1|X_0 = i_0, \ldots, X_n = i_n) = P(Z_{n+1} = i + 1|X_0 = i_0, \ldots, X_n = i_n = p$$

Here, the Z_n variables are independent. The transition matrix is a matrix with finite rows and as many columns, having 0 on the main diagonal, p on the diagonal above the main, q on the diagonal lower than the main, and 0 elsewhere, as shown in the following diagram:

$$P = \begin{bmatrix} \ddots & & & & & & \\ \vdots & \ddots & \cdots & & & & \\ & & q & 0 & p & & \\ & & & q & 0 & p & \\ & & & & q & 0 & p \\ & & & & \vdots & \ddots & \cdots \\ & & & & & & \ddots \end{bmatrix}$$

It is clear that this generalization greatly simplifies the problem.

Transition diagram

A very intuitive alternative to the description of a Markov chain through a transition matrix is associating an oriented graph (transition diagram) to a Markov chain to which the following two statements apply:

- Vertices are labeled by the S_1, S_2,..., S_n states (or, briefly, from the indices 1, 2, ..., *n* of the states)
- There is a directed edge that connects the S_i vertex to the S_j vertex if and only if the probability of transition from S_i to S_j is positive (a probability that is in turn used as a label of the edge itself)

It is clear that the transition matrix and transition diagram provide the same information regarding the same Markov chain. To understand this duality, we can look at a simple example. Say that we have a Markov chain with three possible states—1, 2, and 3—and the following transition matrix:

$$P = \begin{bmatrix} 1/2 & 1/4 & 1/4 \\ 1/5 & 0 & 4/5 \\ 1/3 & 0 & 2/3 \end{bmatrix}$$

The following diagram shows the transition for the preceding Markov chain. In this diagram, there are three possible states—**1**, **2**, and **3**—and the directed edge from each state to other states shows the transition probabilities p_{ij}. When there is no arrow from state *i* to state *j*, it means that p_{ij}=0:

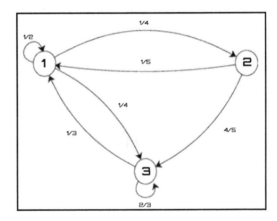

In the previous diagram, we can see that the arrows that come out of a state always sum up exactly at **1**, just as the values of every row in the transition matrix must add up exactly to **1**, which represents the probability distribution. From the comparison between the transition matrix and transition diagram, it is possible to understand the duality between the two resources. As always, a diagram is much more illustrative.

Weather forecasting with Markov chains

We want to build a statistical model to predict the weather. To simplify the model, we will assume that there are only two states: sunny and rainy. Let's further assume that we have made some calculations and discovered that tomorrow's time is somehow based on today's time, according to the following transition matrix:

$$P = \begin{bmatrix} 0.75 & 0.25 \\ 0.30 & 0.70 \end{bmatrix}$$

Recall that this matrix contains the conditional probabilities of the type expressed as $P(A \mid B)$—that is, the probability of A given B. So, this matrix contains the following conditional probabilities:

$$P = \begin{bmatrix} P(Su|Su) & P(Su|Ra) \\ P(Ra|Su) & P(Ra|Ra) \end{bmatrix}$$

In the preceding matrix, **Su** = sunny and **Ra** = rainy. Each row must consist of a complete distribution; thus, all the numbers must be non-negative and sum to 1. Weather has a tendency to resist change—for instance, *P(Sunny | Sunny)* is more likely than *P(Sunny | Rainy)*. Tomorrow's value is not directly related to yesterday's (or an earlier time's) value, so the process is Markovian.

The previous matrix corresponds to the following transition diagram:

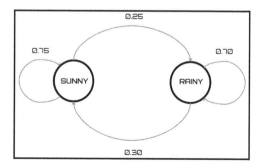

At this point, the following questions come to mind:

- If today is sunny, how can we calculate the probability that it is rainy in the next few days?
- After a certain number of days, what will be the proportion of sunny and rainy days?

Both questions, as well as many others that can come to mind, can be answered through the tools that make Markov chains available to us. The following is the Python code that provides for the alternation between sunny and rainy days starting from a specific initial condition:

```python
import numpy as np
import time
from matplotlib import pyplot

np.random.seed(1)
states = ["Sunny","Rainy"]

TransStates = [["SuSu","SuRa"],["RaRa","RaSu"]]
TransnMatrix = [[0.75,0.25],[0.30,0.70]]

if sum(TransnMatrix[0])+sum(TransnMatrix[1]) != 2:
    print("Warning! Probabilities MUST ADD TO 1. Wrong transition
matrix!!")
    raise ValueError("Probabilities MUST ADD TO 1")

WT = list()
NumberDays = 200
WeatherToday = states[0]
print("Weather initial condition =",WeatherToday)

i = 0
while i < NumberDays:
    if WeatherToday == "Sunny":
        TransWeather = np.random.choice(TransStates[0],
                            replace=True,p=TransnMatrix[0])
        if TransWeather == "SuSu":
            pass
        else:
            WeatherToday = "Rainy"
    elif WeatherToday == "Rainy":
        TransWeather = np.random.choice(TransStates[1],
                            replace=True,p=TransnMatrix[1])
        if TransWeather == "RaRa":
            pass
        else:
```

```
                WeatherToday = "Sunny"
        print(WeatherToday)
        WT.append(WeatherToday)
        i += 1
        time.sleep(0.2)

pyplot.plot(WT)
pyplot.show()

pyplot.hist(WT)
pyplot.show()
```

We will analyze this code line by line. The first lines load the libraries:

```
import numpy as np
import time
from matplotlib import pyplot
```

The first line of this imports the `numpy` library: `numpy` is a library for the Python programming language, adding support for large, multidimensional arrays and matrices, along with a large collection of high-level mathematical functions to operate on these arrays. Two functions will be used: `random.seed()` and `random.choise()`. The second line imports the `time` module which provides various time-related functions. Finally, the `pyplot` module is imported from the `matplotlib` library.

Let's continue analyzing the code:

```
np.random.seed(1)
```

The `random.seed()` function sets the seed of a random number generator, which is useful for creating simulations or random objects that can be reproduced. You have to use this function every time you want to get a reproducible random result. In this case, the random numbers are the same, and they would continue to be the same no matter how far out in the sequence we go. Each seed value will correspond to a sequence of values that are generated for a given random number generator. In the following line, we define the state of the weather condition:

```
states = ["Sunny","Rainy"]
```

As we said, only two states are provided: `Sunny` and `Rainy`. At this point, we have to define the possible transitions of weather conditions:

```
TransStates = [["SuSu","SuRa"],["RaRa","RaSu"]]
```

Only two states allow only four types of transitions: sunny to sunny, sunny to rainy, rainy to rainy, and rainy to sunny. Let's move on to define the transition matrix according to what was established at the beginning of the section:

```
TransnMatrix = [[0.75,0.25],[0.30,0.70]]
```

Remember that this matrix contains the conditional probabilities of the type expressed as *P* (*A* | *B*)—that is, the probability of *A* given *B*. As already mentioned, the rows of this matrix add up to 1. Then we insert the following check to verify that we did not make mistakes in defining the transition matrix:

```
if sum(TransnMatrix[0])+sum(TransnMatrix[1]) != 2:
    print("Warning! Probabilities MUST ADD TO 1. Wrong transition
matrix!!")
    raise ValueError("Probabilities MUST ADD TO 1")
```

Let's move on to creating the main variable using the following code:

```
WT = list()
```

The `WT` phrase will be the variable that will contain the sequence of values that are representative of the weather forecast. This variable will be of a `list` type. Let's now fix the number of days for which we want to forecast the weather conditions using the following code:

```
NumberDays = 200
```

If we wanted to fix another interval, it would be enough to change this value. Let's now fix the initial conditions using the following code:

```
WeatherToday = states[0]
```

In this way, we have selected the first element of the `states` variable. Remember that in Python the first element of a list has an index equal to 0. At this point, we can move on to the weather forecast. But first, we set the initial conditions using the following code:

```
print("Weather initial condition =",WeatherToday)
```

We can now predict the weather conditions for each of the days set by the NumberDays variable. To do this, we will use a while loop. A while loop is different from a for loop, but basically, it performs the same functions. It consists of a control condition and a loop body. At the entrance of the cycle and every time that all the instructions contained in the body are executed, the validity of the control condition is verified. The cycle ends when the condition, consisting of a Boolean expression, returns false. To start, we initialize a counter to allow us to perform the check, as follows:

```
i = 0
```

The exit condition that we impose will be i <NumberDays. This means that when this Boolean expression is false (and this will happen when i = NumberDays), then the loop will not be executed, and it will go to the first statement after the while block, as shown in the following code:

```
while i < NumberDays:
    if WeatherToday == "Sunny":
        TransWeather =
np.random.choice(TransStates[0],replace=True,p=TransnMatrix[0])
        if TransWeather == "SuSu":
            pass
        else:
            WeatherToday = "Rainy"
    elif WeatherToday == "Rainy":
        TransWeather =
np.random.choice(TransStates[1],replace=True,p=TransnMatrix[1])
        if TransWeather == "RaRa":
            pass
        else:
            WeatherToday = "Sunny"
    print(WeatherToday)
    WT.append(WeatherToday)
    i += 1
    time.sleep(0.2)
```

This is the main part of the whole program, so you will need to pay close attention to it. Within the while loop, the prediction of the time for each day in succession occurs through a further conditional structure: the if statement. Starting from a weather condition (remember that we established at the beginning that the weather conditions are sunny), we must provide the weather condition of the next day. We can therefore start from two conditions: Sunny or Rainy.

In fact, the first `if` statement provides two control conditions, as shown in the following screenshot:

```
while i < NumberDays:

    if WeatherToday == "Sunny":
        TransWeather = np.random.choice(TransStates[0],replace=True,p=TransnMatrix[0])
        if TransWeather == "SuSu":
            pass
        else:
            WeatherToday = "Rainy"


    elif WeatherToday == "Rainy":
        TransWeather = np.random.choice(TransStates[1],replace=True,p=TransnMatrix[1])
        if TransWeather == "RaRa":
            pass
        else:
            WeatherToday = "Sunny"


    print(WeatherToday)
    WT.append(WeatherToday)
    i += 1
    time.sleep(0.2)
```

Starting from the weather condition (`Sunny` or `Rainy`), the `random.choice()` function is used for the forecast. As already mentioned, this function generates a random sample from a given 1-D array. The syntax of the function is as follows:

```
numpy.random.choice (a, size = None, replace = True, p = None)
```

Let's look at this code in more detail:

- a: 1-D array-like or `int`—if this is an *ndarray*, a random sample is generated from its elements. If this is an `int`, the random sample is generated as if a were `np.arange (a)`.

- `size`: `int` or tuple of `int` instances. This has an optional output shape. If the given shape is, for example, (m, n, k), then $m * n * k$ samples are drawn. The default is `None`, in which case a single value is returned.

- replace: Boolean. This is optional, whether the sample is with or without a replacement.

- p: 1-D array-like. This is optional. This denotes the probabilities associated with each entry in a. If not given the sample, then it is assumed that there is a uniform distribution over all entries in a.

The generated random samples are returned—in our case, as one of the following values: SuSu, SuRa, RaRa, and RaSu. The first two start from the Sunny condition and the other two start from the Rainy condition. These values are stored in the TransWeather variable.

Within each condition (the if and elif clauses), there is a further if statement. We need this to determine whether to make the transition or to leave the time unchanged (leaving it set to the previous day). For example, in the case of sunny starting conditions, we use the following:

```
if TransWeather == "SuSu":
    pass
else:
    WeatherToday = "Rainy"
```

If the TransWeather variable contains the value SuSu, then the content of the WeatherToday variable (which contains the weather condition of the current day) remains unchanged; otherwise, it is replaced by the Rainy value. Of course, this applies when starting from sunny conditions. For the elif clause, a similar line of reasoning can be made. The last piece of code within the while loop allows us to update the values of the current iteration, as shown in the following code:

```
print(WeatherToday)
WT.append(WeatherToday)
i += 1
time.sleep(0.2)
```

The first line displays the current weather condition on video. The second line stores the current status in a list to memorize the evolution of the weather conditions. These value will return useful information with which to draw a diagram. The third line increases the cycle counter by one unit. The final line adjusts the printing time of the values to make it readable.

At this point, we have generated forecasts for the next 200 days. Let's plot the chart using the following code:

```
pyplot.plot(WT)
pyplot.show()
```

The `pyplot.plot` phrase plots `WT` (a list that contains the weather condition for the next 200 days) on the *y* axis using an array *0 ... N-1* as the *x* axis. The `plot()` phrase is a versatile command, and will take an arbitrary number of arguments. Finally, `pyplot.show` displays the diagram that was created. The following graph shows the weather conditions for the next 200 days, starting from the sunny condition:

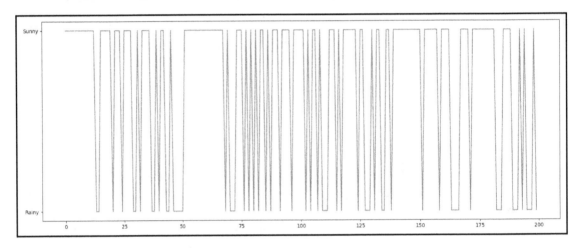

At first sight, it seems that **Sunny** days prevail over rainy ones. To be sure, we can draw a histogram. In fact, a histogram will return the number of values for each of the classes that were counted in the distribution, as shown in the following code:

```
pyplot.hist(WT)
pyplot.show()
```

The following diagram shows a histogram of the weather conditions for the next 200 days:

As anticipated, we have confirmation of the prevalence of **Sunny** days. This result does not seem unexpected because it is based on the transition matrix. In fact, the forecasts are obtained on the basis of this information. If we analyze the transition matrix from which we started again, we can see that the probability of persistence of a **Sunny** condition is greater than that of a **Rainy** condition. Furthermore, the starting condition has been set as a **Sunny** condition. It can be a useful exercise to see what happens when we start from a **Rainy** condition. To do this, just modify the initial conditions.

Generating pseudorandom text with Markov chains

Automatic text generation is one of the challenges that programmers all over the world have wrestled with. The reason for such interest is the demand for automatic systems that can help with text generation. Think of applications that automatically complete words as we type them, or applications that add sentences to our searches as we type them. It follows that the generation of random texts using a given corpus represents a very attractive topic in machine learning algorithms.

Remember that a corpus is a large and structured set of texts, usually electronically stored and processed. Corpora are used to perform statistical analysis and hypothesis testing, checking occurrences, or validating linguistic rules within a specific language territory.

A first approach to the problem could be to use words randomly and compose them together, but the result would be an illegible text. The opposite should be true: the words in the generated text should come in an order that gives the impression that the text was generated by a human being.

One solution to the problem may be the use of Markov chains. As already explained in detail in the previous sections, a Markov chain is a stochastic process with the Markov property. With this property, system state changes depend only on the current state of the system and should not depend on the system state any further than the previous steps.

A procedure for generating a pseudorandom text using Markov chains is summarized in the following steps:

1. Take two consecutive words from the corpus.
2. Build a chain of words. The last two words in the chain represent the current state of the Markov chain.
3. Search all the occurrences of the last two words in the corpus. This will represent the current state. If they appear more than once, then we select one randomly and add the word that follows it to the end of the chain.
4. At this point, the current state is updated; it consists of both the second word of the former chain queue and the new word.
5. Repeat all steps from *Step 3* onward until we reach the desired length of the generated text.

When reading and subdividing a corpus into words, we will not remove commas, punctuation marks, and so on. In this way, we will get a more realistic text.

A text generator based on the Markov chain requires an initial corpus. In fact, as with any machine learning algorithm—even for the text generator—we first have to train our algorithm by providing it with an initial set of data.

For this purpose, we will use a classic of American literature: *The Adventures of Tom Sawyer* by Mark Twain. This will be our corpus; we will save it in text format (using the character set encoding UTF-8).

For the text generation, we will use the `markovify` Python library. Markovify is a simple, extensible Markov chain generator. Its main use is for building Markov models of large corpora of text, and generating random sentences from these.

To get more information, and to download the source code, we can refer to the Markovify project repository at `https://github.com/jsvine/markovify`.

The use of the generator as mentioned is simple. Just be aware of the following simple rules:

- To generate text from a corpus, we use the `markovify.Text` class.
- The text generator works best with large and well-punctuated texts. If the text does not use punctuation to delineate sentences, you will need to separate each sentence on a new line. In this case, you will need to use the `markovify.NewlineText` class.
- By default, `markovify.Text` attempts to execute a sentence that does not overlap with the original text ten times at most. If successful, the method returns the sentence as a string; otherwise, it returns `None`.
- If the text is available as a long sentence, Markovify will not be able to generate new sentences because of the lack of start and end delimiters.
- By default, `markovify.Text` attempts to generate sentences that do not simply return pieces of the original text. The default rule is to delete any generated phrase that exactly overlaps the original text of 15 words or 70% of the word count of the sentence.

To install the Markovify text generator, simply type the following command:

```
pip install markovify
```

The `pip` phrase is a tool for installing Python packages.

The following code shows how to generate pseudorandom text from the masterpiece of Mark Twain:

```
import markovify

with open("corpus.txt") as f:
    CorpusText = f.read()

    TextModel = markovify.Text(CorpusText)

print("Five randomly-generated sentences")
print("----------------------------------")

for i in range(5):
    print(TextModel.make_sentence())

print("----------------------------------")
print("three randomly-generated sentences of no more than 100 characters")
print("----------------------------------")
```

```
for i in range(3):
    print(TextModel.make_short_sentence(100))
```

We will analyze this code line by line. The first line loads the library:

```
import markovify
```

Let's move on to loading the corpus using the following code:

```
with open("corpus.txt") as f:
    CorpusText = f.read()
```

First, we have to open the file. To do this, we have used the `open()` function which returns a `file` object, and is most commonly used with two arguments: `open(filename, mode)`. The first argument is a string containing the filename. The second argument is another string containing a few characters describing the way in which the file will be used. In our case, only the filename is passed.

To read a corpus's contents, we have called the `f.read(size)` function, which reads a quantity of data and returns it as a string. The `size` phrase is an optional numeric argument (in our case, it has been omitted). When `size` is omitted or negative, the entire content of the file will be read and returned.

At this point we can create the model using the following code:

```
TextModel = markovify.Text(CorpusText)
```

This is the main class of the package, and as we have said, it creates the model for generating the text to open from the corpus. This model is trained and ready for use. The most useful `markovify.Text` models you can create are as follows:

- `sentence_split`
- `sentence_join`
- `word_split`
- `word_join`
- `test_sentence_input`
- `test_sentence_output`

Now that the model is ready, we can start generating sentences. Before doing so, we use the `print` function to print the formatting lines on screen to make the output more readable, as shown in the following code:

```
print("Five randomly-generated sentences")
print("--------------------------------")
```

As anticipated, we will first generate five sentences using the following code:

```
for i in range(5):
    print(TextModel.make_sentence())
```

To do this, we first use a `for` loop and then use the `TextModel.make_sentence ()` function. This function generates a sentence from your model. By default, we try ten times to generate a valid sentence, based on the model that we created previously. If successful, it returns the sentence as a string. If not, it returns `None`. Finally, we generate three short sentences of a length no more than `100` characters using the following code:

```
print("--------------------------------")
print("three randomly-generated sentences of no more than 100 characters")
print("--------------------------------")

for i in range(3):
    print(TextModel.make_short_sentence(100))
```

Also, in this case, the main instruction is the one that contains the `TextModel.make_sentence ()` function. All the rest is used only to format the returned sentences. An example of the sentences returned by the code are shown in the following screenshot:

```
Prompt dei comandi                                                    −  □  ×

C:\script\Python\RandomWalk>python MCTextGenGiuseppe.py
Five randomly-generated sentences
-----------------------------------
Blessed are they that shall--they that--a--they that shall mourn, for they--they--" "_Theirs_--" "For _theirs_.
Oh, all right, then.
Not a leaf stirred; not a tombstone on the steps and then broke into a settled melancholy, and her lip trembled.

There was a valued novelty in whistling, which he put the two bereaved women flung themselves into each other an
d be brothers and never regret having driven her poor boy out into the first time, neither.
"You stay here, where there's been pirates on this work or group of boys who had grown plenty strong enough, now
, to think she had discovered him; then he dipped the soap in the early morning recalling the incidents of his f
lower.
-----------------------------------
three randomly-generated sentences of no more than 100 characters
-----------------------------------
A portion of it, even if you're chopped all to flinders, and kill anybody and all the time.
And she put out her hand until all was over.
How many of the great rock stood in.

C:\script\Python\RandomWalk>
```

I must confess, I would have a hard time saying that it is text that is generated by a machine. In this short example, we have seen the enormous potential that this type of algorithm presents. The applications in the real world are varied: the creation of bots that respond to the needs of a human user, creation of poetry and songs starting from a corpus of sentences, creation of a new alias from a name, and so on. Surely these are interesting topics.

Despite this, we must address the shortcomings of text generation through this method. It is inherently stochastic in nature, which can lead to undesirable results at times. It is crucial that the reader knows about this.

Summary

In this chapter, we looked at stochastic processes and their applications. We looked at starting a random walk model. Random walks are mathematical models that are used to describe a path given by a succession of random steps, which, depending on the system we want to describe, may have a certain number of degrees of freedom or direction. We have learned how to deal with one-dimensional random walks, and we have seen how to write a code for the simulation of a random walk in the Python language.

Then we were introduced to Markov chains. To understand this topic, you were briefly introduced to probability calculation. The a priori probability, joint probability, and conditional probability were all defined, with examples of their calculation. We then moved on to the definition of Markov chains. A Markov chain is a mathematical model of a random phenomenon that evolves over time in such a way that the past influences the future only through the present: in other words, it is a stochastic model describing a sequence of possible events in which the probability of each event depends only on the state attained in the previous event. We learned to define and to read a transition matrix and a transition diagram. We used Markov chains for forecasting the weather conditions for 200 consecutive days.

Finally, we used a Markov chains library to generate pseudorandom text using a classic of American literature: *The Adventures of Tom Sawyer* by Mark Twain.

3
Optimal Portfolio Selection

The selection of an optimal portfolio is a typical decision problem, and as such, its solution consists of the following elements: the identification of a set of alternatives, using selection criteria to sort through the different possibilities, and finally the solution of the problem. **Dynamic Programming (DP)** represents a set of algorithms that can be used to calculate an optimal policy given a perfect model of the environment in the form of a **MarkovDecision Process (MDP)**. The DP methods update the estimates of the values of the states—based on the estimates of the values of the successor states—or update the estimates on the basis of past estimates. In DP, an optimization problem is decomposed into simpler subproblems, and the solution for each subproblem is stored so that each subproblem is solved only once. In this chapter, we will learn how to select the optimal portfolio using DP through a Python code implementation.

This chapter covers the following topics:

- DP features
- The DP approach
- Recursion and memoization
- The knapsack problem
- The DP application

By the end of the chapter, the reader will understand the basic concepts of optimization techniques, know how to decompose a problem into subproblems, know how to use the DP approach to reduce the computational cost of the Fibonacci series calculus, understand the difference between recursion and memoization, and understand the basis of the knapsack problem and how to apply it to an optimal portfolio selection problem.

Dynamic Programming

DP is a mathematical methodology developed in the 1950s, mainly by Richard Bellman. It allows us to address certain classes of problems in which a series of interdependent decisions must be taken in sequence. It is based on Bellman's principle of optimality, *Bellman, R.E. 1957. Dynamic Programming. Princeton University Press, Princeton, NJ. Republished 2003: Dover, ISBN 0-486-42809-5*, which states that an optimal policy has the property that whatever the initial state and initial decision are, the remaining decisions must constitute an optimal policy with regard to the state resulting from the first decision.

Consider, for example, the problem of finding the best path that joins two locations. The principle of optimality states that each subpath included in it, between any intermediate location and the final location, must in turn be optimal. Based on this principle, DP solves a problem by taking one decision at a time. At every step, the best policy for the future is determined, regardless of the past choices (it is a Markov process), assuming that the latter choices are also optimal.

DP is, therefore, effectively applicable whenever the original problem can be decomposed into a set of smaller subproblems and when the cost paid or the profit obtained is expressed as a sum of elementary costs associated with each individual decision. More generally, the cost must be expressed, through operators, as a composition of elementary costs, each one dependent on a single decision.

The following diagram shows the best (that is, the shortest) path between two nodes of a network among all those available:

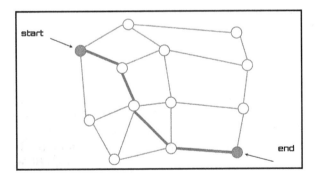

There are many paths available to reach the same destination: only one is the shortest.

Divide and conquer versus Dynamic Programming

To understand the mechanism behind DP, we can compare it with another very common problem-solving mechanism: divide and conquer. With this mechanism, a problem is subdivided into two or more subproblems, and the solution of the original problem is constructed starting from the subproblem solutions. This is a top-down technique that is executed according to the following procedure:

1. Divide the problem instance into two or more subinstances
2. Recursively solve the problem for each subinstance
3. Recombine the subproblem solution in order to obtain the global solution

This mechanism is widely applied for the resolution of multiple problems. The most popular applications are two of the most commonly used sorting algorithms: quick sort and merge sort.

For example, in the quick sort algorithm, the elements of the list to be sorted are divided into two blocks—the smaller ones and the larger ones of a pivot—and the algorithm is called recursively on the two blocks.

There are cases in which divide and conquer is not applicable because we do not know how to obtain the subproblems: the problem does not contain enough information to allow us to decide how to break it into several parts.

In this case, the DP comes into play. We proceed to calculate the solutions of all possible subproblems, and starting from subsolutions we obtain new subsolutions, working up to solve the original problem. Unlike the divide and conquer strategy, the subproblems to be solved are not necessarily disjointed, meaning that the same subproblem can be common to several subproblems. In order to avoid the recalculation of the same subproblem, the subproblems are resolved with a bottom-up strategy—from the smallest subproblem to the largest subproblem—and the solutions to these subproblems are stored in appropriate tables so that they are available for the solution of other subproblems, if necessary.

The following diagram compares these two approaches:

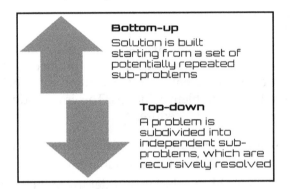

On the basis of what the preceding diagram states, we can deduce that DP is used in cases where there is a recursive definition of the problem, but the direct transformation of this definition into an algorithm generates a program of exponential complexity because of the repeated calculation based on the same subsets of data from the different recursive calls. An example is a calculation of Fibonacci numbers, which we will analyze in detail later.

Memoization

We have seen that DP is a technique for solving recursive problems more efficiently. Why is this the case? Oftentimes in recursive procedures, we solve subproblems repeatedly. In DP, this does not happen: we memorize the solution of these subproblems so that we do not have to solve them again. This is called memoization.

If the value of a variable at a given step depends on the results of previous calculations, and if the same calculations are repeated over and over, then it is convenient to store the intermediate results so as to avoid repeating computationally expensive calculations.

To better understand the difference between recursion and memoization, let's analyze a simple example: the calculation of the factorial of a number. Specifically, this is a factorial of a natural number, n, indicated with $n!$, and is the product of positive integers less than or equal to that number. The calculation of the factorial of n is given in the following formula:

$$n! = \prod_{i=0}^{1} k = n * (n-1) * \ldots * 3 * 2 * 1$$

The calculation of the factorial of a number can also be defined recursively, as follows:

$$n! = \begin{cases} 1, & if \ n = 0 \\ n(n-1)!, & if \ n \geq 1 \end{cases}$$

A function is called recursive if it calls itself. The recursive function can directly solve only particular cases of a problem, called base cases (such as those present in the previous formula); if it is invoked by passing some data that constitutes one of the basic cases, then it returns a result. At each call, the data is reduced, so at a certain point we arrive at one of the basic cases. When the function calls itself, it suspends its execution to make the new call. The execution resumes when the internal call to itself ends. The sequence of recursive calls ends when the innermost one (nested) encounters one of the basic cases.

Let's look at a simple function in Python that calculates the factorial of a number through a recursive procedure:

```
import time
time_start = time.clock()
def factorial (x):
    if x == 0:
        return 1
    else:
        return x * factorial (x-1)
print("Factorial of 10 is: ",factorial (10))
print("Computational time is: ",time.clock() - time_start)
```

Within the function there is an `if` structure with two options: until x is greater than or equal to 1, the function calls itself; when x `== 0`, it stops. The call to the factorial (n-1) asks the function to solve a problem simpler than the initial one (meaning that the value would be lower), but it is always the same problem. The function continues to call itself until it reaches the basic case that it can solve immediately. The `time.clock()` function is used to calculate the computational cost. The results are shown in the following snippet:

```
Factorial of 10 is: 3628800
Computational time is: 0.00022297111682249322
```

Given the nature of the recursive algorithm that was used, this program requires *n + 1* invocations of the factorial function to arrive at a result, and each of these invocations, in turn, has a cost associated with the time taken by the function to return the calculated value.

This program can be improved through memoization using the following method:

1. Create a variable to store temporary results (storeX).
2. Before performing a calculation, find out whether the calculation has already been done. If so, use the stored result.
3. If this is our first time performing a calculation, then store the results for future use.

A memoized version of the program is shown in the following code:

```
import time
time_start = time.clock()

storeX ={}
def factorial (x):
    if x in storeX:
        return storeX[x]
    elif x == 0:
        return 1
    else:
        xt = x * factorial(x-1)
        storeX[x] = xt
        return xt

print("Factorial of 10 is: ",factorial (10))
print("Computational time is: ",time.clock() - time_start)
```

Memoization allows a function to become more time-efficient the more often it is called, resulting in eventual overall speed-up. The following snippet shows the results:

```
Factorial of 10 is: 3628800
Computational time is:0.00012497111682249322
```

From the comparison between the two computational costs, you can see that the version that uses memoization is faster.

Dynamic Programming in reinforcement-learning applications

DP represents a set of algorithms that can be used to calculate an optimal policy given a perfect model of the environment in the form of an MDP. The fundamental idea of DP, as well as reinforcement learning in general, is the use of state values and actions to look for good policies.

The DP method approaches the resolution of Markov decision-making processes through the iteration of two processes called policy evaluation and policy improvement, outlined as follows:

- The policy-evaluation algorithm involves applying an iterative method to the resolution of the Bellman equation. Since convergence is guaranteed to us only for $k \to \infty$, we must be content to have good approximations by imposing a stopping condition.
- The policy-improvement algorithm improves policy based on current values.

A disadvantage of the policy-iteration algorithm is that, at every step, we have to evaluate a policy. This involves an iterative process during which we do not know the time of convergence a priori, which will depend on how the starting policy was chosen, among other things.

One way to overcome this drawback is to cut off the evaluation of the policy at a specific step. This operation does not change the guarantee of convergence to the optimal value. A special case in which the assessment of the policy is blocked at a certain step (also called sweep) defines the value-iteration algorithm. In the value-iteration algorithm, a single iteration of the calculation of the values is performed between each step of the policy improvement.

The DP algorithms are therefore essentially based on two processes that take place in parallel: policy evaluation and policy improvement. The repeated execution of these two processes makes the general process converge toward the optimal solution. In the policy-iteration algorithm, the two phases alternate and each ends before the other begins.

DP methods operate through the entire set of states that can be assumed by the environment, performing a complete backup for each state at each iteration. Each update operation performed by the backup updates the value of a status based on the values of all possible successor states, weighed for their probability of occurrence, and induced by the policy of choice and by the dynamics of the environment. Full backups are closely related to the Bellman equation; they are nothing more than the transformation of the equation into assignment instructions.

When a complete backup iteration does not bring any change to the state values, convergence is obtained, and therefore the final state values fully satisfy the Bellman equation. The DP methods are applicable only if there is a perfect model of the alternator, which must be equivalent to an MDP.

Precisely for this reason, the DP algorithms are of little use in reinforcement learning, both because of their assumption of a perfect model of the environment, and because of their high and expensive computation, but it is still important to mention them because they represent the theoretical basis of reinforcement learning. In fact, all methods of reinforcement learning try to achieve the same goal of the DP methods, only with lower computational cost and without the assumption of a perfect model of the environment.

The DP methods converge to the optimal solution using a number of polynomial operations with respect to the number of states (n) and actions (m) against the number of exponential operations ($m*n$) required by methods based on a direct search.

The DP methods update the estimates of the values of the states—based on the estimates of the values of the successor states—or update the estimates on the basis of past estimates. This represents a special property called bootstrapping. Several methods of reinforcement learning perform bootstrapping, even methods that do not require a perfect model of the environment, as required by the DP methods.

Optimizing a financial portfolio

The management of financial portfolios is an activity that aims to combine financial products in a manner that best represents the investor's needs. This requires an overall assessment of various characteristics, such as risk appetite, expected returns, and investor consumption, as well as an estimate of future returns and risk.

In order to optimize a financial portfolio, we start by measuring the yield and risk of the products available. The risk-return variables can be considered two sides of the same coin, since a certain level of risk will correspond to a given return. The return can be defined as the sum of the results produced by the investment in relation to the capital employed, while the concept of risk can be translated into the degree of variability of returns associated with a given financial instrument.

The following diagram shows the Markowitz efficient frontier:

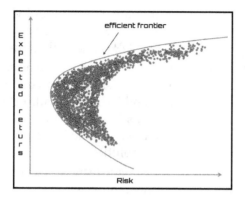

The risk of a portfolio of financial instruments can be reduced through the combination of different activities that are not perfectly correlated with each other; in practice, these are activities whose returns do not move simultaneously over time. This theory was created by the economist Harry Markowitz. Markowitz introduced the concept of diversification in 1952, which states that the risk attributable to a diversified portfolio will be lower than the average risk related to individual assets; this effect is even more pronounced the more that asset returns are decorrelated with each other. Added to this is the need to define the objectives and preferences of the investor.

To build optimized portfolios that guarantee the best risk-return trade-off and at the same time satisfy the objectives and preferences of the investor, we will use an optimization algorithm belonging to a particular class of algorithms that is used in different fields, including artificial intelligence. But before doing so, we will proceed step by step and analyze the basics of process-optimization techniques.

Optimization techniques

An optimization problem is a problem whose solution can be measured in terms of a cost function, also called an objective. The value to look for is normally the minimum value or the maximum value of this function. Optimization problems can be reduced to a sequence of decision problems.

To solve an optimization problem, it is necessary to use an iterative algorithm—that is, a calculation program, given a current approximation of the solution, determines, with an appropriate sequence of operations, a new approximation. Starting from an initial approximation, a succession of possible solutions to the problem is thus determined.

The search algorithms of the optimal solution fall under the following three classes:

- **Enumerative techniques**: Enumerative techniques look for the optimal solution in all points of the function's domain. Simplifications can come from reducing the problem to simpler subproblems. DP is one of these techniques.
- **Numerical techniques**: Numerical techniques use a set of necessary and sufficient conditions that must be satisfied by solving the optimization problem. These can be classified directly and indirectly. Indirect methods look for the least of a function by solving a set of nonlinear functions and searching the solution iteratively until the gradient of the cost function is null. Direct methods make the gradient guide the search for the solution.
- **Probabilistic techniques**: Probabilistic techniques are based on enumerative techniques, but they use additional information to carry out the research and can be seen as evolutionary processes. This category includes the simulated annealing algorithm, which uses a thermodynamic evolutionary process, and genetic algorithms, which exploit biological evolutionary techniques.

In this chapter, we will discuss optimization techniques based on DP.

Solving the knapsack problem using Dynamic Programming

We introduced DP in the previous sections. Now the time has come to tackle a practical case. We will do this by analyzing a classic problem that has been studied for more than a century since 1897: the knapsack problem. The first to deal with it was the mathematician Tobias Dantzig, who based the name on the common problem of packing the most useful items in a knapsack without overloading it.

A problem of this type can be associated with different situations arising from real life. To better characterize the problem, we will propose another, rather unique problem. A thief goes into a house and wants to steal valuables. They put them in their knapsack, but they are limited by the weight. Each object has its own value and weight. He must choose the objects that are of value, but that do not have excessive weight. The thief must not exceed the weight limit in the knapsack, but at the same time, they must optimize their gain.

Now, we will address the problem from a mathematical point of view. Suppose we have a set (X) composed of n objects, labeled with integers from 1 to n: {$1, 2, ..., n$}. These objects meet the following conditions:

- The i-th object has weight ($p[i]$) and value ($v[i]$)
- There is only one instance of each object

We have a container that is able to carry at most a weight equal to P. We want to determine a subset ($Y \subseteq X$) of objects, such that the following criteria are met:

- The total weight of the objects in Y is $\leq P$

- The total value of the objects in Y is the maximum possible value

These last two conditions take the following algebraic forms:

- We want to determine a subset ($Y \subseteq X$) of objects such that the following conditions are met:

$$\sum_{x \in Y} p(x) \leq P$$

- We want to maximize the following overall value:

$$\sum_{x \in Y} v(x)$$

As it has been phrased, this is an optimization problem. In general, an optimization problem consists of two parts:

- A set of constraints (possibly empty) that must be respected
- An objective function that must be maximized or minimized

The mathematical formalism that we have adopted to define the problem unequivocally clarifies these two elements. Many real problems can be formulated relatively simply as optimization problems that can then be solved with a calculator. Reducing a new problem to a known problem allows the use of existing solutions.

As with most problems, even optimization problems, there are different approaches to the problem that allow us to reach the solution. Naturally, they differ with the complexity of each algorithm in terms of time and memory requirements, and in terms of the programming efforts required.

There are two versions of the problem:

- **0–1 knapsack problem**: Each item must be entirely accepted or rejected
- **Fractional knapsack problem**: We can take fractions of items

In other words, in the 0–1 knapsack problem, we are not allowed to break items. We either take the whole item or don't take it. By contrast, in a fractional knapsack, we can break items to maximize the total value of the knapsack's contents.

The problem of the knapsack can be easily applied to the problem of the optimization of a financial portfolio. In fact, we can compare the weight of the objects with the weight of the risk of the financial product that we are considering, and the value of the objects with the expected value of the financial product. Based on these assumptions, it is possible to select financial products that maximize the expected value while keeping the risk below a specific value.

Different approaches to the problem

In the following section, we will address the knapsack problem using three different approaches:

- Brute force
- Greedy algorithms
- Dynamic Programming

We will look at the strengths and weaknesses of each solution in the following sections.

Brute force

Brute force is a very general problem-solving technique that consists of systematically listing all the possible values that could represent a solution and check whether each value satisfies the conditions imposed by the problem.

A brute-force algorithm is simple to implement, and will always find a solution if it exists, but its cost is proportional to the number of possible solutions. Therefore, brute-force research is typically used when the size of the problem is limited or when hypotheses are available that allow us to reduce the set of possible solutions. The method is also used when the simplicity of implementation is more important than speed.

Brute force is the most immediate solution to the knapsack problem: examine all the possible ways to fill the knapsack, which are 2^n, and print an optimal solution (there could be more than one). This approach for $n>15$ is already very slow. This algorithm is usually based directly on the definition of the problem and on the deepening of the concepts involved.

The key elements of this straightforward algorithm are as follows:

- Enumerates every possible combination
- Chooses the best solution (we go through all combinations and find the one with the maximum value and with the total weight less than or equal to P)
- Ensures optimality
- Extremely costly in time, for large n; running time will be $O(2^n)$

The following is an example of the code that is used for solving a 0–1 knapsack problem:

```python
import itertools

objects = [(5, 18),(2, 9), (4, 12), (6,25)]

print("Items available: ",objects)
print("*********************************")

AllCombination = [comb for k in range(0, len(objects)+1) for comb in
itertools.combinations(objects, k)]

print("All combination: ")
for x in range(len(AllCombination)):
    print(AllCombination[x]),

print("*********************************")
def ConditionControl(Subset):
    totweight = totvalue = 0
    for weight, value in Subset:
        totweight += weight
        totvalue += value
    return (totvalue, totweight) if totweight <= 10 else (0, 0)
Subset = max(AllCombination, key=ConditionControl)
print("Subset selected: ",Subset)

value, weight = ConditionControl(Subset)
print("Total value: " ,value)
print("Total weight: ",weight)
```

We will analyze this code line by line. The first line loads the library:

```
import itertools
```

The `itertools` module implements a number of iterator building blocks inspired by constructs from APL, Haskell, and SML. Each has been recast in a form suitable for Python. The module standardizes a core set of fast, memory-efficient tools that are useful by themselves or in combination. Together, they form an iterator algebraic formula, making it possible to construct specialized tools succinctly and efficiently in pure Python. Then, a list of items are passed, as shown in the following code:

```
objects = [(5, 18),(2, 9), (4, 12), (6,25)]
```

Each pair represents the weight and values of each object that the thief finds in the house. These objects have been included in a list. The list type is a container that holds a number of other objects, in a given order. The list type implements the sequence protocol, and also allows you to add and remove objects from the sequence. At this point, the imported objects are printed, as follows:

```
print("Items available: ",objects)
print("*********************************")
```

The following code shows the results that are obtained:

```
Items available: [(5, 18), (2, 9), (4, 12), (6, 25)]
*********************************
```

Now it is necessary to determine all the possible combinations of objects using the following code:

```
AllCombination = [comb for k in range(0, len(objects)+1) for comb in
itertools.combinations(objects, k)]
```

To determine all combinations of objects, the `itertools.combinations()` function is used. This function returns *r* length subsequences of elements from the input iterable. Combinations are emitted in lexicographic order. So, if the input iterable is sorted, the combination tuples will be produced in a sorted order. Elements are treated as unique based on their position, not on their value. So if the input elements are unique, there will be no repeat values in each combination. All the calculated combinations are then printed, as follows:

```
print("All combination: ")
for x in range(len(AllCombination)):
    print(AllCombination[x]),
print("*********************************")
```

To print a combination for each line, a `for` statement is used. Then, some markers are printed to better present the results. Now, a new function definition is needed, as shown in the following code:

```
def ConditionControl(Subset):
    totweight = totvalue = 0
    for weight, value in Subset:
        totweight += weight
        totvalue += value
    return (totvalue, totweight) if totweight <= 10 else (0, 0)
```

The `ConditionControl()` function checks the weight. As we know, the knapsack problem must satisfy the condition where the total weight of the objects must be less than or equal to a weight established beforehand. In our case, we fix it at 10. This check will be carried out for each combination contained in the subset variable. For each combination, the total weight and the total value will be calculated. If the total weight is less than or equal to 10, then the total weight and the total value are returned. It's time to select the combination of items to take away, as shown in the following code:

```
Subset = max(AllCombination, key=ConditionControl)
```

The `max()` function is used to select the best subset. This function returns the largest item in an iterable or the largest of two or more arguments. If one positional argument is provided, it should be an iterable. The largest item in the iterable is returned. If two or more positional arguments are provided, the largest of the positional arguments is returned. There are two optional keyword-only arguments. One of these, the key argument, specifies a one-argument ordering function. A key argument `ConditionControl()` function is passed. To display the selected subset, a `print()` function is invoked, as follows:

```
print("Subset selected: ",Subset)
```

Now that the best combination has been selected, all that remains is to derive the values that are associated with it, as follows:

```
value, weight = ConditionControl(Subset)
```

To extract the total weight and the total value associated with the selected subset, the `ConditionControl()` function is invoked and the selected subset is passed. Finally, the extracted values are displayed, as follows:

```
print("Total value: " ,value)
print("Total weight: ",weight)
```

The following screenshot shows the results of the 0–1 knapsack problem solution that are returned:

```
Prompt dei comandi                                                    –  □  ×
C:\script\Python\DP>python KPBrute9GIUSEPPE2.py
Items available:  [(5, 18), (2, 9), (4, 12), (6, 25)]
*********************************
All combination:
()
((5, 18),)
((2, 9),)
((4, 12),)
((6, 25),)
((5, 18), (2, 9))
((5, 18), (4, 12))
((5, 18), (6, 25))
((2, 9), (4, 12))
((2, 9), (6, 25))
((4, 12), (6, 25))
((5, 18), (2, 9), (4, 12))
((5, 18), (2, 9), (6, 25))
((5, 18), (4, 12), (6, 25))
((2, 9), (4, 12), (6, 25))
((5, 18), (2, 9), (4, 12), (6, 25))
*********************************
Subset selected:  ((4, 12), (6, 25))
Total value:  37
Total weight:  10

C:\script\Python\DP>
```

As anticipated, the optimal solution to the problem that we have just seen is the most immediate, but also the most expensive from a computational point of view. In the following sections, we will look at another solution that is more economical in terms of calculation.

Greedy algorithms

Before introducing a greedy algorithm to find an optimal solution to the problem of the knapsack, it is appropriate to recall the main characteristics of any greedy technique. Any greedy technique proceeds iteratively. Starting from an empty solution, an element *A* is added to the partial solution under construction at each iteration. Of all the possible candidates to be added, element *A* is the most promising one—that is, if chosen, element *A* leads to a greater improvement of the objective function. It is clear that not all problems can be solved with this strategy, but only those for which it is possible to show that making the best choice at the moment leads to an optimal solution globally.

Let's look at an algorithm that simply performs the following operations:

- Discard all objects weighing more than the maximum capacity (preprocessing)
- Sort the objects for a given criterion
- Select the objects one at a time until the weight constraint is respected
- Return the value of the solution and the set of selected objects

Look at the following code which is an example of a greedy algorithm:

```
P = 10
objects = [(5, 18),(2, 9), (4, 12), (6,25)]
print("Items available: ",objects)
print("**********************************")
objects = filter(lambda x: x[0]<=P, objects)
objects = sorted(objects, key=lambda x: x[0])
weight, value, subset = 0, 0, []
print("Items filtered and sorted: ",objects)
print("**********************************")
for item in objects:
    if weight + item[0] <= P:
        weight = weight + item[0]
        value = value + item[1]
        subset.append(item)
print("Subset selected: ",subset)
print("Total value: ",value)
print("Total weight: ",weight)
```

We will analyze this code line by line. The first line sets the weight constraint:

```
P = 10
```

Then a list of items is passed, as follows:

```
objects = [(5, 18),(2, 9), (4, 12), (6,25)]
```

Each pair represents the weight and values of each object that the thief finds in the house. These objects have been included in a list. The `list` type is a container that holds a number of other objects in a given order. The `list` type implements the sequence protocol, and also allows you to add and remove objects from the sequence. At this point, the imported objects are printed, as follows:

```
print("Items available: ",objects)
print("**********************************")
```

The results are shown in the following snippet:

```
Items available: [(5, 18), (2, 9), (4, 12), (6, 25)]
**********************************
```

We used the same dataset as in the previous example to make it easier to compare the different techniques. Now, we will proceed to discard all objects weighing more than the maximum capacity, as follows:

```
objects = filter(lambda x: x[0]<=P, objects)
```

To do this, the `filter()` function is used. The `filter()` function constructs an iterator from the elements of an iterable for which a function returns `true`. In other words, this function filters the given iterable with the help of a function that tests whether each element in the iterable is `true` or not. The syntax of the `filter()` function is as follows:

```
filter(function, iterable)
```

The `filter()` function takes two parameters:

- `function`: This function tests whether elements of an `iterable` return `true` or `false`. If none, the function defaults to the `identity` function, which returns `false` if any elements are `false`.

- `iterable`: This is the iterable that is to be filtered. It could be a set, list, tuple, or container of any iterators.

In our case, the function is `lambda x: x[0]<=P`, which checks the weight limit, and the `iterable` to filter is objects. To optimize the memory space, the `objects` list is updated. We can now dedicate ourselves to the ordering of objects according to a certain criterion, as follows:

```
objects = sorted(objects, key=lambda x: x[0])
```

To sort the elements of the `objects` list in a specific order, the `sorted()` function is used. This function returns a `sorted` list from the given `iterable`. This sorts the elements of a given `iterable` in a specific order—ascending or descending. The default order is ascending. A `lambda` function that serves as a key for the sort comparison is passed. In our case, the list of `objects` is sorted in ascending order according to the first element of each pair of values that represents the weight. At this point, the data preparation phase is over and we can move on to selecting the `objects`, as follows:

```
weight, value, subset = 0, 0, []
print("Items filtered and sorted: ",objects)
print("*********************************")
```

The first line is used to initialize the three variables, `weight`, `value`, and `subset`, that represent respectively the weight, value, and subset of the objects available in the list. Then all the items that have been filtered and sorted are printed to be compared with the starting list printed previously. Now let's take a tour of the list with a `for` loop, as follows:

```
for item in objects:
    if weight + item[0] <= P:
        weight = weight + item[0]
        value = value + item[1]
        subset.append(item)
```

In every turn, an object is considered: if the total weight does not exceed the limit imposed by the condition, then the weight and the total value are updated and this object is added to the knapsack. Finally, the results are printed, as follows:

```
print("Subset selected: ",subset)
print("Total value: ",value)
print("Total weight: ",weight)
```

The results are shown in the following screenshot:

As we can see in the preceding screenshot, a result has been obtained even if it is not the best solution. In fact, compared to the solution obtained with the brute-force algorithm that we looked at in the previous section, the value of the objects inserted in the backpack is much lower (21 versus 37): algorithm improvement is necessary.

One possible improvement of the algorithm is to first perform a descending preorder of the objects based on the density of the value, calculated as follows:

$$density = \frac{value}{weight}$$

This technique is implemented in the following code:

```
P = 10
objects = [(5, 18),(2, 9), (4, 12), (6,25)]
print("Items available: ",objects)
print("**********************************")
objects = filter(lambda x: x[0]<=P, objects)
objects = sorted(objects, key=lambda x: x[1]/x[0], reverse=True)
weight, value, subset = 0, 0, []
print("Items filtered and sorted: ",objects)
print("**********************************")
for item in objects:
    if weight + item[0] <= P:
        weight = weight + item[0]
        value = value + item[1]
        subset.append(item)
print("Subset selected: ",subset)
print("Total value: " ,value)
print("Total weight: ",weight)
```

We will analyze this code line by line. As previously done, in the first line, the weight constraint has been set:

```
P = 10
```

Then a list of items is passed, as follows:

```
objects = [(5, 18),(2, 9), (4, 12), (6,25)]
```

At this point, the imported objects are printed, as follows:

```
print("Items available: ",objects)
print("**********************************")
```

The results are shown in the following code:

```
Items available: [(5, 18), (2, 9), (4, 12), (6, 25)]
********************************
```

We used the same data set as the previous example to make it easier to compare the different techniques. Now, we will proceed to discard all objects weighing more than the maximum capacity, as follows:

```
objects = filter(lambda x: x[0]<=P, objects)
```

To do this, the `filter()` function is used. To optimize the memory space, the `objects` list is updated. We can now dedicate ourselves to the ordering of objects according to a certain criterion, as follows:

```
objects = sorted(objects, key=lambda x: x[1]/x[0], reverse=True)
```

To order the `objects` list, the `sorted()` function is used. The use of the `sorted()` function is slightly different than the previous case. In this case, a `lambda` function orders the data according to a different criterion: `lambda x: x[1]/x[0]`. Finally, a descending order is imposed. At this point, the data preparation phase is over and we can move on to selecting the objects, as follows:

```
weight, value, subset = 0, 0, []
print("Items filtered and sorted: ",objects)
print("**********************************")
```

The first line is used to initialize the three variables, `weight`, `value`, and `subset`, that represent respectively the weight, value, and subset of the objects available in the list. Then all the items that have been filtered and sorted are printed to compare them with the starting list printed previously. Now let's take a tour of the list with a `for` loop, as follows:

```
for item in objects:
    if weight + item[0] <= P:
        weight = weight + item[0]
        value = value + item[1]
        subset.append(item)
```

In every turn, an object is considered: if the total weight does not exceed the limit imposed by the condition, then the weight and the total value are updated and this object is added to the knapsack. Finally, the results are printed, as follows:

```
print("Subset selected: ",subset)
print("Total value: ",value)
print("Total weight: ",weight)
```

The results are shown in the following screenshot:

```
C:\script\Python\DP>python KPGreedy2.py
Items available:  [(5, 18), (2, 9), (4, 12), (6, 25)]
************************************
Items filtered and sorted:  [(2, 9), (6, 25), (5, 18), (4, 12)]
************************************
Subset selected:  [(2, 9), (6, 25)]
Total value:  34
Total weight:  8

C:\script\Python\DP>
```

From the analysis of the preceding screenshot, we can see that not even in this case have we obtained the optimal solution, but on the other hand, a decidedly greater value has been selected (34 versus 21).

Dynamic Programming

In the previous sections, we have seen how the knapsack problem can be solved through different approaches. In particular, we learned to treat this problem with an algorithm called brute force: in this case, we obtained the optimal solution at an extremely heavy computational cost. On the other hand, the greedy solution gave us a lighter algorithm from a computational point of view, but did not allow us to obtain the optimal solution. A solution that combines both these needs—an optimal solution and a fast algorithm—can be provided by DP.

As we said in the section on DP, we subdivide an optimization problem into simpler subproblems and store the solution for each subproblem so that each subproblem is solved only once. The idea behind the method that we will use is to calculate solutions to subproblems once and store the solutions in a table so that they can be reused (repeatedly) later.

The following is a knapsack problem solution using DP:

```
def KnapSackTable(weight, value, P, n):
    T = [[0 for w in range(P + 1)]
             for i in range(n + 1)]
    for i in range(n + 1):
        for w in range(P + 1):
            if i == 0 or w == 0:
```

```
                T[i][w] = 0
            elif weight[i - 1] <= w:
                T[i][w] = max(value[i - 1]
                              + T[i - 1][w - weight[i - 1]],
                                      T[i - 1][w])
            else:
                T[i][w] = T[i - 1][w]
    res = T[n][P]
    print("Total value: " ,res)
    w = P
    totweight=0
    for i in range(n, 0, -1):
        if res <= 0:
            break
        if res == T[i - 1][w]:
            continue
        else:
            print("Item selected: ",weight[i - 1],value[i - 1])
            totweight += weight[i - 1]
            res = res - value[i - 1]
            w = w - weight[i - 1]

    print("Total weight: ",totweight)

objects = [(5, 18),(2, 9), (4, 12), (6,25)]
print("Items available: ",objects)
print("**********************************")
value = []
weight = []
for item in objects:
    weight.append(item[0])
    value.append(item[1])
P = 10
n = len(value)
KnapSackTable(weight, value, P, n)
```

We will analyze this code line by line. This algorithm starts with the definition of a
`KnapSackTable()` function that will choose the optimal combination of the objects
respecting the two constraints imposed by the problem: the total weight of the objects equal
to 10, and the maximum value of the chosen objects, as shown in the following code:

```
def KnapSackTable(weight, value, P, n):
    T = [[0 for w in range(P + 1)]
            for i in range(n + 1)]
```

To start, we define and initialize the table that will contain the values. The table is built in a bottom-up manner, row by row, as shown in the following table:

i \ w	w=0	1	2	3	...	...	10
i= 0	0	0	0	0	...	...	0
1	0						
2	0						
3	0						
4	0						

Then we set an iterative loop on all objects and on all `weight` values, as follows:

```
for i in range(n + 1):
    for w in range(P + 1):
        if i == 0 or w == 0:
            T[i][w] = 0
        elif weight[i - 1] <= w:
            T[i][w] = max(value[i - 1] + T[i - 1][w - weight[i - 1]], T[i -
1][w])
        else:
            T[i][w] = T[i - 1][w]
```

The first `If` statement constructs the first row and the first column of the table. In particular, we initialize the first line to 0, which corresponds to the case in which, for different transportable weights, we have no object (`T[0, w] = 0`). Initialize the first column to 0, which corresponds to the case in which, for several possible objects, I have a backpack of zero capacity (`T [i, 0] = 0`). The `elif` option contains a further check on the weight of the current object. If the control is satisfied, update the current cell according to the following formula: `T [i] [w] = max (value [i - 1] + T [i - 1] [w - weight [i - 1]], T [i - 1] [w])`. Finally, the `else` option does not consider the current object and places it equal to the value it had on the previous line. Once the last cell of the last row of the table has been reached, we can memorize the result obtained, which represents the maximum value of the objects that can be carried in the knapsack, as follows:

```
res = T[n][P]
print("Total value: " ,res)
```

The procedure followed so far does not indicate which subset provides the optimal solution. We must extract this information using a set procedure. We will only analyze the last column of the table (w = P), and we will then run through it from the last value down to the top one.

If the current element is the same as the previous one, we will move on to the next one; otherwise, the current object will be included in the knapsack. This is shown in the following code:

```
w = P
totweight=0
for i in range(n, 0, -1):
    if res <= 0:
        break
```

If the current element is the same as the previous one, we will move on to the next one, as follows:

```
if res == T[i - 1][w]:
    continue
```

It it is not the same, then the current object will be included in the knapsack, and this item will be printed, as follows:

```
else:
    print("Item selected: ",weight[i - 1],value[i - 1])
    totweight += weight[i - 1]
    res = res - value[i - 1]
    w = w - weight[i - 1]
```

Finally, the total included weight is printed, as follows:

```
print("Total weight: ",totweight)
```

In this way, we have defined the function that allows us to build the table. Now we have to define the input variables and pass them to the function, as follows:

```
objects = [(5, 18),(2, 9), (4, 12), (6,25)]
print("Items available: ",objects)
print("**********************************")
```

Now the objects are defined and printed. Let's initialize two variables using the following code:

```
value = []
weight = []
```

At this point, we need to extract the `weight` and `value` variable values from the objects. We put them in a separate array to better understand the steps, as follows:

```
for item in objects:
    weight.append(item[0])
    value.append(item[1])
```

Finally, the total weight that can be carried by the knapsack and the number of available items is set, as follows:

```
P = 10
n = len(value)
```

We just have to invoke the function and pass the data we have just defined, as follows:

```
KnapSackTable(weight, value, P, n)
```

The results are shown in the following screenshot:

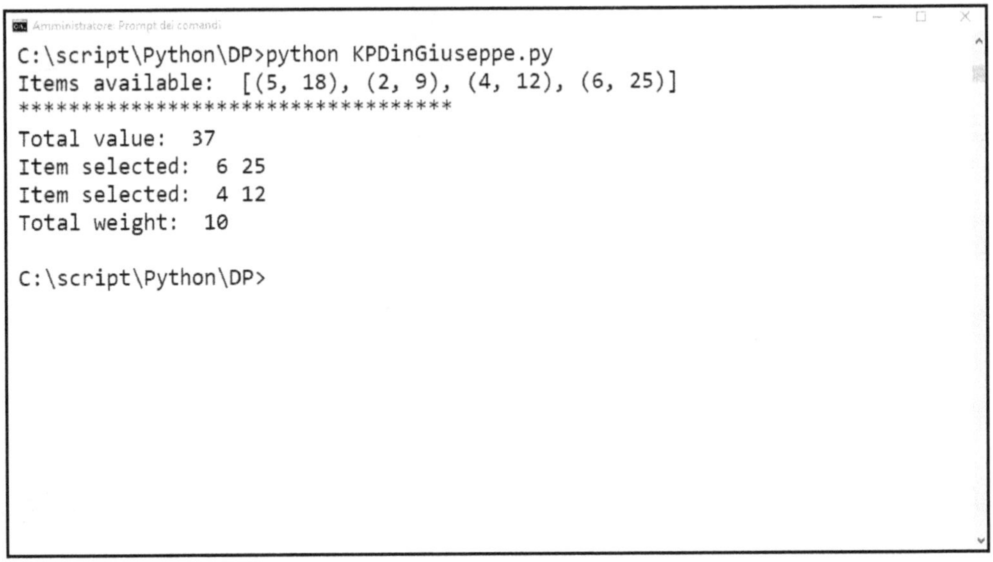

```
Amministratore: Prompt dei comandi                                    —  □  ×
C:\script\Python\DP>python KPDinGiuseppe.py
Items available:  [(5, 18), (2, 9), (4, 12), (6, 25)]
*********************************
Total value:  37
Item selected:  6 25
Item selected:  4 12
Total weight:  10

C:\script\Python\DP>
```

The DP algorithm allowed us to obtain the optimal solution, saving on computational costs.

Summary

In this chapter, we have addressed the basic concepts of the optimization techniques. To start, we learned the essential contents underlying the DP. With DP, we subdivide an optimization problem into simpler subproblems. We then proceed to calculate the solutions of all possible subproblems, and starting from subsolutions, we obtain new subsolutions, and carry on until we solve the original problem.

Then, we looked at the difference between recursion and memoization. In DP, this does not happen: we memorize the solution of these subproblems so that we do not have to solve them again; this is called memoization. The idea behind this method is to calculate solutions to subproblems once and store the solutions in a table so that they can be reused (repeatedly) later. To better understand this technique, we looked at a practical case: the calculation of the factorial of a number. This problem was dealt with by applying both methods: recursion and memoization. The savings from the computational point of view were confirmed.

After this, we looked at the optimization of a financial portfolio. The management of financial portfolios is an activity that aims to seek a combination of financial products that best meets the investor's needs; this requires an overall assessment of various characteristics, such as risk appetite, expected returns, and investor consumption, as well as an estimate of future returns and risk.

Finally, we learned the basics of the knapsack problem and how to apply them to an optimal portfolio selection. This problem was addressed through three different approaches: brute force, greedy algorithms, and DP. For each approach, a solution algorithm was provided and the results were compared.

4
Forecasting Stock Market Prices

Humans have always tried to predict the future. Forecasting has been, therefore, one of the most studied techniques over time. Forecasts cover several fields: weather forecasts, economic and political events, sports results, and more. Because we try to predict so many different events, there are a variety of ways in which predictions can be developed. Monte Carlo methods for estimating the value function and discovering excellent policies do not require the presence of a model of the environment. They are able to learn through the use of an agent's experience alone or from samples of state sequences, actions, and rewards obtained from the interactions between agent and environment. The experience can be acquired by the agent in line with the learning process, or it can be emulated by a previously populated dataset. Stock prices change on a daily basis, changing the value of our investments. It's possible to monitor these changes through a calculation of daily stock returns. The daily return measures the change in a stock's price as a percentage of the previous day's closing price. In this chapter, we will learn how to use Monte Carlo methods for forecasting stock market prices.

We will cover the following topics:

- The basic concepts of forecasting
- The model-free approach
- Estimation of action values
- Off-policy prediction and control
- Monte Carlo methods
- Forecasting stock market prices

By the end of this chapter, the reader will learn the basic concepts of forecasting techniques, and understand the model-free approach to deal with **reinforcement learning (RL)** problems. The reader will also learn how to estimate action values, discover how an off-policy learner learns the value of the optimal policy regardless of an agent's actions, and learn how to apply Monte Carlo methods to forecast environment behavior.

Monte Carlo methods

As we said in Chapter 1, *Overview of Keras Reinforcement Learning*, the goal of RL is to learn a policy that, for each state *s* in which the system is located, indicates to the agent an action to maximize the total reinforcement received during the entire action sequence. To do this, a value function estimation is required, which represents how good a state is for an agent. It is equal to the total reward expected for an agent from the status *s*. The value function depends on the policy with which the agent selects the actions to be performed.

Monte Carlo methods for estimating the value function and discovering excellent policies do not require the presence of a model of the environment. They are able to learn through the use of the agent's experience alone or from samples of state sequences, actions, and rewards obtained from interactions between agent and environment. The experience can be acquired by the agent in line with the learning process, or it can be emulated by a previously populated dataset. The possibility of gaining experience during learning (online learning) is interesting because it allows the obtaining of excellent behavior even in the absence of a priori knowledge of the dynamics of the environment. Even learning through an already-populated experience dataset can be interesting because, if combined with online learning, it makes automatic policy improvement induced by others' experiences possible.

To solve RL problems, Monte Carlo methods estimate the value function on the basis of the total sum of rewards obtained on average in past episodes. This assumes that the experience is divided into episodes, and that all episodes are composed of a finite number of transitions. This is because, in Monte Carlo methods, the policy update and value function estimate take place after an episode is completed. Indeed, Monte Carlo methods iteratively estimate policy and value functions. In this case, however, each iteration cycle is equivalent to completing an episode. So, the policy update and value function estimate occur episode by episode, as we just said.

Historical background

According to some, the historical origins of Monte Carlo methods could be dated back to 1700 D.C., well before the advent of computers. In 1777, the French mathematician George Louis Leclerc de Buffon describes in his work, *Essai d'arithmetique morale,* an experiment to estimate value through a random simulation based on the launch of a needle, obtaining a result of good numerical precision for the time. Suppose we have a floor made of parallel strips of wood, each of the same width and greater than the length of a needle, and we drop that needle onto the floor. What is the probability that the needle will land on a line between two strips? In the following diagram, two possible events are shown:

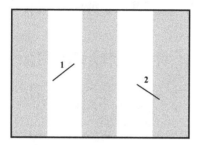

Needle 1 does not lie across a line, while needle 2 needle lies across a line. The solution can be used to design a Monte Carlo method for approximating the number π.

But the true origin of the method, at least for what remains in publications, is due to research conducted during World War II in the Los Alamos laboratories. At Los Alamos, in the 1950s, a group of researchers led by Nicholas Metropolis, including John von Neumann and Stanislaw Ulam, developed the Monte Carlo method. They participated in the Manhattan Project for the study of the dynamics of nuclear explosions. But, these studies had already been initiated by Enrico Fermi (technical director of the Manhattan Project), who at the beginning of the 1930s claimed to use estimates obtained with statistical sampling techniques for the study of neutron motion. In the context of the war, the application of the Monte Carlo method is justified in the need, during an aerial bombardment, to select targets to hit in a large area in a way that is not totally casual. The name "Monte Carlo" was given by Nicholas Constantine Metropolis in reference to the capital of the Principality of Monaco, Monte Carlo, where the famous casino is located, where randomness is the essential component of every activity.

So, the fathers of this method seem to be the people who have made the history of modern physics:

- Enrico Fermi (1901-1954), Italian physicist, winner of the Nobel Prize in Physics in 1938, is remembered mainly for his studies in the field of nuclear physics.
- John von Neumann (1903-1957), Hungarian mathematician, physicist, and computer scientist is known as a multifaceted personality. His main contributions were in the fields of mathematics, economics, information technology, and physics. He is considered the father of modern computers.
- Stanislaw Ulam (1909-1984), Polish mathematician, is known above all for his contribution in the field of impulse nuclear propulsion.

Basic concepts of the Monte Carlo simulation

In everyday life, we often need to know the probability of a certain event, but there are too many variables that influence it and it is not possible to perform analytical calculations. The solution to this problem requires the use of simulated sampling methods, that is, simulating the situation in which the probability of a certain event is to be calculated. Stochastic simulation is carried out by reproducing the mechanism, replacing an analytical—difficult to carry out—with an empirical observation of the phenomenon and taking from it information that is not analytically detectable. This simulation is called the Monte Carlo method.

So, the Monte Carlo method consists of looking for the solution to a problem, representing it as a parameter of a hypothetical population, and estimating this parameter by examining a sample of the population obtained through sequences of random numbers.

The Monte Carlo method is a numerical procedure used in physics to reproduce the state of a system. In general, this method allows the generation of events according to an appropriate probability distribution, so it can be applied to any phenomenon whose probability of occurrence is known.

For example, suppose that I is the unknown value to be calculated and can be interpreted as the average value of a random variable, X. The Monte Carlo method consists, in this case, of estimating I by calculating the average of a constructed sample by determining N values of X; this is achieved using a procedure involving the use of **random numbers**, as shown in the following diagram:

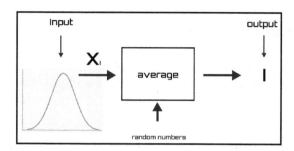

The Monte Carlo method is part of the family of non-parametric statistical methods. It is useful to overcome the computational problems related to the exact tests, which—for large samples—generate a number of excessive permutations.

The method is used to derive estimates through simulations. It is based on an algorithm that generates a series of uncorrelated numbers, which follow the probability distribution that is supposed to have the phenomenon to be investigated.

The Monte Carlo simulation calculates a series of possible realizations of the phenomenon under investigation, with the weight of the probability of such event, trying to explore the whole space of the parameters of the phenomenon. Once this representative sample has been calculated, the simulation performs measurements of the quantities of interest on this sample. The Monte Carlo simulation is well-executed if the average value of these measurements on system achievements converges to the true value.

Monte Carlo applications

The Monte Carlo simulation is suitable for solving two orders of problems:

- Probabilistic problems in which phenomena are involved related to the stochastic fluctuation of random variables
- Deterministic problems, completely devoid of aleatory components , but whose solution strategy can be reformulated in such a way as to be equivalent to determining the expected value of one function of stochastic variables

The conditions necessary for the application of the Monte Carlo method are independence and the analogy of experiments. By independence, we mean that the results of each repetition of the experiment should not be able to influence each other. By analogy, it is understood that, for the observation of the feature, the same experiment is repeated n times. In the following sections, we will see an application of the method.

Numerical integration using the Monte Carlo method

Monte Carlo simulations are nothing more than a numerical technique for calculating integrals. The Monte Carlo algorithm is a numerical method that is used to find solutions to mathematical problems, which can have many variables and cannot be solved easily, for example, integral calculus. The efficiency of this method increases compared to other methods when the size of the problem grows.

In the simplest cases, the integration operation can be carried out through the use of methods such as integration by parts, substitution, and series. In the less immediate situations, however, it is necessary to resort to the use of a computer, and the Monte Carlo simulation offers a simple solution, especially useful in cases of multidimensional integrals. It is, however, important to note that the result provided by this simulation represents only an approximation of the integral and not its precise value.

Let an integral I of the function f be limited to the interval $[a, b]$:

$$I = \int_a^b f(x)dx$$

Let U be an upper bound of the function f on the interval $[a, b]$. To delimit the approximation, it's necessary to draw a basic rectangle $[a, b]$ with the height, U. In this way, in fact, the area subtended by the function $f(x)$, that is, the integral of $f(x)$, will certainly be smaller than the area of the aforementioned rectangle. Now comes into play the Monte Carlo simulation. We define the following variables:

- $x \in [a,b]$
- $y \in [0,U]$

Here, x and y are both random numbers.

Now, consider a point in the Cartesian coordinate plane $(x; y)$. What interests us is to know the probability that this point is inside the graph of the function f, that is, the probability that $y \leq f(x)$. This probability coincides with the relationship between the following:

- The area subtended by the function f, which coincides with the definite integral I
- Area A of the rectangle with the base $[a, b]$ and height U: $A= (b-a)U$

The following diagram shows the area subtended by the function f and the area A of the rectangle with the base $[a, b]$ and height U:

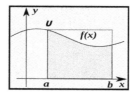

Therefore, we can write the following:

$$P(y \leq f(x)) = \frac{I}{A} = \frac{I}{(b-a)U}$$

Since the goal is to find I, the only unknown term is $P(y \leq f(x))$. The Monte Carlo simulation estimates this probability. N pairs of random numbers are generated (x_i, y_i), with the following:

- $i = 1, \ldots, n$
- $x_i \, \varepsilon \, [a, b]$
- $y_i \, \varepsilon \, [0, U]$

Based on the generation of such two-dimensional vectors of random numbers, there will be a certain amount of cases for which $y_i \leq f(x_i)$. We will indicate this quantity with R and this varies with the variations of the generated vectors. It is therefore good to note that this is not a certain number, but an approximation whose accuracy increases with the increase in the number of generated vectors. The approximation of $P(y \leq f(x))$ will therefore be equal to the following:

$$\rho = \frac{R}{n}$$

Having found the value of the last unknown, it is possible to proceed with the estimate of the integral I:

$$I \cong \rho(b-a)U = \frac{R}{n}(b-a)U = \frac{R}{n}A$$

The problem, from the mathematical point of view, is defined, and now we have to implement a Python code that follows this procedure. The following is the code:

```
import random as rm
rm.seed(3)

f = lambda x: x**2
```

```
a = 0.0
b = 3.0

NumSteps = 1000000
ymin = f(a)
ymax = ymin
for i in range(NumSteps):
    x = a + (b - a) * float(i) / NumSteps
    y = f(x)
    if y < ymin: ymin = y
    if y > ymax: ymax = y

A = (b - a) * (ymax - ymin)
n = 1000000
R = 0
for j in range(n):
    x = a + (b - a) * rm.random()
    y = ymin + (ymax - ymin) * rm.random()
    if abs(y) <= abs(f(x)):
        if f(x) > 0 and y > 0 and y <= f(x):
            R += 1
            if f(x) < 0 and y < 0 and y >= f(x):
                R -= 1

NumIntegral = R / n * A
print ("Numerical integration = " + str(NumIntegral))
```

We will analyze this code line by line. The first line loads the library:

```
import random as rm
```

The `random` module in Python contains a number of random number generators for various distributions. For integers, there is a uniform selection from a range. For sequences, there is a uniform selection of a random element, a function to generate a random permutation of a list in-place, and a function for random sampling without replacement. Two functions are used from this module: `seed` and `random`. The `seed` function sets the seed of random number generator, which is useful for creating simulations or random objects that can be reproduced. You have to use this function every time you want to get a reproducible random result. In this case, the random numbers are the same, and they would continue to be the same no matter how far out in the sequence we go. Each seed value will correspond to a sequence of values generated for a given random number generator. That is, if you supply the same seed twice, you get the same sequence of numbers twice. The `random` function returns the next random floating point number in the range (0.0, 1.0).

After correctly importing the library, we pass to analyze the individual operations. Let's start with setting `seed`:

```
seed(3)
```

Recall that, if you supply the same seed twice, you get the same sequence of numbers twice. Let's move on to define the function used to calculate the integral:

```
f = lambda x: x**2
```

A simple quadratic function is used. Now, we will define the integration interval:

```
a = 0.0
b = 3.0
```

Let's now fix the number of steps in which to divide the integration interval:

```
NumSteps = 1000000
```

The greater the number, the better the simulation will be, even if the algorithm becomes slower. Now, we evaluate the function at the end of each step:

```
ymin = f(a)
ymax = ymin
for i in range(NumSteps):
    x = a + (b - a) * float(i) / numSteps
    y = f(x)
    if y < ymin: ymin = y
    if y > ymax: ymax = y
```

Without this, we have all the data to proceed: we can apply the Monte Carlo method. To start, calculate the area of the rectangle:

```
A = (b - a) * (ymax - ymin)
```

Now, we set the number of pairs of random numbers that we have to generate:

```
n = 1000000
```

Finally, we calculate `R`:

```
R = 0
for j in range(n):
    x = a + (b - a) * random.random()
    y = ymin + (ymax - ymin) * random.random()
    if abs(y) <= abs(f(x)):
        if f(x) > 0 and y > 0 and y <= f(x):
            R += 1
```

```
if f(x) < 0 and y < 0 and y >= f(x):
    R -= 1
```

We just have to calculate the numerical integral and print it:

```
NumIntegral = R / n * A
print ("Numerical integration = " + str(NumIntegral))
```

The result is shown as follows:

```
Numerical integration = 9.007802984367009
```

From the integral calculation, we know that the exact value is 9 so the solution obtained works (error = 0.08%).

In summary, the Monte Carlo integration estimates the value of an integral using random sampling. This algorithm gives the correct value of an integral on average, and only requires a function to be evaluated at random points on its domain. This method is really useful in cases of functions with discontinuities—functions that are impossible to integrate directly. The error of estimate results independent of dimensionality of integrand, and show a faster convergence in the estimation of high-dimensional integrals compared to non-random quadrature methods. In return, it suffers from noise due to variance in estimates; to reduce this problem, more samples and the variance reduction method can help.

Monte Carlo for prediction and control

So far, we have seen the problem-solving approach of Monte Carlo methods. But, our goal is to manage the interaction with the environment with this technology. In the previous sections, we said that Monte Carlo methods do not require the presence of a model of the environment to estimate the value function and discover excellent policies. This means that Monte Carlo is model-free: no knowledge of **Markov Decision Process** (**MDP**) transitions/rewards is required. So, we do not need to have previously modeled the environment, but the necessary information will be collected during interaction with the environment (online learning). Monte Carlo methods learn directly from episodes of experience, where an episode of experience is a series of tuples (state, action, reward, and next state).

 Monte Carlo prediction is used to estimate the value function. Monte Carlo control is used to optimize the value function so as to make the value function more accurate than the estimation.

In general, Monte Carlo methods rely on repeated random sampling to obtain numerical results. To do this, they use randomness to solve deterministic problems. In our case, we will use random sampling of states and action-state pairs, we will look at the rewards, and then we will review the policy in an iterative way. The iteration of the process will converge on optimal policy as we explore every possible action-state pair.

For example, we could use the following procedure:

- We assign a reward of +1 to a right action, -1 to a wrong action, and 0 to a draw
- We establish a table in which each key corresponds to a particular state-action pair and each value is the value of that pair. This represents the average reward received for that action in that state

To solve the RL problems, Monte Carlo methods estimate the value function on the basis of the total sum of rewards, obtained on average in past episodes. This assumes that the experience is divided into episodes, and that all episodes are composed of a finite number of transitions. This is because, in Monte Carlo methods, the estimate of the new values and the modification of the policy takes place once an episode is completed. Monte Carlo methods iteratively estimate policy and value function. In this case, however, each iteration cycle is equivalent to completing an episode—the new estimates of **policy** and **value function** occur episode by episode, as shown in the following diagram:

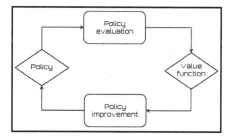

The workflow includes the sampling of experience episodes and the subsequent updating of estimates at the end of each episode. Because of the many random decisions within each episode, these methods have a high variance, although these are unbiased.

You may recall two processes, called **policy evaluation** and **policy improvement**:

- Policy evaluation algorithms consist of applying an iterative method to the resolution of the Bellman equation. Since convergence is guaranteed to us only for $k \rightarrow \infty$, we must be content to have good approximations by imposing a stopping condition.
- Policy improvement algorithms improve policy based on current values.

As we said, the new estimates of policy and value function occur episode by episode; so the policy is updated only at the end of an episode.

The following shows a pseudocode for Monte Carlo policy evaluation:

```
Initialize
    arbitrary policy π
    arbitrary state-value function
Repeat
    generate episode using π
    for each state s in episode
        the received reinforcement R is added to the set of
        reinforcers obtained so far
        estimate the value function on the basis on the average
        of the total sum of rewards obtained
```

Usually, the term "Monte Carlo" is used for estimation methods, the operations of which involve random components; in this case, the term "Monte Carlo" refers to RL methods based on total reward averages. Unlike DP methods, which calculate the values for each state, Monte Carlo methods calculate values for each state-action pair because, in the absence of a model, only state values are not sufficient to decide which action is best performed in a certain state.

Amazon stock price prediction using Python

The stock market forecast has always been a very popular topic: this is because stock market trends involve a truly impressive turnover. The interest that this topic arouses in public opinion is clearly linked to the opportunity to get rich through good forecasts of a stock market title. A positive difference between the purchased stock price and that of the sold stock price entails a gain on the part of the investor. But, as we know, the performance of the stock market depends on multiple factors. In this section, we'll see how Monte Carlo methods can be applied to predict the future stock price of a very popular company: I refer to Amazon, the US e-commerce company, based in Seattle, Washington, which is the largest internet company in the world.

Amazon has been listed on Wall Street since 1997 with the AMZN symbol; its title is included in the NASDAQ index, which gathers companies in technology and IT sectors. Founded in the 1990s, Amazon was among the first major companies to sell products using the internet; its business strategy has been set with a long-term perspective, with the proviso from the beginning that it won't generate profits for several years and instead focusing on a rapid expansion of the business and the conquest of new market areas.

To analyze the performance of Amazon stock prices, we will use the data relating to the stock prices in the time interval from 2000-06-05 to 2018-06-05 on NASDAQ GS stock quote (it is possible to set a different interval from the one displayed by default).

This data was downloaded from the Yahoo Finance website at the following web address:
`https://finance.yahoo.com/quote/AMZN/history/`

The following screenshot shows the Yahoo Finance website:

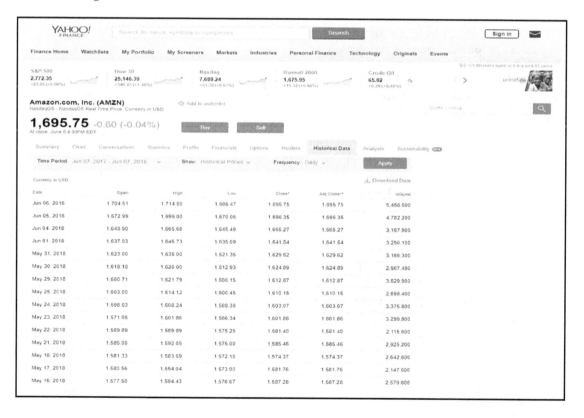

The file downloaded (in `.csv` format) contains the following features:

- **Date**: Date of quote
- **Open**: Open price
- **High**: High price
- **Low**: Low price
- **Close**: Close price adjusted for splits
- **Adj Close**: Close price adjusted for both dividends and splits
- **Volume**: Exchange volume

Data is available in the CSV file named `AMZN.csv`. To start, let's see how to import data into Python. The first thing to do is to import the library that we will use:

```
import pandas as pd
```

With this code, we imported the `pandas` library. Now, let's see how to import the data contained in the dataset in Python:

```
dataset = pd.read_csv('AMZN.csv',header=0, usecols=['Date',
'Close'],parse_dates=True,index_col='Date')
```

To import a dataset, we used the `read_csv` module of the `pandas` library. The `read_csv` method loads the data in a pandas `DataFrame` we named `dataset`. The following arguments are used:

- `header`: The row number(s) used as the column names and the start of the data. Default behavior is to infer the column names; if no names are passed the behavior is identical to `header=0` and column names are inferred from the first line of the file. If column names are passed explicitly, then the behavior is identical to `header=None`.
- `usecols`: This returns a subset of the columns. If list-like, all elements must either be positional (that is, integer indices into the document columns) or strings that correspond to column names, provided either by the user in names or inferred from the document header row(s). In our case, we have collected only two columns (`Date` and `Close`).
- `parse_dates`: This is a Boolean. If `True`, try parsing the index.
- `index_col`: This is the column to use as the row labels of the `DataFrame`. If a sequence is given, a MultiIndex is used.

The data necessary for the simulation have been correctly imported; we can proceed with our analysis.

Exploratory analysis

Before starting with data prediction using the Monte Carlo method, we will conduct an exploratory analysis to understand how the data is distributed and extract preliminary knowledge. To extract preliminary information about the imported dataset, we can invoke the `info()` function:

```
print(dataset.info())
```

This function prints information about a `DataFrame`, including the index and column `dtypes`, non-null values, and memory usage. The following results are returned:

```
<class 'pandas.core.frame.DataFrame'>
DatetimeIndex: 4529 entries, 2000-06-05 to 2018-06-05
Data columns (total 1 columns):
Close     4529 non-null float64
dtypes: float64(1)
memory usage: 70.8 KB
```

From the analysis of the results obtained, we can see that the dataset contains `4529` observations of Amazon stock prices in the period from `2000-06-05` to `2018-06-05`. To display on video the first five rows of the imported `DataFrame`, we can use the `head()` function, as follows:

```
print(dataset.head())
```

This function returns the first *n* rows for the object based on position. It is useful for quickly testing if your object has the right type of data in it. By default (if *n* is omitted), the first five rows are displayed. The following results are returned:

```
              Close
Date
2000-06-05   54.5000
2000-06-06   50.5625
2000-06-07   51.8125
2000-06-08   51.875020
00-06-09   52.1875
```

To get a preview of the data contained in it, we can calculate a series of basic statistics. To do so, we will use the `describe()` function in the following way:

```
print(dataset.describe())
```

This function generates descriptive statistics that summarize the central tendency, dispersion, and shape of a dataset's distribution, excluding NaN (not a number) values. It analyzes both numeric and object series, as well as `DataFrame` column sets of mixed data types. The output will vary depending on what is provided. The following results are returned:

```
              Close
count   4529.000000
mean     243.952496
std      323.696425
min        5.970000
25%       38.740002
50%       87.269997
75%      306.540009
max     1696.349976
```

From an initial analysis of the results obtained, we can see that Amazon stock prices have made a noticeable change over the last 18 years. In fact, the minimum value is equal to $5.97, while the maximum value is equal to $1696.35. To confirm this, the standard deviation values are high, indicating a high volatility: the value of the examined data deviates significantly from its average.

After having taken a look at the content of the dataset, we are going to perform an initial visual exploratory analysis. To do it, we will use the `matplotlib` library:

```
import matplotlib.pyplot as plt
```

So, the `pyplot` module is imported from the `matplotlib` library, and we just have to draw the graph:

```
plt.figure(figsize=(10,5))
plt.plot(dataset)
plt.show()
```

Three functions have been used: `figure()`, `plot()`, and `show()`. Let's analyze the operation in detail. The first one creates a new figure, empty for now, and we need to set the size of the frame that will contain it. In fact, we use the `figsize` parameter, which sets the width and height in inches. Then, the `plot()` function is used, which plots the dataset, and finally the `show()` function is used to display the plot. The `show()` function, when running in IPython with its PyLab mode, displays all figures and returns to the IPython prompt.

In non-interactive mode, it displays all figures and block until the figures have been closed; in interactive mode, it has no effect unless figures were created prior to a change from non-interactive to interactive mode (not recommended). In that case, it displays the figures but does not block. In the following graph, Amazon stock prices from 2000-06-05 to 2018-06-05 are shown:

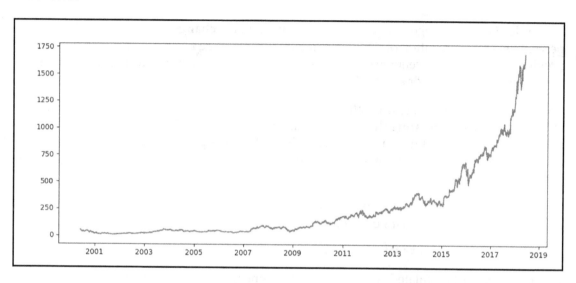

From the analysis of the previous graph, we can see that prices have increased considerably over time. In particular, starting from **2015**, this increase has shown an exponential trend. But, let's try to deepen the change that Amazon stock has recorded over time.

Very often, it is interesting to study the evolution of a phenomenon not only through the graph of its time series but also by making comparisons between the intensity of the phenomenon at different times, that is, calculating the variations of intensity from one period to another. Furthermore, it can be interesting to analyze the trend of the variations of the phenomenon occurred between adjoining periods of time.

We indicate with $Y1, ..., Y_t, ..., Y_n$ a time series. A time series is the chronological recording of experimental observations of a variable, such as price trends, stock market indices, spreads, and unemployment rates. It is therefore a succession of data ordered over time from which we want to extract information for the characterization of the phenomenon under observation, and for the prediction of future values.

The variation occurred between two different times (let's indicate them with t and $t + 1$) and can be measured using the following ratio:

$$\frac{Y_{t+1} - Y_t}{Y_t}$$

This index is a percentage ratio and is called a **percentage change**. In particular, this is the percentage rate of variation of the phenomenon Y of the time $t + 1$ with respect to the previous time t. The percentage change method gives a more precise description as to how the data has changed over a period of time.

This method is used both to track the prices of individual securities and of large market indices, as well as comparing the values of different currencies. Balance sheets with comparative financial statements will generally include the prices of specific assets at different points in time, along with the percentage changes over the accompanying periods of time.

To calculate percentage change in Python, we will use the `pct_change()` function. This function returns percent change over a given number of periods:

```
DataPctChange = dataset.pct_change()
```

What we have just calculated coincides with the concept of return: why do we want to use the returns instead of prices? The benefit of using returns, versus prices, is normalization: measuring all variables in a comparable metric, hence enabling evaluation of analytic relationships among two or more variables despite originating from a price series of unequal values. This is a requirement for many multidimensional statistical analysis and machine learning techniques.

In particular, we will calculate the logarithm of returns. Also, in this case, we have clear benefits:

- **Log-normality**: If we assume that prices are distributed log normally, then $log(1 + ri)$ is conveniently normally distributed
- **Approximate raw-log equality**: When returns are very small results, $log(1 + r)$ is roughly equal to r
- Logarithmic returns are additive over time

To calculate the logarithm of returns, we will use the `log()` function from numpy. First, we import the numpy library:

```
import numpy as np
```

Then, we apply the `log` function, as follows:

```
LogReturns = np.log(1 + DataPctChange)
```

To get a preview of what we've got, let's print the tail:

```
print(LogReturns.tail(10))
```

The `tail()` function returns the last *n* rows from the object based on position. It is useful for quickly verifying data, for example, after sorting or appending rows. The following values are returned (the last ten rows of the `LogReturns` object):

```
Date
2018-05-22  -0.002564
2018-05-23   0.012855
2018-05-24   0.000755
2018-05-25   0.004407
2018-05-29   0.001688
2018-05-30   0.007425
2018-05-31   0.002907
2018-06-01   0.007288
2018-06-04   0.014352
2018-06-05   0.018492
```

Now, we will draw a diagram with the logarithm of the returns we have calculated:

```
plt.figure(figsize=(10,5))
plt.plot(LogReturns)
plt.show()
```

As we have already done previously, we first set the dimensions of the graph, then we plotted the graph, and finally we visualized it. The following graph shows the logarithm of the returns:

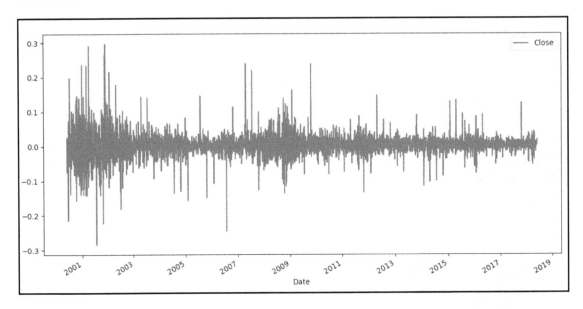

Analyzing the previous graph, we can see that the returns are normally distributed and have a stable mean.

The Geometric Brownian motion model

The geometric Brownian motion is a stochastic process defined in the continuum in which the logarithm of the random variable over time follows a Brownian motion. This process is particularly important in the financial sector, particularly in the option pricing, as the **Black-Scholes-Merton (BSM)** model assumes that the price of the underlying asset follows such a process.

This model takes its name from the botanist Robert Brown (1828), who observed in 1827 that particles of pollen suspended in water moved irregularly on a microscopic scale. Later, it was discovered that the movement was due to the water molecules that accidentally hit the pollen particles and put them in motion. Brown posed the problem of describing the observed movement mathematically, but did not solve the problem alone. Several scientists list made further simplifications to the model. These included L. Gouy, A. Einstein, M. Smoluchowski, P. Langevin, and N. Wiener.

The Brownian motion has the following properties:

- **Continuity**: $B(t)$ has a continuous path and B $(t=0) = 0$.
- **Normality**: The increment of the Brownian process in the interval of time of length t between t and t-1 is Bt-Bt-1. This increment is normally distributed with a mean of zero and variance equal to the time increment, dt.
- **Markov property**: The conditional distribution $B(t)$ given information up to time $t<t$-1 depends only on $B(t$-1$)$.

The starting point of this model is the hypothesis that, under a particular probability measure, the expected return of the underlying asset (the asset on which the derivative depends, that is, the security whose price is based on the market value of another financial instrument) is equal to the non-risky interest rate r.

This model lends itself well to modeling the returns on a logarithmic scale (log returns) of an asset. Suppose we observe a title at the instants: t (0), t (1) ,.., t (n). We indicate with s (i) = S (ti) the value of an asset at the time, $t(i)$.

Returns are then given using the following:

$$y(i) = [s(i) - s(i - 1)]/s(i - 1), \ i = 1, 2, \ldots, n$$

Passing to the logarithmic scale, we have the following:

$$x(i) = \ln s(i) - \ln s(i - 1), \ i = 1, 2, \ldots, n$$

If prices are not very variable, that is, s (i) - s (i - 1) is kept small, the difference between x (i) and y (i) is not appreciable. This derives from the fact that $\ln$ (1 + z) is approximately equal to z if z is small. On the basis of the BSM model of geometric Brownian motion, the price of the underlying will satisfy the following stochastic differential equation:

$$dS(t) = \sigma S(t)dB(t) + \mu S(t)dt$$

Here, $dB(t)$ is a standard Brownian motion and μ and σ are real constants. The equation has an analytical solution in the following form:

$$S(t) = S(0)e^{(\alpha t + \sigma B(t))}$$

In logarithmic form, we write the previous equation as follows:

$$ln\frac{S(t)}{S(0)} = \alpha t + \sigma B(t)$$

Here, the following is applicable:

- α is a drift
- $B(t)$ is a standard Brownian motion

We will try to define the concept of drift by analogy. Imagine pouring a drop of dye into a tin: the dye molecules will slowly spread in the water without following a precise direction until the dye is more or less uniformly dripped. This is a classic example of Brownian motion. Now, imagine pouring a drop of dye in a river: the drop will always be distributed randomly in the water, but following a precise direction, which is the movement of the river current. This is the drift. In the stock market, the drift is similar to the process that creates a long-term trend.

Now that we have defined a Brownian motion, we will return to our needs: to predict stock price.

Monte Carlo simulation

The daily price of an asset is obtained as an exponential raise of the previous day's price using a certain value: r. The r is a periodic rate of return. So, we can say that the asset increases or decreases in a day according to the following formula:

$$Stockprice(t) = Stockprice(t-1) * exp(r)$$

The exponential term is called daily return. Since the rate of return of an asset is a random number, to model the movement and determine possible future values, we must use a formula that shapes random movement. This model was formulated by Louis Bachelier. His work has been expanded and has eventually become fundamental in many areas of finance, hence the BSM formula.

This model is based on the following assumptions:

- The changes in stock price depend on the expected return over time and the effect of the constant volatility of the people who buy and sell at random over time have on that expected return

- This price is made up of two contributions: fixed drift rate and random stochastic variable
- The two contributions include the certainty of the movement and the uncertainty caused by the volatility

Let's analyze these two components in detail. For the drift, we will use the expected rate of return—in other words, the rate we expect to change every day. The expected rate is the rate most likely to occur. To calculate it, we will use the historical mean of the log returns and the variance. So, let's say the following:

$$drift = mean\ value\ of\ the\ log\ returns - (0.5 * variance\ to\ the\ log\ returns)$$

As a result, the rate we expect the asset to change every day is the average of the past periodic day of returns minus one half of the variance over time. This is known as an assets drift.

The assets drift is the expected rate of change for price, but it is not necessarily the price of the rate that actually changes every day; it is only the rate that is most likely to occur. This rate price is an unknown random number. We can determine the probabilities of using the rate based on the expected rate of return, that is, the drift and historical volatility also known as standard deviation.

r can assume any value, being able to grow and decrease. If we report the values d and r over time in a graph, we obtain a normal distribution, a bell-shaped curve (the same applies to log returns). Hence, the Brownian motion has a normal distribution using the drift as an average and using the historical standard deviation as a future standard deviation. The area under the normal distribution curve represents the total probability of the event occurring.

Finally, to create a Monte Carlo simulation, we can perform the following steps:

1. Import the closing prices of an asset
2. Find the periodic log returns
3. Find the mean, variance, and standard deviation of the log returns
4. Calculate the drift as a mean of -0.5 variance
5. Calculate a random stochastic offset as *standard deviation * random term (B)*
6. Calculate the daily returns as *e(drift + stdev * B)*
7. Calculate the stock price (*t*) as *stock price (t-1) * daily returns*

A number of these steps have already been performed. In fact, we have already calculated the log returns, so we can resume our algorithm starting from Step 3. Then, we will calculate the mean, variance, and standard deviation of the log returns.

To do this, the following functions are used: `mean()`, `var()`, and `std()`. The `mean()` function computes the arithmetic mean along the specified axis and returns the average of the array elements. The average is taken over the flattened array by default, otherwise it is taken over the specified axis. `float64` intermediate and return values are used for integer inputs. In the following code, the mean value of `LogReturns` is calculated:

```
MeanLogReturns = np.array(LogReturns.mean())
```

The `var()` function computes the variance along the specified axis: it returns the variance of the array elements, a measure of the spread of a distribution. The variance is computed for the flattened array by default, otherwise over the specified axis. In the following code, the variance to the `LogReturns` is calculated:

```
VarLogReturns = np.array(LogReturns.var())
```

The `std()` function computes the standard deviation along the specified axis: it returns the standard deviation, a measure of the spread of a distribution of the array elements. The standard deviation is computed for the flattened array by default, otherwise over the specified axis. In the following code, the standard deviation of the `LogReturns` is calculated:

```
StdevLogReturns = np.array(LogReturns.std())
```

At this point, we have the tools to calculate the two contributions that will form the price estimate: *drift* and a random component. To calculate the *drift*, as previously stated, we will use the following formula:

$$drift = mean - 0.5 * variance$$

In Python, it becomes the following:

```
Drift = MeanLogReturns - (0.5 * VarLogReturns)
```

Let's print the `Drift` value obtained:

```
print("Drift = ",Drift)
```

The result is shown as follows:

```
Drift = [0.00023356]
```

In this way, we have obtained the first contribution of the Brownian motion: the fixed part. The drift compensates for the asymmetry in results compared to straight Brownian motion; in other words, it indicates the annualized change in expected value. Now, we have to calculate the second component of the Brownian motion, that is, a number corresponding to the distance between the mean and the events, expressed as the number of standard deviations.

To do this, we must first set some parameters: first, we must specify the time intervals that we will use. These intervals will be `4529` as many as the observations contained in the original dataset. Our intention is to predict the price trend of the shares and compare it to the real one. Therefore, we will have to fix the number of iterations, that is, how many simulations will be carried out in order to choose the trend that best approximates the real data. In this case, we have decided to perform `20` simulations. So, let's see this in Python code:

```
NumberIntervals = 4529
Iterations = 20
```

Then, we will evaluate the random term, B. To do so, we will use two functions: `np.random.rand` and `norm.ppf`. The `np.random.rand()` function computes random values in a given shape: it creates an array of the given shape and populates it with random samples from a uniform distribution over *[0, 1)*. The `norm.ppf()` function gives the value of the variate for which the cumulative probability has the given value. This function is contained in the `norm` package, which we have to import:

```
from scipy.stats import norm
```

The following line shows the command to evaluate the random term, B:

```
B = norm.ppf(np.random.rand(NumberIntervals, Iterations))
```

Stock prices change on a daily basis, changing the value of our investments. It's possible to monitor these changes through a calculation of daily stock returns. The daily return measures the change in a stock's price as a percentage of the previous day's closing price. A positive return means the stock has grown in value, while a negative return means it has lost value. To calculate daily returns, the following formula is used:

$$exp(drift + stdev * B)$$

In Python code, it becomes the following:

```
DailyReturns = np.exp(Drift + StdevLogReturns * B)
```

The `np.exp()` function calculates the exponential of all elements in the input array. The time has come to predict the stock prices. To start, we will recover the first value of the historical data that we have recovered:

```
StockPrices0 = dataset.iloc[0]
```

To do this, the pandas `iloc()` function has been used. This function returns a purely integer location-based indexing for selection by position. `iloc[0]` is primarily integer position-based (from 0 to length -1 of the axis), but can also be used with a boolean array. The first data is selected from the dataset available (stock price at 2000-06-05).

Now, let's initialize the matrix that will contain the price forecasts. Recall that this matrix will have 4529 rows and 20 columns: each row will contain 4529 price forecasts (one for each monitoring day), while each column will be a different list of forecasts:

```
StockPrice = np.zeros_like(DailyReturns)
```

The NumPy `.zeros_like()` function returns an array of zeros with the same shape and type as a given array, `(DailyReturns)`. We set the starting value:

```
StockPrice[0] = StockPrices0
```

Now, we just have to set a `for` loop that will update the price of the shares for each day (`NumberIntervals`) and for the different simulations (iterations):

```
for t in range(1, NumberIntervals):
    StockPrice[t] = StockPrice[t - 1] * DailyReturns[t]
```

At this point, we can trace the obtained curves:

```
plt.figure(figsize=(10,5))
plt.plot(StockPrice)
```

To perform a simple comparison between a forecast curve and the real trend of Amazon stock, we will add this trend:

```
df1 = np.array(dataset.iloc[:, 0:1])
plt.plot(df1,'bs')
```

The last curve has been highlighted to make the comparison easier. Finally, we visualize everything using `plt.show()`.

The following graph shows a forecast curve and the real trend of Amazon stock prices:

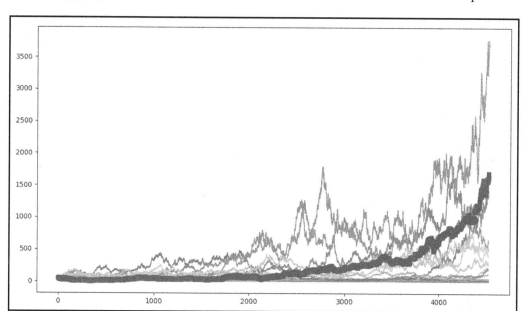

As already stated, the highlighted curve shows the real trend of the stock. It is clear that not all of the simulations adapt to this trend but, in some cases, we can say that the simulations do not differ much.

Summary

In this chapter, the basic concepts of the Monte Carlo method have been explored. The Monte Carlo method consists of looking for the solution of a problem, representing it as a parameter of a hypothetical population, and of estimating this parameter by examining a sample of the population obtained through sequences of random numbers. To understand the basic concepts, a numerical integration using the Monte Carlo method was performed. Then, Monte Carlo techniques for prediction and control were explored.

Subsequently, a practical case was addressed: Amazon stock price prediction using Python. To analyze the performance of Amazon stock prices, we used data relating to the stock prices in the time interval from 2000-06-05 to 2018-06-05 on NASDAQ GS stock quote. This data was downloaded from the Yahoo Finance website. Then, a model based on a BSM formula was fit. Finally, a forecast curve and the real trend of Amazon stock prices were compared.

5
Delivery Vehicle Routing Application

The **Vehicle Routing Problem** (VRP) is a typical distribution and transport problem, which consists of optimizing the use of a set of vehicles with limited capacity to pick up and deliver goods or people to geographically distributed stations. Managing these operations in the best possible way can significantly reduce costs. **Temporal difference** (TD) learning algorithms are based on reducing the differences between estimates made by the agent at different times. It is a combination of the ideas of the **Monte Carlo** (MC) method and **Dynamic Programming** (DP). It can learn directly from raw data, without a model of the dynamics of the environment (such as MC). Update estimates are based in part on other learned estimates, without waiting for the final result (bootstrap, like in DP). In this chapter, we will learn how to use TD learning algorithms to manage warehouse operations through Python and the Keras library.

The following topics will be covered in this chapter:

- Temporal difference algorithms
- Planning and learning with tabular methods
- Q-learning
- Optimal action
- Grid world environment

By the end of this chapter, the reader will have learned the different types of TD learning algorithms, and discovered how to use TD algorithms to predict the future behavior of a system. The reader will also have learned the basic concepts of the Q-learning algorithm, and how to use the current best policy estimate to generate system behavior through the Q-learning algorithm. Finally, the reader will understand how to deal with the **Delivery Vehicle Routing** (DVR) application through Q-learning techniques.

Temporal difference learning

TD learning algorithms are based on reducing the differences between estimates made by the agent at different times. Q-learning, which we will discuss in the following section, is a TD algorithm, but it is based on the difference between states in immediately adjacent instants. TD is more generic and may consider moments and states further away.

TD is a combination of the ideas of the MC method and DP, both of which can be summarized as follows:

- MC methods allow the solving of reinforcement learning problems based on the average of the obtained results
- DP represents a set of algorithms that can be used to calculate an optimal policy given a perfect model of the environment in the form of a **Markov Decision Process** (**MDP**)

The following can be said of TD methods:

- They inherit from MC methods the idea of learning directly from experience accumulated by interacting with the system, without the dynamics of the system itself
- They inherit from DP methods the idea of updating the estimation of functions in a state from estimates made in other states (bootstrap)

TD methods are suitable for learning without a model of dynamic environments. They converge using a fixed policy if the time step is sufficiently small or if it reduces over time.

Such methods differ from other techniques because they try to minimize the error of consecutive time forecasts. To achieve this goal, these methods rewrite the update of the value function in the form of a Bellman equation, improving the prediction by bootstrap. In this, the variance of the forecast is reduced in each update step. To get a backpropagation of updates, in order to save memory, an eligibility vector is applied. Example trajectories are used more efficiently, resulting in good learning rates.

The methods based on time differences allow us to manage the problem of control (that is, to search for the optimal policy) by updating the value functions based on the results of the transition to the next state. At every step, the Q function (action-value function) is updated on the basis of the value it has assumed for the next state-action pair and the reward obtained through the following equation, by adopting a one-step look-ahead:

$$Q(s_t, a_t) = r + \gamma * \max_{a_{t+1}} \big(Q(s_{t+1}, a_{t+1}) \big)$$

Look-ahead is the generic term for a procedure that attempts to foresee the effects of choosing a branching variable to evaluate one of its values. The two main aims of look-ahead are to choose a variable to evaluate next, and to choose the order of values to assign to it.

It is clear that a two-step formula can also be used, as shown in the following line:

$$Q(s_t, a_t) = r_t + \gamma * r_{t+1} + \gamma^2 * \max_{a_{t+2}} \left(Q(s_{t+2}, a_{t+2}) \right)$$

More generally, with the n-step look-ahead, we obtain the following formula:

$$Q(s_t, a_t) = r_t + \gamma * r_{t+1} + ... +$$
$$\gamma^{(n-1)} * r_{t+n-1} + \gamma^n * \max_{a_{t+n}} \left(Q(s_{t+n}, a_{t+n}) \right)$$

An aspect characterizing the different types of algorithms based on TD is the methodology of choosing an action. There are on-policy methods, in which the update is made on the basis of the results of actions determined by the selected policy, and off-policy methods, in which various policies can be assessed through hypothetical actions, which are not actually undertaken. Unlike on-policy methods, the latter can separate the problem of exploration from that of control, and learning tactics not necessarily applied during the learning phase.

SARSA

As we anticipated in Chapter 1, *Overview of Keras Reinforcement Learning*, the **State-Action-Reward-State-Action (SARSA)** algorithm implements an on-policy TDs method, in which the update of the action value function (Q) is performed based on the results of the transition from the state $s = s$ *(t)* to the state $s' = s$ *(t + 1)* by the action a *(t)*, taken on the basis of a selected policy: π *(s, a)*.

There are policies that always choose the action that provides the maximum reward, and non-deterministic policies (ε-greedy, ε-soft, and softmax), which ensure an element of exploration in the learning phase.

In SARSA, it is necessary to estimate the action-value function $q(s, a)$, because the total value of a state $v(s)$ (value function) is not sufficient in the absence of an environment model to allow the policy to determine, given a state, which action is best performed. In this case, however, the values are estimated step-by-step following the Bellman equation with the update parameter $v(s)$, considering, however, in place of a state, the state-action pair.

Being of an on-policy nature, SARSA estimates the action-value function based on the behavior of the π policy, and at the same time modifies the greedy behavior of the policy with respect to the updated estimates from the action-value function. The convergence of SARSA, and more generally of all TD methods, depends on the nature of politics.

The following shows a pseudocode for a SARSA algorithm:

```
Initialize
    arbitrary action-value function

Repeat (for each episode)
    Initialize s
    choose a from s using policy from action-value function
    Repeat (for each step in episode)
        take action a
        observe r, s'
        choose a' from s' using policy from action-value function
        update action-value function
        update s,a
```

The update rule of the `action-value` function uses all five elements (s_t, a_t, r_{t+1}, s_{t+1}, and a_{t+1}) and, for this reason, it is called **State-Action-Reward-State-Action (SARSA)**.

Q-learning

Q-learning is one of the most-used reinforcement learning algorithms. This is due to its ability to compare the expected utility of the available actions without requiring an environment model. Thanks to this technique, it is possible to find an optimal action for every given state in a finished MDP.

A general solution to the reinforcement learning problem is to estimate, thanks to the learning process, an evaluation function. This function must be able to evaluate, through the sum of the rewards, the convenience or otherwise of a particular policy. In fact, Q-learning tries to maximize the value of the Q function (action-value function), which represents the maximum discounted future reward when we perform actions a in the state s.

Q-learning, like SARSA, estimates the function value $q(s, a)$ incrementally, updating the value of the state-action pair at each step of the environment, following the logic of updating the general formula for estimating the values for the TD methods. Q-learning, unlike SARSA, has off-policy characteristics; that is, while the policy is improved according to the values estimated by $q(s, a)$, the value function updates the estimates following a strictly greedy secondary policy: given a state, the chosen action is always the one that maximizes the value $maxq (s, a)$. However, the π policy has an important role in estimating values because, through it, the state-action pairs to be visited and updated are determined.

The following shows a pseudocode for a Q-learning algorithm:

```
Initialize
    arbitrary action-value function
Repeat (for each episode)
    Initialize s
    choose a from s using policy from action-value function
    Repeat (for each step in episode)
        take action a
        observe r, s'
        update action-value function
        update s
```

Q-learning uses a table to store each state-action couple. At each step, the agent observes the current state of the environment and, using the π policy, selects and executes the action. By executing the action, the agent obtains the reward R_{t+1} and the new state S_{t+1}. At this point, the agent is able to calculate $Q(S_t, a_t)$, updating the estimate.

Basics of graph theory

As anticipated at the beginning of this chapter, what we will face is an optimization problem or (what is the same) we will try to identify the shortest path. Graphs are data structures that are widely used in optimization problems. A graph is graphically represented by a vertex and edge structure. The vertices can be seen as events from which different alternatives (the edge) depart. Typically, graphs are used to represent a network in an unambiguous way: vertices represent individual calculators, road intersections, or bus stops, and edges are electrical connections or roads. Edges can connect vertices in any way possible.

 Graph theory is a branch of mathematics that allows you to describe sets of objects together with their relationships; it was born in 1700 with Leonhard Euler.

A graph is indicated in a compact way, with $G = (V, E)$, where V indicates the set of vertices and E the set of edges that constitute it. The number of vertices is $|V|$, and the number of edges, $|E|$.

The number of vertices of the graph, or of a subpart of it, is obviously the fundamental quantity to define its dimensions; the number and distribution of edges describe their connectivity.

There are different types of edges (we are talking about undirected edges for which the edges do not have a direction, in comparison with those directed). A directed edge is called an **arc** and the relative graph is called a **digraph**. For example, undirected edges are used to represent computer networks with synchronous links for data transmission (as shown in the following diagram), and directed graphs can represent road networks, allowing the representation of double-senses and unique senses.

The following diagram shows a simple graph:

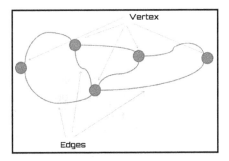

We speak of connected graphs if we can reach all the other vertices of the graph from any specific vertex. We speak of weighted graphs if a weight is associated with each edge, normally defined by a weight function (w). The weight can be seen as a cost or the distance between the two knots that the bow unites. The cost can be dependent on the flow that crosses the edge through a law. In this sense, the function w can be linear or not, and it depends on the flow that crosses the edge (non-congested networks) or also on the flow of nearby edges (congested networks).

A vertex is characterized by its degree, which is equal to the number of edges that end on the vertex itself. Depending on the degree, vertices are named as follows:

- A vertex of the order 0 is called an isolated vertex
- A vertex of the order 1 is called a leaf vertex

In the following diagram, a graph is shown with vertices labeled by degree:

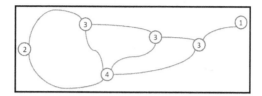

In a directed graph, one can distinguish the outdegree (number of outgoing edges), from the indegree (number of incoming edges). Based on this assumption, the following names are used:

- A vertex with an indegree of zero is called a source vertex
- A vertex with an outdegree of zero is called a sink vertex

Finally, a simplicial vertex is one whose neighbors form a clique: every two neighbors are adjacent. A universal vertex is a vertex that is adjacent to every other vertex in the graph.

To represent a graph, different approaches are available:

- Graphic representation (which we have seen in the preceding diagram)
- An adjacency matrix
- A list of vertices *V* and of arcs *E*

The first way to represent a graph was clearly introduced through a practical example (see the preceding diagram). Visual representation of graphs is obtained by drawing a dot or circle for every vertex, and drawing an edge between two vertices if they are connected by an edge. If the graph is directed, the direction is indicated by drawing an arrow. In the following sections, we will analyze the other two ways.

The adjacency matrix

So far, we have represented a graph through vertices and edges. When the number of vertices is small, this way of representing a graph is the best one because it allows us to analyze its structure in an intuitive way. When the number of vertices becomes large, the graphic representation becomes confusing. In this case, it is better to represent the graph using the adjacency matrix. By adjacency matrix or connection matrix, we mean a particular data structure commonly used in graph representation. In particular, it is widely used in the drafting of algorithms that operate on graphs and in general in their computer representation. If it is a sparse matrix, the use of the adjacency list is preferable to the matrix.

Given any graph, its adjacency matrix is made up of a square binary matrix that has the names of the vertices of the graph as rows and columns. In the (*i, j*) place of the matrix, there is a *1* if and only if there exists in the graph an edge that goes from the *i* vertex to the *j* vertex; otherwise there is a *0*. In the case of the representation of undirected graphs, the matrix is symmetric with respect to the main diagonal. For example, see the graph represented in the following diagram:

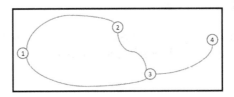

This can be represented through the following adjacency matrix:

$$
\begin{matrix}
0 & 1 & 1 & 0 \\
1 & 0 & 1 & 0 \\
1 & 1 & 0 & 1
\end{matrix}
$$

As anticipated, the matrix is symmetric with respect to the main diagonal being the undirected one. If there are numbers instead of the *1* in the matrix, these are to be interpreted as the weight attributed to each connection (edge), and the matrix is called Markov's matrix, as it is applicable to a Markov process. For example, if the set of vertices of the graph represents a series of points on a map, the weight of the edges can be interpreted as the distance of the points that they connect.

One of the fundamental characteristics of this matrix is to make it possible to obtain the number of paths from node *i* to node *j*, which must cross *n* vertices. To obtain all this, it is sufficient to make the *n* power of the matrix and to see the number that appears in the place *i, j*.

Adjacency lists

Adjacency lists are a mode of graph representation in memory. It is probably the most immediate representation to think about and the simplest to implement, even if in general not the most efficient in terms of occupied space.

Let's analyze a simple graph; next to each vertex is its list of adjacencies. The idea of representation is simply that a list is associated with every V_i vertex, containing all the V_j vertices so that there is an edge from V_i to V_j.

Assuming all pairs of the type (V_i, L), where L is the adjacency list of the V_i vertex, are stored, we obtain a unique description of the graph. Alternatively, if you decide to sort adjacency lists, you do not need to explicitly store the vertexes as well.

Let's look at an example. We will use the same graph we adopted in the previous section, which is represented in the following diagram:

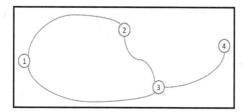

We will then build the list of adjacencies based on what has been said so far. The following table represents the graph in the preceding diagram:

1	adjacent to	2,3
2	adjacent to	1,3
3	adjacent to	1,2,4
4	adjacent to	3

An adjacency list is made up of pairs. There is a pair for each vertex in the graph. The first element of the pair is the vertex that is being analyzed, and the second is the set formed by all the vertices adjacent to it, which is connected to it by one side.

Assuming that we have a graph with n vertices and m edges (directed) that unite them, and supposing we store the adjacency lists in order (so as not to explicitly memorize the indices), we will have each edge appear in one and only one list of adjacencies. Each edge appears as the number of the vertex to which it points. It is therefore necessary to store a total of m numbers less than or equal to n, for a total cost of $m log_2 n$.

There is no obvious way to optimize this representation for non-oriented graphs; each arc must be stored in the adjacency lists of both vertices that it connects, hence halving the efficiency. The same argument holds if the graph is oriented, but we need an efficient method to know the arcs entering a certain vertex; in this case, it is convenient to associate two lists with each vertex: that of the incoming arcs and that of the outgoing arcs.

As far as time efficiency is concerned, representation by adjacency lists behaves quite well both in access and in insertion, carrying out the main operations in time $O(n)$.

Graphs as data structures in Python

Python has no built-in data type or class for representing graphs, but it is easy to implement them. Data structures are ideal for representing graphs in Python, for example, it is very simple to implement them through dictionaries.

Dictionaries are associative arrays, therefore objects that are substantially similar to arrays but that use different indices. In fact, unlike lists that use only whole numbers, dictionaries can adopt as indices any Python object as long as it's immutable, for example, strings, tuples, and numbers. We will then be able to use the key-value structure of dictionaries to represent any graph, using as few lines of code as possible.

Dictionaries represent only one of the data structures we can use to represent graphs. It is important to emphasize that, after choosing the basic data structure to represent the model, we will be bound to it, since all the functions implemented later will refer to it.

Let's analyze the simple graph of the following diagram:

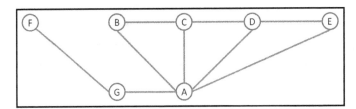

This graph can be implemented through the following data structure:

```
graph = { "a" : ["b", "c", "d", "e", "g"],
          "b" : ["c", "a"],
          "c" : ["a", "b", "d"],
          "d" : ["a", "c", "e"],
          "e" : ["a", "d"],
          "f" : ["g"],
          "g" : ["a", "f"]
          }
```

The keys of the dictionary (called `graph`) are the vertices of our graph. The corresponding values are lists with the vertices, which are connected by an edge. An edge will be expressed through a 2-values tuple that will contain the two connected vertices inside it. The dictionary, as defined, does not contain the connections between the various vertices. To obtain this information, we have to implement a function that generates the list, passing as the argument the graph, as shown in the following code:

```
def EdgesList (graph):
    edges = []
    for vertex in graph:
        for neighbour in graph[vertex]:
            edges.append((vertex, neighbour))
    return edges
```

At this point, it will be enough to print the list of connections among the nodes of the graph:

```
print (EdgesList (graph))
```

In the following, the obtained results are shown:

```
[('a', 'b'), ('a', 'c'), ('a', 'd'), ('a', 'e'), ('a', 'g'), ('b', 'c'),
('b', 'a'), ('c', 'a'), ('c', 'b'), ('c', 'd'), ('d', 'a'), ('d', 'c'),
('d', 'e'), ('e', 'a'), ('e', 'd'), ('f', 'g'), ('g', 'a'), ('g', 'f')]
```

As it is possible to verify, since these connections are undirected, the same edge appears twice. For example, the connection between *A* and *B* appears twice: `('a', 'b')` and `('b', 'a')`. To remove this redundancy, a simple change to the code is necessary:

```
def EdgesList (graph):
    edges = []
    for vertex in graph:
        for neighbour in graph[vertex]:
            if (neighbour, vertex) not in edges
                edges.append((vertex, neighbour))
    return edges
```

It was enough to add a control, with an `if` conditional structure, to check if the current connection is not present in the list.

Graphs using the NetworkX package

NetworkX is a Python package for the creation, manipulation, and study of the structure, dynamics, and functions of complex networks. The NetworkX package contains several standard network algorithms extremely useful for storing, analysis, and visualization of graphs.

The following are some features of the package:

- Data structures for graphs, digraphs, and multigraphs
- Many standard graph algorithms
- Network structure and analysis measures
- Generators for classic graphs, random graphs, and synthetic networks
- Several types of vertices can be represented
- Edges can hold arbitrary data
- An open source 3-clause BSD license
- It's well-tested with over 90% code coverage

The NetworkX package supports four types of graphs:

- **Undirected graphs**: `nx.Graph()`
- **Directed graphs**: `nx.DiGraph()`
- **Undirected multigraphs**: `nx.MultiGraph()`
- **Directed multigraphs**: `nx.MultiDiGraph()`

To understand how to use the methods available in the package, we will use a practical example. We will try to represent the graph already seen in the previous section and that is represented graphically in the following diagram:

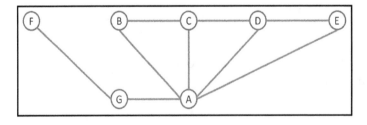

To start, we will import the libraries we will use in the example:

```
import networkx as nx
import matplotlib.pyplot as plt
```

First, we import the `networkx` library that we will use to build the graph, so we import `matplotlib.pyplot` that we will use to plot the graph. This is due to the fact that `networkx` is not a graphic design package so for this task it relies on the `matplotlib` library and offers an interface to use the open source Graphviz software package. The first thing to do is to create an empty `Graph` object with no vertices and no edges:

```
G = nx.Graph()
```

A `Graph` object is a collection of vertices along with identified pairs of vertices, called edges. Now, we can start defining the vertices:

```
G.add_node('A')
G.add_node('B')
G.add_node('C')
G.add_node('D')
G.add_node('E')
G.add_node('F')
G.add_node('G')
```

To add vertices (nodes) to the `Graph` object, the `add_node` method has been used. This method adds a single node and updates node attributes. Another way to add nodes to the `Graph` object is to add a list of nodes, as follows:

```
G.add_node(['A', 'B'])
```

Now that we have the list of nodes, we can insert the connections between them (edges):

```
G.add_edge('A', 'B')
G.add_edge('A', 'C')
G.add_edge('A', 'D')
G.add_edge('A', 'E')
G.add_edge('A', 'G')
G.add_edge('B', 'C')
G.add_edge('C', 'D')
G.add_edge('D', 'E')
G.add_edge('F', 'G')
```

To add edges to the `Graph` object, the `add_edge` method has been used. This method adds an edge between two vertices. The vertices will be automatically added if they are not already in the graph. Edge attributes can be specified with keywords or by directly accessing the edge's attribute dictionary. At this point, we just have to trace the graph:

```
nx.draw(G,with_labels=True, font_weight='bold')
```

To do this, the nx.draw method has been used. This method draws the G graph with the matplotlib library, as a simple representation with no node labels or edge labels and using the full Matplotlib figure area and no axis labels, by default. Two parameters have been added: with_labels=True and font_weight='bold'. The first one adds the name of the vertex and the second one traces it in bold. Now, we just have to visualize it:

```
plt.show()
```

The following screenshot shows the obtained graph:

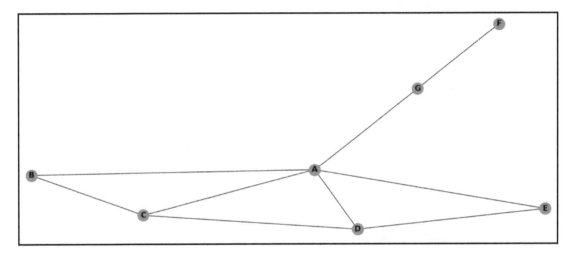

Comparing the obtained graph with the one from which we started, it is easy to understand that it is the same graph: just turn it over.

Finding the shortest path

So far, we have only dealt with creating a graph by defining the list of vertices and the connections between them. But, we haven't said anything about the characteristics of these connections. We can state that it is precisely the characteristics of the connections that have made the graphs particularly useful for the representation of a very large number of problems.

Regarding the edge, we have only distinguished between undirected and directed edges. We can add to them another type: weighted edges. Directed or undirected edges can also have a weight or a quantitative value associated with them. This property can be used to define characteristics such as distances between the nodes of a road network, the costs necessary to find a specific resource, the capacity of a line, and the energy required to move between locations along a route. Edges can also be weighted based on their center values or many other topological parameters.

Given a weighted graph and a designated vertex X, it is often requested to find the path from X to each of the other vertices in the graph. Identifying a path connecting two or more nodes of a graph appears as a subproblem of many other problems of discrete optimization and has, in addition, numerous applications in the real world.

Consider, for example, the problem of identifying a route between two locations shown on a road map, where the vertices are the localities, while the edges are the roads that connect them. In this case, each cost is associated with a cost that may be the length in kilometers of the road or the average time needed to cover it. If, instead of any path, one wants to identify one of minimum total cost, then the resulting problem is known as the problem of the shortest path in a graph. In other words, the shortest path between two vertices of a graph is that path that connects these vertices and that minimizes the sum of the costs associated with crossing each edge.

So, let's take a practical example: consider a tourist visiting Italy by car who wants to reach Venice from Rome. Having a map of Italy available in which for each direct link between the cities is marked its length, how can the tourist find the shortest path?

The system can be schematized with a graph in which each city corresponds to a vertex and the roads correspond to the connecting arcs between the vertices. You need to determine the shortest path between the source vertex and the target vertex of the graph.

A solution to the problem is to number all possible routes from Rome to Venice and, for each, calculate the total length and then select the shortest. This solution is not the most efficient because there are millions of paths to analyze.

In practice, modeling the map of Italy as a weighted oriented graph, $G = (V, E)$, where each vertex represents a city, each edge (u, v) represents a direct path from u to v and each weight $w (u, v)$ corresponding to an edge (u, v) represents the distance between u and v, the problem to be solved is that of finding the shortest path that connects the vertex corresponding to Rome with that corresponding to Venice.

Given a weighted directed graph $G = (V, E)$, the weight of a path $p = (v_0, v_1, ..., v_k)$ is given by the sum of the weights of the edges that constitute it, as shown in the following formula:

$$w(p) = \sum_{i=1}^{k} w(v_{i-1}, v_i)$$

A shortest path from node u to node v of V is a path $p = (u, v_1, v_2, ..., v)$ so that $w(p)$ is minimal, as follows:

$$min \sum_{i=1}^{k} w(v_{i-1}, v_i)$$

The cost of the minimum path from u to v is denoted by $\delta(u, v)$. If there is no path from u to v then $\delta(u, v) = \infty$.

Given a connected weighted graph, $G = (V, E)$ and a source node s of V, there are several algorithms to find the shortest path from s toward each other node of V. In the next section, we will analyze the Dijkstra algorithm.

The Dijkstra algorithm

The Dijkstra algorithm is able to solve the problem of finding the shortest path from the source s to all of the nodes. The algorithm maintains a label $d(i)$ to the nodes representing an upper bound on the length of the shortest path of the node i.

At each step, the algorithm partitions the nodes in V into two sets: the set of permanently labeled nodes and the set of nodes that are still temporarily labeled. The distance of permanently labeled nodes represents the shortest path distance from the source to these nodes, whereas the temporary labels contain a value that can be greater than or equal to the shortest path length.

The basic idea of the algorithm is to start from the source and try to permanently label the successor nodes. At the beginning, the algorithm places the value of the source distance to zero and initializes the other distances to an arbitrarily high value (by convention, we will set the initial value of the distances $d[i] = +\infty$, $\forall i \in V$).

At each iteration, the node label i is the value of the minimum distance along a path from the source that contains, apart from i, only permanently labeled nodes. The algorithm selects the node whose label has the lowest value among those labeled temporarily, labels it permanently, and updates all the labels of the nodes adjacent to it. The algorithm terminates when all the nodes have been permanently labeled.

From the execution of this algorithm, we obtain, for each destination node v of V, a shortest path p (from s to v), and we calculate the following:

- d $[v]$: The distance of node v from source node s long p

- π $[v]$: The predecessor of node v long p

Initialization for each node v of V:

- d $[v]$: ∞ if $v \neq s$, otherwise d $[s] = 0$

- π $[v] = \emptyset$

During the execution, we use the relaxation technique of a generic edge (u, v) of E, which serves to improve the estimation of d.

The relaxation of an edge (u, v) of E, consists in evaluating if, using u as a predecessor of v, the current value of distance d $[v]$ can be improved and, in this case, they update d $[v]$ and π $[v]$. The procedure is as follows:

1. If $d[v] > d[u] + w (u, v)$, then

2. $d[v] = d[u] + w (u, v)$

3. π $[v] = u;$

The operations performed by the algorithm are basically two: a node selection operation and an operation to update the distances. The first selects, at each step, the node with the value of the lowest label and the other verifies the condition $d[v] > d[u] + w(u, v)$ and, if so, updates the value of the label placing $d[v] = d[u] + w (u, v)$.

The following is a simple code that implements the Dijkstra algorithm:

```python
import heapq
inf = float('Inf')

def dijkstra(G, s):
    n = len(G)
    Q = [(0, s)]
    d = [inf for i in range(n)]
    d[s]=0
    while len(Q)!=0:
        (cost, u) = heapq.heappop(Q)
        for v in range(n):
            if d[v] > d[u] + G[u][v]:
                d[v] = d[u] + G[u][v]
                heapq.heappush(Q, (d[v], v))
    return d
```

As always, we will analyze the code line-by-line, starting with the first line:

```python
import heapq
```

The `heapq` library provides an implementation of the heap queue algorithm, also known as the priority queue algorithm. A priority queue is an abstract data type, which is like a regular queue or stack data structure, but where additionally each element has a priority associated with it. In a priority queue, an element with high priority is served before an element with low priority. If two elements have the same priority, they are served according to their order in the queue. Let's move on to the next line of code:

```python
inf = float('Inf')
```

This command defines an unbounded upper value for comparison. This is useful for finding the lowest values for something, as for our case, calculating path costs when traversing all the possible solutions. Then, we pass to define the function that will calculate the distance between the source node and the other nodes:

```python
def dijkstra(G, s):
```

Two parameters have passed: the G graph and the s source node. The first part of the function is destined to initialize the variables:

```python
n = len(G)
Q = [(0, s)]
d = [inf for i in range(n)]
d[s]=0
```

The first line measure the length of the list that represents the graph. The second initializes the Q heap to zero. The third sets all distances from the source to the upper bond, `inf`. Finally, the fourth sets the distance of the path to zero. Let's move on to the next line:

```
while len(Q)!=0:
```

A `while` loop is a control flow statement that allows code to be executed repeatedly based on a given condition. In our case, the condition is set on the length of the Q heap. The cycle will be repeated until values remain into the heap. We start working on the queue:

```
(cost, u) = heapq.heappop(Q)
```

The `heappop` function pops and returns the smallest item from the heap, maintaining the heap invariant. At this point, we apply the relaxation of an edge technique:

```
for v in range(n):
    if d[v] > d[u] + G[u][v]:
        d[v] = d[u] + G[u][v]
        heapq.heappush(Q, (d[v], v))
```

As anticipated, the relaxation of an edge (u, v) of *E*, consists of evaluating `if`, using u as a predecessor of v. The current value of distance, `d[v]`, can be improved and, in this case, they update `d[v]` and the heap. To do this, the `heappush` function has been used: this function pushes the value `(d[v], v)` onto the heap, maintaining the heap invariant. Finally, for all vertices, the distance of the path is returned:

```
return d
```

Let's now look at a practical application of this algorithm. As already mentioned, the `dijkstra` function needs two parameters: the graph, G, and the source node, s. To define the graph G we will use the adjacency matrix. We recall in this regard that if instead of the *1* in the matrix, there are numbers, these are to be interpreted as Markov's matrix, as it is applicable to a Markov process.

This is precisely our case because we want to insert the weight of each connection:

```
G = [\
    [0.0, 2.0, 5.0, inf],\
    [2.0, 0.0, 2.0, 6.0],\
    [5.0, 2.0, 0.0, 3.0],\
    [inf, 6.0, 3.0, 0.0]]
```

The following is the graph represented by the previous adjacency matrix:

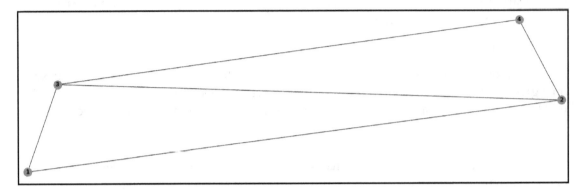

Now, we just have to call the function passing this adjacency matrix and the source node:

```
d = dijkstra(G, 0)
print(d)
```

The following results are returned:

```
[0, 2.0, 4.0, 7.0]
```

By analyzing the preceding graph, it is possible to confirm the correctness of the results.

The Dijkstra algorithm using the NetworkX package

In the previous section, *Graphs using the NetworkX package*, we have used the `networkx` package to represent graphs in Python. Using this tool, the search for the shortest paths becomes extremely simple and equally rapid. Let's analyze the following code:

```
import networkx as nx
import matplotlib.pyplot as plt

G = nx.Graph()
G.add_node(1)
G.add_node(2)
G.add_node(3)
G.add_node(4)
G.add_edge(1, 2, weight=2)
G.add_edge(2, 3, weight=2)
G.add_edge(3, 4, weight=3)
G.add_edge(1, 3, weight=5)
G.add_edge(2, 4, weight=6)
```

```
pos = nx.spring_layout(G, scale=3)
nx.draw(G, pos,with_labels=True, font_weight='bold')
edge_labels = nx.get_edge_attributes(G,'r')
nx.draw_networkx_edge_labels(G, pos, labels = edge_labels)
plt.show()

print(nx.shortest_path(G,1,4,weight='weight'))
print(nx.nx.shortest_path_length(G,1,4,weight='weight'))
```

First, we import the libraries we have used in the example:

```
import networkx as nx
import matplotlib.pyplot as plt
```

Then, a graph object is created and the vertices are added:

```
G = nx.Graph()
G.add_node(1)
G.add_node(2)
G.add_node(3)
G.add_node(4)
```

Subsequently, the weighted edges are added:

```
G.add_edge(1, 2, weight=2)
G.add_edge(2, 3, weight=2)
G.add_edge(3, 4, weight=3)
G.add_edge(1, 3, weight=5)
G.add_edge(2, 4, weight=6)
```

At this point, we have drawn the graph by adding labels to the edges with the indication of weight:

```
pos = nx.spring_layout(G, scale=3)
nx.draw(G, pos,with_labels=True, font_weight='bold')
edge_labels = nx.get_edge_attributes(G,'r')
nx.draw_networkx_edge_labels(G, pos, labels = edge_labels)
plt.show()
```

To do this, the `draw_networkx_edge_labels` function has been used. In the following screenshot, the result is shown:

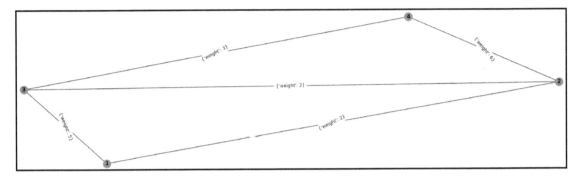

Finally, the shortest path from 1 to 4 nodes has been calculated:

```
print(nx.shortest_path(G,1,4,weight='weight'))
```

The `shortest_path` function computes the shortest paths and path lengths between nodes in the graph. The following are the results:

```
[1, 2, 3, 4]
```

Finally, the length of the shortest paths has been calculated:

```
print(nx.nx.shortest_path_length(G,1,4,weight='weight'))
```

The following is the result:

```
7
```

As it is possible to verify, we have obtained the same result.

The Google Maps algorithm

Google Maps is one of the most famous geospatial applications of all time, having transformed the way we navigate using a digital map to get from point A to point B. Before Google Maps, most people used paper maps to navigate and then started using digital maps. In the following screenshot, we can see the different route options offered by Google Maps to reach Venice from Rome:

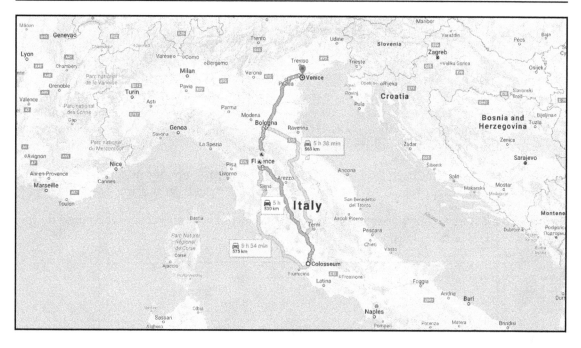

Digital maps immediately appeared to have different advantages compared to the equivalent of printing—different levels of zoom, the possibility of adding personal points of interest, and so on, but perhaps the most interesting feature was the possibility of using the computer to calculate the shorter distance from point A to point B without needing to understand it yourself or ask someone who has lived in a place long enough to derive it from experience.

The algorithm on which the service offered by Google is based originates from graph theory and, in particular, from the initial navigation algorithm of Edsger W. Dijkstra.

The core of this algorithm is that which still powers the functionality to navigate on Google Maps, on Apple Maps, HERE WeGo maps, OpenStreetMap maps, and certainly any other digital map. Obviously, the necessary variations and optimizations occurred over time, but certainly all referred to the initial Dijkstra algorithm, which at the time solved the problem of finding the shortest and most efficient route possible between two nodes of a structured graph network.

The Vehicle Routing Problem

As anticipated at the beginning of the chapter, the VRP is a typical distribution and transport problem, which consists of optimizing the use of a set of vehicles with limited capacity to pick up and deliver goods or people to geographically distributed stations. Managing these operations in the best possible way can significantly reduce costs. Before tackling the problem with Python code, let's analyze the basic characteristics of the topic in order to understand possible solutions.

On the basis of what has been said so far, it is clear that a problem of this type is configured as a path optimization procedure that can be conveniently dealt with using graph theory.

Suppose we have the following graph, with the distances between vertices indicated on the edges (6 vertices and 7 edges):

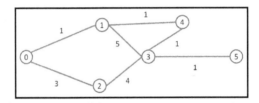

It is easy to see that the shortest path from **0** node to **5** node is **0 – 1 – 4 – 3 – 5**.

We want to implement a Python code that allows us to research this path through the technique of Q-learning. We analyze the code line-by-line, starting with importing the libraries:

```
import numpy as np
```

Only the numpy library is imported. Let's move on to the reward matrix setting:

```
RMatrix = np.matrix([ [-1,50,1,-1,-1,-1],
                      [-1,-1,-1,1,50,-1],
                      [-1,-1,-1,1,-1,-1],
                      [-1,-1,-1,-1,-1,100],
                      [-1,-1,-1,50,-1,-1],
                      [-1,-1,-1,-1,-1,100] ])
```

The `numpy` library's `matrix` function is used, which returns a matrix from an array-like object, or from a string of data. Let's try to understand how we set this matrix: it's all very simple—we have associated a high reward at the most convenient edges, that is, those with a lower weight (which means shorter). We then associated the highest reward (**100**) to the edge that leads us to the goal. Finally, we associated a negative reward to non-existent links. The following diagram shows how we set the rewards:

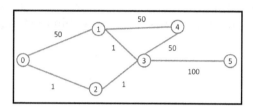

Let's move forward and define `QMatrix`:

```
QMatrix = np.matrix(np.zeros([6,6]))
```

A matrix of `zeros` is defined using, once again, `numpy` library's `matrix` function. Recall, `QMatrix` contains the information that the agent is able to learn during the process (action-value function). In this matrix, the rows represent the current status of the agent, and the columns represent the possible actions that lead to the next state. Now, let's define the discount factor:

```
gamma = 0.9
```

The discount factor is a number between 0 and 1 and determines the importance of future rewards. A factor equal to 0 will make the agent opportunistic, making it consider only the current rewards, while a factor tending to 1 will make the agent also attentive to the rewards they will receive in a long-term future. Let's move on to initialize the state of the environment:

```
InitialState = 0
```

At this point, it is necessary to define all the possible actions available in the current state. To do so, we will define a function that just given a state of the environment returns all available actions:

```
def AllActions(state):
    CurrentState = RMatrix[state,]
    AllAct = np.where(CurrentState >= 0)[1]
    return AllAct
```

The state of the environment is passed and the `numpy` library's `where` function is used to select all the available actions contained in the `RMatrix` row specified by the `state` that satisfies the `CurrentState >= 0` condition. We use the newly defined function to recover all possible actions available in the initial state:

```
AvAct = AllActions(InitialState)
```

In the training phase, we will have to make choices of actions that will then be evaluated by the agent through the reward. To do so, it will be necessary to define a function that will choose at random which action must be performed within the range of all the available actions:

```
def NextAction(AvActRange):
    NextAct = int(np.random.choice(AvAct,1))
    return NextAct
```

Now, we begin to choose the next action to be performed:

```
Action = NextAction(AvAct)
```

After making the appropriate initial choices, it is time to experiment the paths. To do so, we will define a new function that will update the `QMatrix` matrix based on the selected path and the Q-learning algorithm:

```
def Update(CurrentState, Action, gamma):
    MaxIndex = np.where(QMatrix[Action,] == \
                    np.max(QMatrix[Action,]))[1]

    if MaxIndex.shape[0] > 1:
        MaxIndex = int(np.random.choice(MaxIndex, size = 1))
    else:
        MaxIndex = int(MaxIndex)
        MaxValue = QMatrix[Action, MaxIndex]
        QMatrix[CurrentState, Action] = \
            RMatrix[CurrentState, Action] + gamma * MaxValue
```

In this function, lies the heart of the Q-learning algorithm. At every step, the Q function (action-value function) is updated on the basis of the value it has assumed for the next state-action pair and the reward obtained through the following equation:

$$Q(s_t, a_t) = r + \gamma * \max_{a_{t+1}} \left(Q(s_{t+1}, a_{t+1}) \right)$$

Let's move on to update `QMatrix` using the following function:

```
Update(InitialState,Action,gamma)
```

Now that we have defined all the tools for training the system, we just have to do it:

```
for i in range(10000):
    CurrentState = np.random.randint(0, int(QMatrix.shape[0]))
    AvAct = AllActions(CurrentState)
    Action = NextAction(AvAct)
    Update(CurrentState,Action,gamma)
```

The training performs `10000` iterations updating the `QMatrix`. We can then print the definitive matrix that defines the action-value function:

```
print("Q matrix trained :")
print(QMatrix/np.max(QMatrix)*100)
```

In practice, what we have printed is the normalized version of `QMatrix`. Now that the model is ready, we can test it by evaluating the shortest path from node 0 to node 5:

```
CurrentState = 0
Steps = [CurrentState]
```

After defining the starting node, we will walk through all the nodes:

```
while CurrentState != 5:
    NextStepIndex = np.where(QMatrix[CurrentState,] ==
np.max(QMatrix[CurrentState,]))[1]
    if NextStepIndex.shape[0] > 1:
        NextStepIndex = int(np.random.choice(NextStepIndex, size = 1))
    else:
        NextStepIndex = int(NextStepIndex)
        Steps.append(NextStepIndex)
        CurrentState = NextStepIndex
```

Finally, we will print the shortest path:

```
print("Shortest path:")
print(Steps)
```

The following `Q matrix` is returned:

```
Q matrix trained :
[[  0.    86.45  81.19   0.     0.     0.  ]
 [  0.     0.     0.    90.1   90.5    0.  ]
 [  0.     0.     0.    90.1    0.     0.  ]
 [  0.     0.     0.     0.     0.   100.  ]
 [  0.     0.     0.    95.     0.     0.  ]
 [  0.     0.     0.     0.     0.   100.  ]]
```

To find the shortest path from `Q matrix`, just follow the following procedure:

1. We start from the starting node
2. In the row relating to this node, the column relative to the maximum value is identified, and this is the next node
3. Repeat the procedure from Step 2 until reaching the target

The shortest path returned is in the following:

```
Shortest path:
[0, 1, 4, 3, 5]
```

The result is in agreement with what we had assumed at the beginning of the section.

Summary

In this chapter, TD learning algorithms were introduced. TD learning algorithms are based on reducing the differences between estimates made by the agent at different times. The SARSA algorithm implements an on-policy TDs method, in which the update of the action value function (Q) is performed based on the results of the transition from the state $s = s\ (t)$ to the state $s' = s\ (t + 1)$ by the action $a\ (t)$, taken on the basis of a selected policy $\pi\ (s, a)$. Q-learning, unlike SARSA, has off-policy characteristics, that is, while the policy is improved according to the values estimated by $q(s, a)$, the value function updates the estimates following a strictly greedy secondary policy: given a state, the chosen action is always the one that maximizes the value $max_{q\ (s,\ a)}$.

Then, the basics of graph theory were addressed: the adjacency matrix and adjacency list topics were covered. We have seen how to represent graphs in Python using the dictionary data structure. Later, we learned how to represent graphs using the NetworkX package.

We therefore addressed the shortest path problem. Given a weighted graph, and a designated vertex X, it is often requested to find the path from X to each of the other vertices in the graph. Identifying a path connecting two or more nodes of a graph is a problem that appears as a subproblem of many other problems of discrete optimization and has, in addition, numerous applications in the real world. We also analyzed the Dijkstra algorithm in Python.

Finally, VRP was resolved using the Q-learning algorithm.

6
Continuous Balancing of a Rotating Mechanical System

The automatic control of a dynamic system—for example, a motor, an industrial plant, or a biological function, such as a heartbeat—aims to modify the behavior of the system that is to be controlled, or its outputs, through the manipulation of appropriate quantities of the inputs into the system.

Neural networks are exceptionally effective at generating results that meet the criteria for highly structured data. We could then represent our Q-function with a neural network, which takes the status and action as inputs and then outputs (gives) the corresponding Q-value. Deep reinforcement learning methods use deep neural networks to approximate the reinforcement learning components of the value function, policy, and model. In this chapter, we will learn how to use deep reinforcement learning methods for balancing a rotating mechanical system.

This chapter will cover the following topics:

- Neural network basic concepts
- The Keras neural network model
- Deep reinforcement learning
- The Keras–RL package
- Actor–critic methods

At the end of the chapter, you will know the basic concepts of artificial neural networks, how to apply neural network methods to your data, how neural network algorithms work, the basic concepts that deep neural networks use to approximate reinforcement learning components, how to implement a Deep Q-network using Python and Keras features, and know how to implement a DQN to balance a rotating mechanical system.

Neural network basic concepts

Artificial neural networks (**ANN**) are mathematical models for the simulation of typical human brain activities, such as image perception, pattern recognition, language understanding, sense–motor coordination, and so on. These models are composed of a system of nodes, equivalent to the neurons of a human brain, which are interconnected by weighted links, equivalent to the synapses between neurons, as shown in the following diagram:

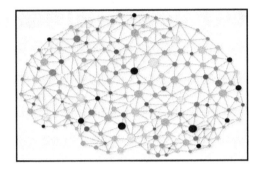

The output of the network is iteratively changed from the link weights up to the convergence. The original data is provided to the input layer and the result of the network is returned from the output level. The input nodes represent the independent or predictor variables that are used to predict the dependent variables—that is, the output neurons.

Serial computers and their programs are very powerful tools that are used to perform tasks that require the repetition of a number of well-defined operations where accuracy, reliability, and speed are the most important features. These information-processing systems are very useful, but not intelligent; the only element of intelligence in the whole process is the programmer who has analyzed the task and created the program. For an artificial system to be intelligent, it should at least be able to solve problems that humans find simple, trivial, and natural.

ANNs are information-processing systems that try to simulate within a computer system the functioning of biological nervous systems that are made up of a large number of nerve cells, or neurons, connected to each other in a complex network. Each neuron is connected, on average, with tens of thousands of other neurons, with hundreds of billions of connections. Intelligent behavior emerges from the many interactions between these interconnected units.

Some of these units receive information from the environment, others emit responses to the environment, and others—if they are present—communicate only with the units within the network. These three types of units are defined as input units, output units, and hidden units, respectively.

The following diagram shows a generic neural network architecture:

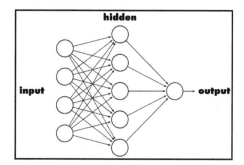

Each unit performs a very simple operation that is activated if the total amount of signals received exceeds an activation threshold. If a unit becomes active, it emits a signal that is transmitted along the communication channels to other units to which it is connected. Each connection point acts as a filter that transforms the received message into an excited or inhibitory signal, increasing or decreasing the intensity at the same time, according to its individual characteristics. The input–output link (in other words, the network transfer function) is not programmed, but is simply obtained from a learning process based on empirical data that may involve supervised, unsupervised, or reinforcement learning.

Neural networks work in parallel, and are therefore able to deal with lots of data at the same time, as opposed to serial computers, where each piece of data is processed individually and in succession. Although each individual neuron is relatively slow, parallelism partly explains the faster speed of the brain in performing tasks that require the simultaneous processing of a large amount of data, such as visual object recognition. This is essentially a complicated statistical system with good noise immunity.

If some of the system's units malfunction, the network as a whole has performance reductions, but is unlikely to encounter a system shutdown. The following diagram shows a comparison between **serial processing** and **parallel processing**:

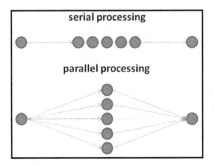

Models produced by neural networks, though very efficient, cannot be explained in human symbolic language; the results must be accepted as they are, as a kind of black box.

As with any modeling algorithm, neural networks are also efficient only if the predictive variables are carefully chosen. They require a system-training phase that sets the weights of individual neurons, and this phase can take a long time if the number of records and variables analyzed is very large. There are no theorems or models that allow us to define the network, so the success of a network depends greatly on the creator's experience.

Neural networks are usually used in situations where data may be partially incorrect, or where no analytic models are available to deal with the problem. Their typical use is in OCR software, facial recognition systems, and, more generally, in systems dealing with handling data that is subject to error or noise. They are also one of the most used tools in data-mining analysis. Neural networks are also used as a means of forecasting financial or meteorological analysis. In recent years, their significance has increased considerably in the field of bioinformatics, where they are used to find functional and/or structural patterns in nucleic acids and proteins. By providing a long set of input data, the network is able to return the most likely output.

The Keras neural network model

Keras is a high-level neural network API, written in Python and capable of running on top of TensorFlow, CNTK, or Theano. It was developed with a focus on enabling fast experimentation. With the use of Keras, we will be able to move from idea to result in the shortest possible time so you can spend more time analyzing results.

Keras owes its widespread use to its extreme ease of use. Keras follows best practices to reduce the workload on the user. It provides consistent and simple APIs, minimizes the number of user actions needed for common use cases, and provides clear and viable feedback in the event of a network error.

Another feature of Keras that has ensured its success is its modularity. A model is intended as a sequence of autonomous and fully configurable modules that can be connected with the least possible number of restrictions—in particular, the neural layers, the cost functions, the optimizers, the initialization schemes, the activation functions, and the regularization schemes are all independent modules that can be combined to create new models.

Keras is also easily extensible: the new modules are easy to add (like new classes and functions), and existing modules provide numerous examples. The possibility to easily create new modules allows a wide diffusion of the library, making Keras suitable for the most varied tasks.

Finally, as we just said, Keras is written in Python: no separate template configuration files in a declarative format are needed. The models are described in Python code, which is compact, easier to debug, and allows maximum extensibility.

The Keras model implementation provides the following steps:

1. Prepare the input and specify the input dimension.
2. Define the model architecture and build the computational graph.
3. Specify the optimizer and configure the learning process.
4. Specify the inputs and outputs of the computational model and the loss function.
5. Train and test the model on the dataset.

Now, we analyze this procedure through the required code. The simplest type of model is the `Sequential` model, a linear stack of layers. The steps listed in the procedure we have just seen translate into the following few lines of code:

```
from keras.models import Sequential
model = Sequential()
```

To start, we have imported a `Sequential` class from the `keras.models`, and we have set the kind of model that we are going to define. Now, we will stack the layers, as follows:

```
from keras.layers import Dense
model.add(Dense(units=64, activation='relu', input_dim=100))
model.add(Dense(units=10, activation='softmax'))
```

To stack the layers, the `.add()` method is used. This method simply adds layers to the model. Two dense layers have been added: first, a dense layer with 100 input nodes, 64 output nodes, and a `'relu'` activation function, and second, a layer with 10 output nodes and a `'softmax'` activation function. At this point we can configure the model, as follows:

```
model.compile(loss='categorical_crossentropy',
              optimizer='sgd',
              metrics=['accuracy'])
```

To configure the learning process, the `.compile` method has been used. The following arguments are passed:

- `loss`: String (name of the objective function) or objective function. You can use this to see the losses. If the model has multiple outputs, you can use a different loss on each output by passing a dictionary or a list of losses. The loss value that will be minimized by the model will then be the sum of all individual losses.
- `optimizer`: String (name of optimizer) or optimizer instance. An optimizer is one of the two arguments required for compiling a Keras model. You can either instantiate an optimizer before passing it to `model.compile()`, as in the preceding example, or you can call it by its name. In the latter case, the default parameters for the optimizer will be used.
- `metrics`: List of metrics to be evaluated by the model during training and testing. Typically, you will use `metrics=['accuracy']`. To specify different metrics for different outputs of a multioutput model. You could also pass a dictionary, such as `metrics={'output_a': 'accuracy'}`.

The time has come to train the model, as follows:

```
model.fit(x_train, y_train, epochs=5, batch_size=32)
```

The `.fit` method trains the model for a given number of epochs (iterations on a dataset). The following arguments are passed:

- `x_train`: NumPy array of training data (if the model has a single input), or list of NumPy arrays (if the model has multiple inputs). If input layers in the model are named, you can also pass a dictionary for mapping input names to NumPy arrays. The `x` parameter can be `None` (default) if feeding on framework-native tensors.

- y_train: NumPy array of target (label) data (if the model has a single output), or list of NumPy arrays (if the model has multiple outputs). If output layers in the model are named, you can also pass a dictionary mapping output names to NumPy arrays. The y parameter can be None (default) if feeding on framework-native tensors.
- epochs: Integer. This states the number of epochs to train the model. An epoch is an iteration over the entire x and y data provided. Note that in conjunction with the initial_epoch, epochs is to be understood as the "final epoch". The model is not trained for a number of iterations given by epochs, but merely until the epoch of index epochs is reached.
- batch_size: Integer or None. This indicates the number of samples per gradient update. If unspecified, batch_size will default to 32.

We can now evaluate the performance of the model, as follows:

```
loss_and_metrics = model.evaluate(x_test, y_test, batch_size=128)
```

The .evaluate method returns the loss value and metric values for the model in test mode. Finally, we can generate predictions on new data, as follows:

```
classes = model.predict(x_test, batch_size=128)
```

The .predict method generates output predictions for the input samples. Computation is done in batches. The following arguments are available:

- x_test: The input data, as a NumPy array (or list of NumPy arrays, if the model has multiple inputs).
- batch_size: Integer. If unspecified, it will default to 32.
- verbose: Verbosity mode, 0 or 1.
- steps: Total number of steps (batches of samples) before declaring the prediction round finished. Ignored with the default value of None.

As we have seen, the definition of a model of artificial neural networks using Keras is really a breeze.

Classifying breast cancer using the neural network

The breast is made up of a set of glands and adipose tissue, and is situated between the skin and the chest wall. It is, in fact, not a single gland, but a set of glandular structures, called lobules, joined together to form a lobe. In a breast, there are 15 to 20 lobes. The milk reaches the nipple from the lobules through small tubes called milk ducts.

Breast cancer is a potentially serious disease if it is not detected and treated for a long time. It is caused by the uncontrolled multiplication of some of the cells in the mammary gland that have transformed into malignant cells. This means that they have the ability to detach themselves from the tissue that has generated them to invade the surrounding tissues, and eventually the other organs of the body. In theory, cancers can be formed from all types of breast tissue, but the most common ones are from glandular cells or from those forming the walls of the ducts.

The objective of the following example is to identify each of a number of benign or malignant cases of possible breast cancer. To do this, we will use the data contained in the dataset named `BreastCancer` (from the Wisconsin Breast Cancer database). This data has been taken from the UCI Repository of Machine Learning databases. This database is continually expanding as +DNA samples arrive periodically when Dr. Wolberg reports his clinical cases. The database, therefore, reflects this chronological grouping of the data. This grouping information appears immediately, having been removed from the data itself. Each variable, except for the first, was converted into 11 primitive numerical attributes with values ranging from 0 through to 10.

To get the data, we draw on the large collection of data available in the UCI Machine Learning Repository at `http://archive.ics.uci.edu/ml`.

The data frames contain 699 observations on 11 variables—1 factor, 9 integers, and 1 target class—as shown in the following list:

- `Id`: Sample code number
- `Cl.thickness`: Clump thickness
- `Cell.size`: Uniformity of cell size
- `Cell.shape`: Uniformity of cell shape
- `Marg.adhesion`: Marginal adhesion
- `Epith.c.size`: Single epithelial cell size

- `Bare.nuclei`: Bare nuclei
- `Bl.cromatin`: Bland chromatin
- `Normal.nucleoli`: Normal nucleoli
- `Mitoses`: Mitoses
- `Class`: Class (0 for benign, 1 for malignant)

As said previously, the objective of this example is to identify each of a number of benign or malignant classes. The following code is for classifying a case as breast cancer:

```
import numpy
from sklearn.model_selection import train_test_split
from keras.models import Sequential
from keras.layers import Dense
numpy.random.seed(1)
dataset = numpy.loadtxt("BreastCancer.csv", delimiter=",")
X = dataset[:,1:10]
Y = dataset[:,10]
X = (X - numpy.min(X, 0)) / (numpy.max(X, 0) - numpy.min(X, 0))
X_train, X_test, Y_train, Y_test = train_test_split(X, Y, test_size=0.2,
random_state=1)
model = Sequential()
model.add(Dense(10, input_dim=9, activation='relu'))
model.add(Dense(1, activation='sigmoid'))
model.compile(loss='binary_crossentropy', optimizer='adam',
metrics=['accuracy'])
model.fit(X_train, Y_train, epochs=200, batch_size=10)
ResultEval = model.evaluate(X_test, Y_test)
print("\n%s: %.2f%%" % (model.metrics_names[1], ResultEval [1]*100))
```

I already know that you are wondering why there is so little code. This is because Keras does everything with as little code as possible. As we have already done in all the examples that we have seen so far, we will analyze this code line by line to understand its operating principle. The first part of the code is used to import libraries, as follows:

```
import numpy
```

First, we import the `numpy` library that will be used to set the seed value, and for scaling the data. Then the `train_test_split()` function is imported from the `sklearn.model_selection` library, as follows:

```
from sklearn.model_selection import train_test_split
```

The `sklearn` phrase refers to a free machine-learning library for the Python programming language. It features various classification, regression, and clustering algorithms, including support vector machines, random forests, gradient boosting, *k*-means, and DBSCAN, and it is designed to interoperate with the Python numerical and scientific libraries NumPy and SciPy.

Then, the model and layer are imported from Keras, as follows:

```
from keras.models import Sequential
from keras.layers import Dense
```

For now, let's limit ourselves to importing; we will deepen this code when we come to use it. To set the seed value, the `numpy.random.seed()` function is used, as follows:

```
numpy.random.seed(1)
```

The `seed` function sets the seed of the random number generator, which is useful for creating simulations or random objects that can be reproduced. You have to use this function every time you want to get a reproducible random result. Now, we have to load the dataset, as follows:

```
dataset = numpy.loadtxt("BreastCancer.csv", delimiter=",")
```

The `numpy.loadtxt()` function has been used to load the dataset. This function loads data from a text file. Each row in the text file must have the same number of values. Our data is contained in a `.csv` file named `BreastCancer.csv`. The `delimiter` argument is passed, which specifies the string that is used to separate values (in our case, a comma). For backward compatibility, byte strings will be decoded as `"latin1"`. The default is whitespace. Now, we have to split the dataset into the input (`X`) and output (`Y`) variables, as follows:

```
X = dataset[:,1:10]
Y = dataset[:,10]
```

The first variable is omitted because it represents the ID that no information adds to the data. Before using the data, a clarification is necessary. Oftentimes, the data will contain variables with different ranges. When the predictors have different ranges, the impact of the feature having a greater numeric range on the response variables could be more than one having a less numeric range, and this could, in turn, impact the prediction's accuracy. Our goal is to improve the predictive accuracy and not allow a particular feature to impact the prediction because of a large numeric value range. Thus, we may need to scale values under different features so that they fall under a common range. Through this statistical procedure, it is possible to compare identical variables belonging to different distributions and also different variables, or variables expressed in different units.

Remember, it is good practice to rescale the data before training a machine learning algorithm. With rescaling, data units are eliminated, allowing you to easily compare data from different locations.

In this case, we will use the *min-max* method (usually called feature scaling) to get all the scaled data in the range (0, 1). The formula to achieve this is as follows:

$$x1_{scaled} = \frac{x - x_{min}}{x_{max} - x_{min}}$$

The following command performs feature scaling:

```
X = (X - numpy.min(X, 0)) / (numpy.max(X, 0) - numpy.min(X, 0))
```

The `numpy.min()` and `numpy.max()` functions are used to calculate the minimum and maximum values of each database column.

Let's now split the data for the training and the test models. Training and testing the model forms the basis of the further usage of the model for prediction in predictive analytics. Given a dataset of 100 rows of data, which includes the predictor and response variables, we split the dataset into a convenient ratio (say 80:20), and allocate 80 rows for training and 20 rows for testing. The rows are selected at random to reduce bias. Once the training data is available, the data is fed to the machine-learning algorithm to get the massive universal function in place. To split the dataset, we will use the `sklearn.model_selection.train_test_split()` function, as follows:

```
X_train, X_test, Y_train, Y_test = train_test_split(X, Y, test_size=0.2,
random_state=1)
```

The `train_test_split()` function splits arrays or matrices into random `train` and `test` subsets. The first two arguments are X (predictors) and Y (target) NumPy arrays. The allowed inputs are lists, NumPy arrays, SciPy-sparse matrices, or pandas data frames. Then, two options are added:

- `test_size`: This should be between 0.0 and 1.0, and represents the proportion of the dataset to include in the test split
- `random_state`: This is the seed used by the random-number generator

After properly preparing the data, the time has come to define our model based on neural networks. As already expected, we will do this using the Keras liberia. Models in Keras are defined as a sequence of levels. To start creating a sequential model, use the following:

```
model = Sequential()
```

Now, let's add the levels one at a time until we are satisfied with the architecture of our network, as follows:

```
model.add(Dense(10, input_dim=9, activation='relu'))
```

The first level to add will define the input level—you need to make sure that it has the right number of inputs. This can be specified when creating the first layer with the `input_dim` argument. In our case, having already given the first variable (ID), we have set it to 9 to indicate that there are nine input variables. After setting the number of input variables, it is necessary to establish how many neurons will have to possess this level and how many levels our network must be composed of.

Before proceeding with the code analysis, a clarification should be made. The attentive reader can ask what the reason for our choice of the number of hidden layers and the number of neurons for each hidden layer. Unfortunately, there is no precise rule or even a mathematical formula that allows us to determine which numbers are appropriate for that specific problem. This is because every problem is different from every other problem, and each network approximates a system differently. So, what is the difference between one model and another? The answer is obvious and once again very clear—the researcher's experience.

The advice I can give, which stems from my vast experience in data analysis, is to try, try, and try again. The secret to experimental activity is just that. In the case of neural networks, this consists of trying to set up different networks and then verifying their performance.

However, there are some things that can be said, for example, about the optimum choice of the number of neurons that we need, such as the following:

- A small number of neurons will lead to a high error rate for your system, as the predictive factors might be too complex for a small number of neurons to capture
- A large number of neurons will over fit to your training data, and will not generalize well
- The number of neurons in each hidden layer should be somewhere between the size of the input and the output layer, potentially the mean
- The number of neurons in each hidden layer shouldn't exceed twice the number of input neurons, as you will probably be grossly overfitting at this point

In our case, we have used a fully connected network structure with two levels. In the first level, 10 neurons are set. Let's add the second layer, as follows:

```
model.add(Dense(1, activation='sigmoid'))
```

This layer defines the output, with 1 neuron to predict the class. Before proceeding, let's talk about the `activation` functions chosen. We have used the rectifier (`'relu'`) activation function on the first layer and the `'sigmoid'` function in the output layer. We used a `'sigmoid'` on the output layer to ensure that our network output is between 0 and 1. Now, we will compile the model, as follows:

```
model.compile(loss='binary_crossentropy', optimizer='adam',
metrics=['accuracy'])
```

The `.compile` method has been used to configure the learning process. The following arguments are passed:

- `loss`: By using `binary_crossentropy`, we have used logarithmic loss, which for a binary classification problem is defined in Keras as `'binary_crossentropy'`.
- `optimizer`: The `'adam'` optimizer has been used, and this is the default parameter to use when following those provided in the original paper.
- `metrics`: By using `'accuracy'`, we have collected and reported the classification accuracy as the metric because this is a classification problem.

The model fitting is performed using the following command:

```
model.fit(X_train, Y_train, epochs=200, batch_size=10)
```

The `.fit` method trains the model for a given number of epochs (iterations on a dataset). The following arguments are passed:

- `x_train`: NumPy array of training data returned from the splitting operation performed on the initial dataset
- `y_train`: NumPy array of target data returned from the splitting operation performed on the initial dataset
- `epochs`: In this case, 200, the number of epochs to train the model
- `batch_size`: In this case, 10, number of samples per gradient update

Finally, all we have to do is evaluate the network performance on the dataset that we set aside for the test phase. This will give us an idea of how well we have modeled the dataset and how much the model is able to generalize. The .evaluate method has been used to evaluate the model, as follows:

```
ResultEval = model.evaluate(X_test, Y_test)
print("\n%s: %.2f%%" % (model.metrics_names[1], ResultEval [1]*100))
```

The .evaluate method returns the loss and metrics values for the model in test mode. The metric was set when the model was compiled. We have set the classification accuracy as the metric because this is a classification problem. The following result is returned:

```
acc: 96.43%
```

The result is really good; an accuracy of 96.43% tells us that the model was able to recognize breast cancer in 96.43% of cases. In fact, the accuracy of a classifier is defined as the number of samples correctly classified with respect to the total number of samples classified.

Deep reinforcement learning

In the examples of the previous chapters, the estimates of the value function were made using a table, in which each box represents a state or a state–action pair. The use of a table to represent the value function allows the creation of simple algorithms and, if the environmental conditions are Markovian, allows to accurately estimate the value function because it assigns the expected return learned during policy iterations to every possible configuration from the environment. The use of the table, however, also leads to limitations; in fact, these methods are applicable only to environments with a reduced number of states and actions. The problem is not limited to the large amount of memory required to store the table, but also to the large amount of data and time required to estimate each state–action pair accurately. In other words, the main problem is generalization.

To solve this problem, we can adopt a method based on the combination of reinforcement learning methods with function approximation methods. The following diagram shows a Deep Q-learning scheme:

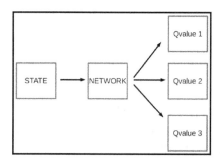

The term Deep Q-learning refers to a reinforcement learning method that adopts a neural network as a function approximation. It therefore represents an evolution of the basic Q-learning method since the state–action table is replaced by a neural network, with the aim of approximating the optimal value function.

Compared to the approaches seen in the previous chapters, where it was used to structure the network in order to request both input and action, and provide its expected return, Deep Q-learning revolutionizes the structure in order to request only the status in the input environment and provide as many status–action values as there are actions that can be performed in the environment.

The Keras–RL package

In the previous sections, we learned how to make a simple neural network with Keras. But, our goal is to develop algorithms based on reinforcement learning in the Keras environment. To do this, a valid tool that can be used is the `keras-rl` package. This package implements some deep reinforcement learning algorithms in Python, and integrates seamlessly with Keras's in-depth learning library.

Furthermore, `keras-rl` works immediately with OpenAI Gym. OpenAI Gym is a library that helps you implement algorithms based on reinforcement learning. It includes a growing collection of benchmark issues that expose a common interface and a website where people can share their results and compare algorithm performance. This library will be adequately addressed in the next chapter—for now, we will limit ourselves to using it.

These prerogatives do not limit the use of the `keras-rl` package, in the sense that the uses of `keras-rl` can be easily adapted to our needs. You can use the built-in Keras callbacks and metrics, or define others. For this reason, it is easy to implement your own environments and even algorithms simply by extending some simple abstract classes.

Currently, the following algorithms have been implemented:

- **Deep Q-learning (DQN)**
- Double DQN
- **Deep deterministic policy gradient (DDPG)**
- **Continuous DQN (CDQN or NAF)**
- The **cross-entropy method (CEM)**
- **Dueling network DQN (dueling DQN)**
- Deep SARSA
- **Asynchronous advantage actor–critic (A3C)**
- **Proximal policy optimization algorithms (PPO)**

The `keras-rl` package has been implemented by Matthias Plappert, a researcher scientist at the Karlsruhe Institute of Technology (in Karlsruhe, Germany) working on machine learning, particularly deep reinforcement learning in robotics.

 You can learn more at his GitHub section at `https://github.com/matthiasplappert`.

Installing `keras-rl` is easy. Just run the following commands and you should be good to go:

```
pip install keras-rl
```

This will install `keras-rl` and all necessary dependencies. In the following section, we will analyze an example of continuous Deep Q-learning using `keras-rl`.

Continuous control with deep reinforcement learning

In this example, we will address the problem of an inverted pendulum swinging up—this is a classic problem in control theory. In this version of the problem, the pendulum starts in a random position, and the goal is to swing it up so that it stays upright. Torque limits prevent the agent from swinging the pendulum up directly. The following diagram shows the problem:

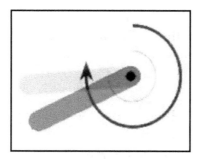

The problem is addressed using an environment available in the OpenAI Gym library (Pendulum-v0) with the help of the DDPG agent of the keras-rl library (DDPGAgent).

OpenAI Gym is a library that helps us to implement algorithms based on reinforcement learning. It includes a growing collection of benchmark issues that expose a common interface and a website where people can share their results and compare algorithm performance. For the moment, we will imitate the use of the OpenAI Gym library; for more details, we will deepen the concepts that we will soon be looking at in Chapter 7, *Dynamic Modeling of a Segway as an Inverted Pendulum System*. The Pendulum-v0 environment is very similar to the CartPole environment (which we will use in the following chapter), but with an essential difference—we are expanding from a discrete environment (CartPole) to a continuous environment (Pendulum-v0).

The DDPG agent is based on an adaptation of Deep Q-learning to the domain of continuous action. This is an actor–critic algorithm, devoid of models, based on a deterministic policy gradient that can operate on continuous action spaces. Using the same learning algorithm, network architecture, and hyperparameters, this algorithm effectively solves several simulated physical activities, including classic problems, such as the inverted pendulum problem.

Actor–critic methods implement a generalized policy iteration, alternating between a policy evaluation and a policy improvement step. There are two closely related processes of actor improvement that aim at improving the current policy and critic evaluation, evaluating the current policy. If the critic is modeled by a bootstrapping method, it reduces the variance so that the learning is more stable than pure policy gradient methods.

Let's analyze the code in detail. As always, we will start with importing of the library necessary for our calculations, as follows:

```
import numpy as np
import gym
```

As shown in the following code, first we import the numpy library, which will be used to set the seed value. Then, we import the gym library, that will help us to define the environment. Having done this, we import some functions of the keras library to build a neural network model:

```
from keras.models import Sequential, Model
from keras.layers import Dense, Activation, Flatten, Input, Concatenate
from keras.optimizers import Adam
```

First, the Sequential model is imported, and the Sequential model is a linear stack of layers. Then, some keras layers are imported—Dense, Activation, Flatten, Input, and Concatenate. A Dense model is a fully connected neural network layer. The Activation layer applies an activation function to an output. The Flatten layer flattens the input—this does not affect the batch size. The Input layer is used to instantiate a Keras tensor. A Keras tensor is a tensor object from the underlying backend (Theano, TensorFlow, or CNTK), which we augment with certain attributes that allow us to build a Keras model just by knowing the inputs and outputs of the model. Finally, the Concatenate layer concatenates a list of inputs. It takes as an input a list of tensors, that are all of the same shape except for the concatenation axis, and returns a single tensor, the concatenation of all inputs.

Let's import the keras-rl library, as follows:

```
from rl.agents import DDPGAgent
from rl.memory import SequentialMemory
from rl.random import OrnsteinUhlenbeckProcess
```

The DDPGAgent, a memory, and a random model are imported. Now, we will define the environment, as follows:

```
ENV_NAME = 'Pendulum-v0'
gym.undo_logger_setup()
```

In this way, we have set the name of the environment. Then, gym.undo_logger_setup() is called to undo Gym's logger setup and configure things manually. The default should be fine, most of the time. Let's get the environment, as follows:

```
env = gym.make(ENV_NAME)
```

The NumPy random.seed() function is used to set the seed value, as follows:

```
np.random.seed(123)
```

The `seed` function sets the seed of the random-number generator, which is useful for creating simulations or random objects that can be reproduced. You have to use this function every time you want to get a reproducible random result. The `seed` function must also be set for the environment, as follows:

```
env.seed(123)
```

Now, we will extract the actions that are available to the agent, as follows:

```
assert len(env.action_space.shape) == 1
nb_actions = env.action_space.shape[0]
```

When it encounters an `assert` statement, Python evaluates the accompanying expression, which is hopefully `true`. If the expression is `false`, Python raises an `AssertionError` exception. The `nb_actions` variable now contains all the actions available in the selected environment. `gym` will not always tell you what these actions mean, but only which ones are available. Now, we will build a simple neural network model using the Keras library, starting from the `actor` model definition, as shown in the following code:

```
actor = Sequential()
actor.add(Flatten(input_shape=(1,) + env.observation_space.shape))
actor.add(Dense(16))
actor.add(Activation('relu'))
actor.add(Dense(16))
actor.add(Activation('relu'))
actor.add(Dense(16))
actor.add(Activation('relu'))
actor.add(Dense(nb_actions))
actor.add(Activation('linear'))
print(actor.summary())
```

The `actor` model, given the current state of the environment, determines the best action to take. In this phase, only numeric data is treated, so there will be no more complex layers in the network than the dense/fully connected layers we've been using thus far. It follows that the `actor` model is quite simply a series of fully connected layers that map from the environment observation to a point in the environment space. Now, let's move on to the critic network, as follows:

```
action_input = Input(shape=(nb_actions,), name='action_input')
observation_input = Input(shape=(1,) + env.observation_space.shape,
name='observation_input')
flattened_observation = Flatten()(observation_input)
x = Concatenate()([action_input, flattened_observation])
x = Dense(32)(x)x = Activation('relu')(x)
x = Dense(32)(x)
x = Activation('relu')(x)
```

```
x = Dense(32)(x)
x = Activation('relu')(x)
x = Dense(1)(x)
x = Activation('linear')(x)
critic = Model(inputs=[action_input, observation_input], outputs=x)
print(critic.summary())
```

In this case, we are essentially faced with the opposite issue. That is, the network definition is slightly more complicated, but its training is relatively straightforward. The critic network is intended to take both the environment state and action as inputs and calculate a corresponding valuation. Now that the neural network model is ready to use, let's configure and compile our agent. One problem with using the DQN is that the neural network used in the algorithm tends to forget previous experiences because it overwrites them with new experiences. So, we need a list of previous experiences and observations to reform the model with previous experiences. For this reason, a memory variable is defined that will contain the previous experiences, as follows:

```
memory = SequentialMemory(limit=100000, window_length=1)
```

Now, we will define a random_process, as follows:

```
random_process = OrnsteinUhlenbeckProcess(size=nb_actions, theta=.15,
mu=0., sigma=.3)
```

So now, we just have to define the agent, as follows:

```
agent = DDPGAgent(nb_actions=nb_actions, actor=actor, critic=critic,
critic_action_input=action_input, memory=memory,
nb_steps_warmup_critic=100, nb_steps_warmup_actor=100,
random_process=random_process, gamma=.99, target_model_update=1e-3)
```

Let's compile the model using the following code:

```
agent.compile(Adam(lr=.001, clipnorm=1.), metrics=['mae'])
```

This command compiles an agent and the underlying models to be used for training and testing. Now that the agent is ready, we can train it, as follows:

```
agent.fit(env, nb_steps=50000, visualize=True, verbose=1,
nb_max_episode_steps=200)
```

The `fit()` function trains the `agent` on the given environment. At the end of the training, we have to save the weights that we obtained, as follows:

```
agent.save_weights('ddpg_{}_weights.h5f'.format(ENV_NAME), overwrite=True)
```

Saving the weight of a network or an entire structure takes place in an HDF5 file, an efficient and flexible storage system that supports complex multidimensional datasets. Finally, we will evaluate our algorithm for 10 episodes, as follows:

```
agent.test(env, nb_episodes=10, visualize=True, nb_max_episode_steps=200)
```

From the simulation, we can verify that our agent was able to balance the system with a good approximation.

Summary

In this chapter, we learned the basic concepts of artificial neural networks. We also learned how to apply neural network methods to our data, and how neural network algorithms work. We learned about the basic concepts that deep neural networks use to approximate reinforcement learning components.

Then, we looked at the basics of the Keras neural network model, as well as a practical example of the Keras neural network model. Then, we moved on to explore the Deep Q-learning concepts. The term "Deep Q-learning" refers to a reinforcement learning method that adopts a neural network as a function approximation. It therefore represents an evolution of the basic Q-learning method, as the state–action table is replaced by a neural network, with the aim of approximating the optimal value function. This network have the current state as input, and the corresponding Q-value for each of the action as output.

Then, we introduced the `keras-rl` package, which implements some deep reinforcement learning algorithms in Python and integrates seamlessly with Keras's in-depth learning library. Lastly, we looked at a practical example of deep reinforcement learning algorithms using Keras and `keras-rl`.

7
Dynamic Modeling of a Segway as an Inverted Pendulum System

A Segway is a personal transport device that exploits an innovative combination of computer science, electronics, and mechanics. It functions as an extension of the body; as with a partner in a dance, it is able to anticipate every move. The operating principle is based on the reverse pendulum system. The reverse pendulum system is an example commonly found in textbooks on control and research literature. Its popularity derives in part from the fact that it is unstable without control and has a non-linear dynamic, but above all, because it has several practical applications, such as controlling a takeoff rocket or a Segway.

In this chapter, we will analyze the functioning of a physical system made by connecting a rigid rod to a cart, modeling the system using different approaches. The rod is connected through a pivot hinged on the carriage and is free to rotate around it. This mechanical system, which is called the reverse pendulum, is a classic problem in control theory. Generally, it is widely used to evaluate the performance of various algorithms (PID controllers, neural networks, fuzzy logic, genetic algorithms, and so on).

The following are the topics covered in the chapter:

- Inverted pendulum system
- OpenAI Gym library
- Q-learning
- CartPole environment

By the end of the chapter, the reader will have learned the basic concepts of Q-learning and how to use this technique to control a mechanical system. They will have discovered the meaning of the most used terms, such as force equilibrium, pendulum mass, and moment of inertia. They will have learned the basics of the OpenAI Gym library, as well as how to use Q-learning to solve the CartPole problem.

How Segways work

The Segway was invented by Dean Kamen, who presented the prototype in 2001. It is an electric traction-transport vehicle for individual locomotion, a very advanced technological concept, initially called Ginger. It is a sort of intelligent scooter that can start, stop, and reverse with simple movements of the passenger-driver body, slight bending forward or backward, and making curves with the help of a knob on the left-hand side of the handlebar. In the following model, called Segway PT, the steering was entrusted to the column that is no longer rigid, but tilt able to the right or left to induce the desired direction changes. The model equipped with the old steering system (Segway HT) is no longer in production. In the following photograph, a Segway PT is shown:

One day, inventor Dean Kamen saw a young man in a wheelchair who was trying to get onto the sidewalk. He understood that the problem was not due to the poor quality of the wheelchair, but from the fact that the world was built for people who managed to keep their balance. Following this, he and his team created the INDEPENDENCE™ iBOT™ Mobility System, a self-balancing machine that allowed users to climb stairs and tackle uneven surfaces. After this, it increased the belief that a balanced vehicle could be a far-reaching solution for all mobility in general. The name Segway derives from the English word "segue," intended as a gradual transition from one state to another. Segway transforms people into enhanced pedestrians, allowing them to go further, do it faster, and carry more things.

After presenting the model to the press, for which it received a very positive reception, the manufacturing company began mass production with the hope of selling an average of 50,000 pieces per year; unfortunately, after 21 months of production, only 6,000 were sold. In September 2003, the manufacturer recalled all the specimens built to remedy a design error, having presented a safety problem in the presence of almost discharged batteries.

Numerous public organizations have considered the possibility of having this type of transportation for use in large cities. For example, they have been tested by police forces and are often used by railway police in stations, although one of the great limits encountered is often having both hands engaged for driving, making it impossible to be able to hold an umbrella, for example. A second criticism has been moved to the autonomy and reliability of the batteries—problems that should be solved with the adoption of new types of batteries.

The functioning of the PT is very similar to that of the human body. It applies a technology called dynamic stabilization to maintain its balance, move forward, or back away. When a person walks, if they shift the weight of their body forward, they tend to take a step forward to keep themselves balanced; in the same way, when they move the weight of their body backward, they tend to take a step backward. On board the PT, the forward displacement of the body drives the wheels of the vehicle, which begin to advance in that direction. In the following picture, we have a physic of walking:

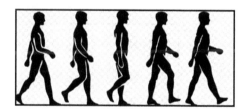

When you lean forward, you only move your center of gravity beyond the point of contact (the point where the tires are in contact with the ground). As a result, the PT tilts slightly forward. The PT systems detect this change and operate the wheels to keep them constantly below the center of gravity of the person on board.

By tilting the LeanSteer to the left, the PT turns left in the same way, by tilting it to the right, the PT turns to the right. To make a curve, direct the LeanSteer in the desired direction, keeping the handlebars aligned to the body. Returning the LeanSteer to the center, the PT resumes traveling in a straight line.

The dynamic stabilization technology of the PT provides dynamic stability when moving back and forth, but does not act on lateral stability, thereby unbalancing the PT on a wheel. This will not compensate for any loss of lateral balance and the person on board could fall.

The user is required to remain stable laterally on the PT, keeping the body in line with the LeanSteer. Tilt into the curves and lean forward to maintain lateral balance.

System modeling basics

A simple pendulum is constituted by an inextensible thread to which a mass material point can be hung that can oscillate around a fixed point called a pole. The component of the weight force along the wire counterbalances the tension of the wire itself, while the component of the weight force perpendicular to the wire acts as a return force and produces the oscillatory motion of the pendulum.

The reverse pendulum represents a simple inverted pendulum, rigid, and without a fixed point. The lower part can therefore move to balance the oscillations of the highest part and thus ensure equilibrium; the control problem therefore leads back to wanting to stabilize the position of a rod constrained to a carriage free to move along a guide.

The modeling of the inverted pendulum is certainly a well-known problem, and there are many sources that report studies that derive models with different levels of approximation. The inverted pendulum system is a popular demonstration of using feedback control to stabilize an open-loop unstable system. A model scheme is shown in the following diagram:.

In this case, the system to be analyzed consists of a reverse pendulum mounted on a motorized trolley. The aim of the control system is to balance the reverse pendulum by applying a torque to the wheels of the carriage to which the pendulum is connected. The control input is the force that moves the carriage horizontally while the output is the angular position of the pendulum. In particular, we considered a two-dimensional problem in which the pendulum is unable to move in the vertical plane. Another example of a real system that can be assimilated to a reverse pendulum consists of a rocket launcher battery placed on a mobile vehicle.

In order to determine the model, it is necessary to analyze the forces acting on the inverted pendulum; for greater clarity, the study of the equations of motion has been divided into the two parts that make up the system. The terms in question are shown in the following list:

- Mass of the cart
- Pendulum mass
- Friction coefficient of the cart
- Length up to the center of mass of the pendulum
- Moment of inertia of the pendulum
- Driving force applied to the cart
- Angle of the pendulum from the vertical
- Cart position coordinate

In the following diagram, a model scheme is shown:

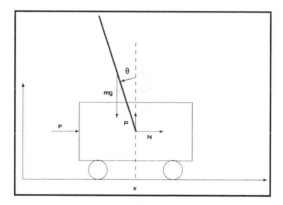

The equations of the system are those of balancing the horizontal and vertical components of the acting forces. Indicate respectively with P and N the vertical and horizontal force exerted by the cart on the rod, with L the distance of the center of gravity of the rod from the hinge and with I the moment of inertia of the rod with respect to the center of gravity. Let it also be the acceleration of gravity. The motion of the rod's barycenter is described by the following equations:

$$N(t) = m\frac{d^2}{dt^2}(x(t) - Lsin(\theta(t)))$$

$$P(t) - mg = m\frac{d^2}{dt^2}(Lcos(\theta(t)))$$

The rotation motion relative to the center of gravity is described by the following equation:

$$LP(t)sin(\theta(t)) + LN(t)cos(\theta(t)) = I\frac{d^2}{dt^2}(\theta(t))$$

Finally, the motion of the cart is described by the following equation:

$$M\frac{d^2}{dt^2}(x(t)) = -N(t) + F(t) - (b\frac{d}{dt}x(t)))$$

In the previous equation, we took into account the presence of a viscous friction of coefficient b.

It is immediately evident how having perfect control of the instrument is not at all easy. On the contrary, it requires a thorough study and many experiments before being able to have a positive response.

OpenAI Gym

OpenAI Gym is a library that helps us to implement algorithms based on reinforcement learning. It includes a growing collection of benchmark issues that expose a common interface, and a website where people can share their results and compare algorithm performance.

OpenAI Gym focuses on the episodic setting of reinforced learning. In other words, the agent's experience is divided into a series of episodes. The initial state of the agent is randomly sampled by a distribution, and the interaction proceeds until the environment reaches a terminal state. This procedure is repeated for each episode, with the aim of maximizing the total reward expectation per episode and achieving a high level of performance in the fewest possible episodes.

Gym is a toolkit for developing and comparing reinforcement-learning algorithms. It supports the ability to teach agents everything from walking to playing games such as Pong or Pinball. The library is available at https://gym.openai.com/.

The following screenshot shows the home page of the OpenAI Gym project site:

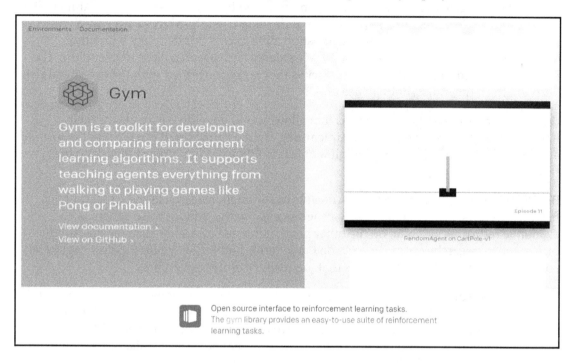

OpenAI Gym includes a growing collection of environments that address the most common problems in reinforcement learning. OpenAI Gym is supported by a website where each user has the possibility to publish the results obtained on a certain environment, in order to compare the performance of the different algorithms with the community. Furthermore, users are encouraged to also share the source code that allowed them to obtain the results loaded, with detailed instructions for easy reproduction of the results obtained from them.

OpenAI Gym also provides abstractions and interfaces for the creation of new environments, and is able to manage rendering, preventing the developer from worrying about it. Since the framework was created specifically for the study of reinforcement-learning algorithms, the interfaces proposed for the interactions between environment and agent exactly match the elements required by the problem.

OpenAI Gym assumes that the environment is episodic in nature and that the agent interacts with it at each step by performing one of the possible actions. Interacting with the environment, the agent obtains information such as status, reward, and a flag indicating the eventual completion of the episode, used by the agent to determine when it is appropriate to reset the environment and start a new episode.

OpenAI Gym is part of a much more ambitious project: the OpenAI project. OpenAI is an **artificial intelligence** (**AI**) research company founded by Elon Musk and Sam Altman. It is a non-profit project that aims to promote and develop friendly AI in such a way as to benefit humanity as a whole. The organization aims to collaborate freely with other institutions and researchers by making their patents and research open to the public. The founders decided to undertake this project as they were concerned with the existential risk deriving from the indiscriminate use of AI.

OpenAI Gym is a library of programs that allow you to develop AIs, measure their intellectual abilities, and enhance their learning abilities. In short, it is a Gym in the form of algorithms that trains the present digital brains to OpenAI Gym project them into the future.

But there is also another goal. OpenAI wants to stimulate research in the AI sector by funding projects that make humanity progress even in those fields where there is no economic return. With Gym, on the other hand, it intends to standardize the measurement of AI so that researchers can compete on equal terms and know where their colleagues have come but, above all, focus on results that are really useful for everyone.

The tools available are many. From the ability to play old video games such as Pong to that of fighting in the GO to control a robot, we just enter our algorithm in this digital place to see how it works. The second step is to compare the benchmarks obtained with the other ones to see where we stand compared to others, and maybe we can collaborate with them to get mutual benefits. In the following list are some environments available in the library (the environments are grouped by category to simplify the search):

- **Algorithms**: Perform computations such as adding multi-digit numbers and reversing sequences. One might object that these tasks are easy for a computer. The challenge is to learn these algorithms purely from examples. These tasks have the nice property that it's easy to vary the difficulty by varying the sequence length.
- **Atari**: Play classic Atari games. We've integrated the Arcade Learning Environment (which has had a big impact on reinforcement learning research) in an easy-to-install form.
- **Box2D**: Continuous control tasks in the Box2D simulator.
- **Classic control**: Complete small-scale tasks, mostly from the reinforcement learning literature. They're here to get you started.
- **MuJoCo**: Continuous control tasks, running in a fast physics simulator. This task use the MuJoCo physics engine, which was designed for fast and accurate robot simulation.

- **Robotics**: Simulated goal-based tasks for the Fetch and ShadowHand robots.
- **Toy text**: Simple text environments to get you started.

In particular, the classic control category offers very useful environments to reproduce the scenarios of important physical experiments, as shown in the following screenshot:

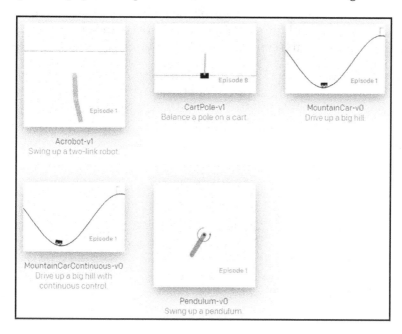

OpenAI Gym makes no assumptions about the structure of our agent and is compatible with any numerical computation library, such as TensorFlow or Theano. The Gym library is a collection of test problems—environments—that we can use to work out our reinforcement-learning algorithms. These environments have a shared interface, allowing you to write general algorithms.

OpenAI Gym methods

OpenAI Gym provides the `Env` class, which encapsulates the environment and its possible internal dynamics. The class has different methods and attributes to implement to create a new environment. The most important methods are called `reset`, `step`, and `render`.

The `reset` method has the task of resetting the environment, initializing it to the initial state. Within the `reset` method, the definitions of the elements that make up the environment must be contained, in this case the definition of the mechanical arm, of the object to be grasped and its support.
The `step` method has the task of moving the environment forward by one step. It requires the action to be performed as input and returns the new observation to the agent. Within the method, the management of the dynamics of the movements, the calculation of the status and of the reward, and the controls for completing the episode must be defined.

The third and last method is to render to which interior must be defined as the elements at each step must be represented. The method involves different types of rendering, such as `human`, `rgb_array`, or `ansi`. With the `human` type, the rendering is done on the screen or command-line interface and the method does not return anything; with the `rgb_array` type, invoking the method returns an *n*-dimensional array representing the RGB pixels of the screen; choosing the third type, the `return` method returns a string containing a textual representation. To render, OpenAI Gym provides the `viewer` class, through which you can draw the elements of the environment as a set of polygons and circles.

Regarding the attributes of the environment, the `Env` class provides the definition of action space, observation space, and reward range. The action space attribute represents the action space, which is the set of possible actions that the agent can perform within the environment. Using the observation space attribute, the number of parameters that make up the state is defined, and for each of them the range of values that can be assumed. The reward `range` attribute contains the minimum and maximum rewards obtainable in the environment, by default set to $(-\infty, +\infty)$.

Using the `Env` class proposed by the framework as a basis for new environments, the common interface provided by the toolkit is adopted. In this way, the environments created can be integrated into the `toolkit` library and their dynamics can be learned from algorithms already implemented by users of the OpenAI Gym community.

OpenAI Gym installation

To install OpenAI Gym, make sure you have previously installed a Python 3.5+ version; then simply type the following command:

```
pip install gym
```

Once this is done, we will be able to insert the tools made available by the library in a simple and immediate way.

The library also offers the possibility to directly clone the Gym's Git repository. This may be necessary if you want to change an environment or add other environments. To clone the Git repository, execute the following commands:

```
git clone https://github.com/openai/gym
cd gym
pip install -e .
```

Next, execute the following command:

```
pip install -e .[all]
```

In this way, we perform a full installation that contains all environments. This requires installing several more involved dependencies, including cmake and a recent pip version.

The CartPole system

The CartPole system is a classic problem of reinforced learning. The system consists of a pole (which acts like an inverted pendulum) attached to a cart via a joint, as shown in the following diagram:

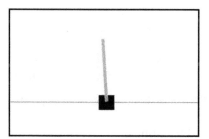

The system is controlled by applying a force of +1 or -1 to the cart. The force applied to the cart can be controlled, and the objective is to swing the pole upward and stabilize it. This must be done without the cart falling to the ground. At every step, the agent can choose to move the cart left or right, and it receives a reward of 1 for every time step that the pole is balanced. If the pole ever deviates by more than 15 degrees from upright, the procedure ends.

To run the CartPole example using the OpenAI Gym library, simply type the following code:

```
import gym
env = gym.make('CartPole-v0')
env.reset()
```

```
for i in range(1000):
    env.render()
    env.step(env.action_space.sample())
```

As always, we will explain the meaning of each line of code in detail. The first line is used to import the `gym` library:

```
import gym
```

Then we move on to create the environment by calling the `make` method:

```
env = gym.make('CartPole-v0')
```

This method creates the environment that our agent will run in. An environment is a problem with a minimal interface that an agent can interact with. The environments in OpenAI Gym are designed to allow the objective testing and benchmarking of an agent's abilities. The `gym` library comes with a diverse suite of environments, which range from easy to difficult and involve many different kinds of data.

For a list of the available environments, refer to `https://gym.openai.com/envs`.

The most-used environments are listed here:

- **Classic control and toy text**: Completes small-scale tasks, mostly from the reinforcement learning literature. They're here to get you started.
- **Algorithmic**: Performs computations such as adding multi-digit numbers and reversing sequences.
- **Atari**: Plays classic Atari games.
- **2D and 3D robots**: Controls a robot in simulation.

In our case, we have called the CartPole-v0 environment. The `make` method returns an `env` object that we will use to interact with the game. But let's go back to analyzing the code.

Now we have to initialize the system using the `reset()` method:

```
env.reset()
```

This method puts the environment into its initial state, returning an array that describes it. At this point, we will use a `for` loop to run an instance of the CartPole-v0 environment for `1000` time steps, rendering the environment at each step:

```
for i in range(1000):
    env.render()
    env.step(env.action_space.sample())
```

Calling the `render()` method will visually display the current state, while subsequent calls to `env.step()` will allow us to interact with the environment, returning the new states in response to the actions with which we call it.

In this way, we have adopted random actions at each step. At this point, it is certainly useful to know what actions we are doing on the environment to decide future actions. The `step()` method returns exactly this. In effect, this method returns the following four values:

- `observation`: An environment-specific object representing your observation of the environment.
- `reward`: Amount of reward achieved by the previous action. The scale varies between environments, but the goal is always to increase your total reward.
- `done`: Whether it's time to reset the environment again. Most (but not all) tasks are divided into well-defined episodes, and `done` being `True` indicates that the episode has terminated.
- `info`: Diagnostic information useful for debugging. It can sometimes be useful for learning.

To run this simple example, save the code in a file named `cart.py` and type the following command in the Terminal window:

```
python cart.py
```

In this way, a window will be displayed containing our system that is not stable and will soon go out of the screen. This is because the push to the cart is given randomly, without taking into account the position of the pole.

To solve the problem, that is, to balance the pole, it is therefore necessary to set the push in the opposite direction to the inclination of the pole. So, we have to set only two actions, -1 or +1, pushing the cart to the left or the right. But in order to do so, we need to know at all times the data deriving from the observation of the environment. As we have already said, these pieces of data are returned by the `step()` method, in particular, they are contained in the observation object.

This object contains the following parameters:

- Cart position
- Cart velocity
- Pole angle
- Pole velocity at tip

These four values become the input of our problem. As we have also anticipated, the system is balanced by applying a push to the cart. There are two possible options:

- Push the cart to the left (0)
- Push it to the right (1)

It is clear that this is a binary classification problem: four inputs and a single binary output.

Let's first consider how to extract the values to be used as input. To extract these parameters, we just have to change the preceding proposed code:

```
import gym
env = gym.make('CartPole-v0')
observation = env.reset()
for i in range(1000):
    env.render()
    print(observation)
    observation, reward, done, info = env.step(env.action_space.sample())
```

By running the code, we can see that the values contained in the observation object are now printed on the screen. All this will be useful soon.

Using values returned from the environment observations, the agent has to decide on one of two possible actions: to move the cart left or right.

Q-learning solution

Now we have to face the most demanding phase: the training of our system. In the previous section, we said that the gym library is focused on the episodic setting of reinforced learning. The agent's experience is divided into a series of episodes. The initial state of the agent is randomly sampled by a distribution and the interaction proceeds until the environment reaches a terminal state. This procedure is repeated for each episode with the aim of maximizing the total reward expectation per episode and achieving a high level of performance in the fewest possible episodes.

In the learning phase, we must estimate an evaluation function. This function must be able to evaluate, through the sum of the rewards, the convenience or otherwise of a particular policy. In other words, we must approximate the evaluation function. How can we do this? One solution is to use an artificial neural network as a function approximator.

Recall that the training of a neural network aims to identify the weights of the connections between neurons. In this case, we will choose random values with weights for each episode. At the end, we will choose the combination of weights that will have collected the maximum reward.

The state of the system at a given moment is returned to us by the observation object. To choose an action from the actual state, we can use a linear combination of the weights and the observation. This is one of the most important special cases of function approximation, in which the approximate function is a linear function of the weight vector, w. For every state, s, there is a real-valued vector, $x(s)$, with the same number of components as w. Linear methods approximate the state-value function by the inner product between w and $x(s)$.

In this way, we have specified the methodology that we intend to adopt for the solution of the problem. Now, to make the whole training phase easily understandable, we report the whole code block and then comment on it in detail on a line-by-line basis:

```
import gym
import numpy as np
env = gym.make('CartPole-v0')
HighReward = 0
BestWeights = None
for i in range(200):
    observation = env.reset()
    Weights = np.random.uniform(-1,1,4)
    SumReward = 0
    for j in range(1000):
        env.render()
        action = 0 if np.matmul(Weights,observation) < 0 else 1
        observation, reward, done, info = env.step(action)
        SumReward += reward
        print( i, j, Weights, observation, action, SumReward, BestWeights)
    if SumReward > HighReward:
        HighReward = SumReward
        BestWeights = Weights
```

The first part of the code deals with importing the libraries:

```
import gym
import numpy as np
```

Then we move on to create the environment by calling the `make()` method:

```
env = gym.make('CartPole-v0')
```

This method creates the environment that our agent will run in. Now let's initialize the parameters we will use:

```
HighReward = 0
BestWeights = None
```

The `HighReward` variable will contain the maximum reward obtained up to the current episode; this value will be used as a comparison value. The `BestWeights` variable will contain the sequence of weights that will have registered the maximum reward. We can now implement the best weight sequence search through an iterative procedure for episodes:

```
for i in range(200):
```

We decide to execute the procedure 200 times, so we initialize the system using the `reset()` method:

```
observation = env.reset()
```

In each episode, we use a sequence of weights equal in number to the observations of the environment, which as previously said is four (cart position, cart velocity, pole angle, and pole velocity at tip):

```
Weights = np.random.uniform(-1,1,4)
```

To fix the weights, we have used the `np.random.uniform()` function. This function draws samples from a uniform distribution. Samples are uniformly distributed over the half-open interval (low and high). It includes low but excludes high.

In other words, any value within the given interval is equally likely to be drawn by a uniform distribution. Three parameters have been passed: the lower boundary of the output interval, its upper boundary, and the output shape. In our case, we requested four random values in the interval (-1, 1). After doing this, we initialize the sum of the rewards:

```
SumReward = 0
```

At this point, we implement another iterative cycle to determine the maximum reward we can get with these weights:

```
for j in range(1000):
```

Calling the `render()` method will visually display the current state:

```
env.render()
```

Now, we have to decide the action:

```
action = 0 if np.matmul(Weights,observation) < 0 else 1
```

As we said, to decide the action we have used a linear combination of two vectors: `Weights` and `observation`. To perform a linear combination, we have used the `np.matmul()` function; it implements a matrix product of two arrays. So, if this product is <0, the action is 0 (move left); otherwise, the action is 1 (move right).

It should be noted that a negative product means that the pole is tilted to the left, so in order to balance this trend, it is necessary to push the cart toward the left. A positive product means the pole is tilted to the right, so in order to balance this trend, it is necessary to push the cart toward the right.

Now we use the `step()` method to return the new states in response to the actions with which we call it. Obviously, the action we pass to the method is the one we have just decided:

```
observation, reward, done, info = env.step(action)
```

As we said, this method returns the following four values:

- `observation`: An environment-specific object representing your observation of the environment.
- `reward`: The amount of reward achieved by the previous action. The scale varies between environments, but the goal is always to increase your total reward. It is of the `float` type.
- `done`: Whether it's time to reset the environment again. Most (but not all) tasks are divided into well-defined episodes, and `done` being True indicates that the episode has terminated. It is of the `Boolean` type.
- `info`: Diagnostic information useful for debugging. It can sometimes be useful for learning. It is of the `dict` type.

We can then update the sum of the rewards with the one just obtained. Remember that, for every time step where we keep the pole straight, we get +1 reward:

```
SumReward += reward
```

We just have to print the values obtained in this step:

```
print ( i, j, Weights, observation, action, SumReward, BestWeights)
```

At the end of the current iteration, we can make a comparison to check whether the total reward obtained is the highest one obtained so far:

```
if SumReward > HighReward:
```

If it is the highest reward obtained so far, update the `HighReward` parameter with this value:

```
HighReward = SumReward
```

Once this is done, fix the sequence of `Weights` of the current step as the best one:

```
BestWeights = Weights
```

With this instruction, the training phase ends, which will give us the sequence of weights that best approximate the evaluation function. We can now test the system.

When the training phase is achieved, in practice it means that we have found the sequence of weights that best approximates this function, that is, the one that has returned the best reward achievable. Now we have to test the system with these values to check whether the pole is able to stand for at least 100 time steps.

Now, as we are already done in the training phase, to make the whole testing phase easily understandable, we report the whole code block and then comment on it in detail on a line-by-line basis:

```
observation = env.reset()
for j in range(100):
    env.render()
    action = 0 if np.matmul(BestWeights,observation) < 0 else 1
    observation, reward, done, info = env.step(action)
    print ( j, action)
```

First, we have to initialize the system once again, using the `reset()` method:

```
observation = env.reset()
```

Then, we have to run an iterative cycle to apply the results obtained in the training phase:

```
for j in range(100):
```

For each step, we will call the `render()` method to visually display the current state:

```
env.render()
```

Now, we have to decide the action to perform on the system based on the best weights obtained in the training phase and on the observations of the current state:

```
action = 0 if np.matmul(BestWeights,observation) < 0 else 1
```

Now we use the `step()` method that returns the new states in response to the actions with which we call it. The action passed to the method is the one we have just decided:

```
observation, reward, done, info = env.step(action)
```

Finally, we print the step number and the action decided for visual control of the flow. By running the proposed code, we can verify that, after the training phase, the system is able to keep the pole in equilibrium for 100 time steps.

Deep Q-learning solution

As we said in `Chapter 1`, *Overview of Keras Reinforcement Learning*, the term Deep Q-learning identifies a reinforcement-learning method of the approximation of a function. It therefore represents an evolution of the basic Q-learning method since the state-action table is replaced by a neural network, with the aim of approximating the optimal value function.

Compared to the previous approaches, where it was used to structure the network in order to request both input and action, and providing its expected return, Deep Q-learning revolutionizes the structure in order to request only the state of the environment and supplying as many status-action values as there are actions that can be performed in the environment.

In the following code, a Deep Q-learning solution for the CartPole problem is proposed:

```
import numpy as np
import gym

from keras.models import Sequential
from keras.layers import Dense, Activation, Flatten
from keras.optimizers import Adam

from rl.agents.dqn import DQNAgent
from rl.policy import BoltzmannQPolicy
from rl.memory import SequentialMemory

ENV_NAME = 'CartPole-v0'

env = gym.make(ENV_NAME)
np.random.seed(123)
env.seed(123)
```

```python
nb_actions = env.action_space.n

model = Sequential()
model.add(Flatten(input_shape=(1,) + env.observation_space.shape))
model.add(Dense(16))
model.add(Activation('relu'))
model.add(Dense(16))
model.add(Activation('relu'))
model.add(Dense(16))
model.add(Activation('relu'))
model.add(Dense(nb_actions))
model.add(Activation('linear'))
print(model.summary())

memory = SequentialMemory(limit=50000, window_length=1)
policy = BoltzmannQPolicy()

dqn = DQNAgent(model=model, nb_actions=nb_actions, memory=memory,
               nb_steps_warmup=10, target_model_update=1e-2,
               policy=policy)

dqn.compile(Adam(lr=1e-3), metrics=['mae'])

dqn.fit(env, nb_steps=1000, visualize=True, verbose=2)

dqn.save_weights('dqn_{}_weights.h5f'.format(ENV_NAME), overwrite=True)

dqn.test(env, nb_episodes=5, visualize=True)
```

As already done in all the examples proposed so far, we will analyze this code line by line to understand its operating principle. The first part of the code is used to import libraries:

```python
import numpy as np
import gym
```

First, we import the numpy library, which will be used to set the seed value. So we import the gym library that will help us to define the environment. Having done this, we import some functions of the keras library to build a neural network model:

```python
from keras.models import Sequential
from keras.layers import Dense, Activation, Flatten
from keras.optimizers import Adam
```

Keras is a high-level neural network API, written in Python and capable of running on top of TensorFlow, CNTK, or Theano. It was developed with a focus on enabling fast experimentation. With the use of Keras, we will be able to move from idea to result in the shortest possible time so you can spend more time analyzing results. First the `Sequential` model is imported; the `Sequential` model is a linear stack of layers. Then some Keras `layers` are imported: `Dense`, `Activation`, and `Flatten`. A `Dense` model is a fully connected neural network layer. The `Activation` layer applies an activation function to an output. The `Flatten` layer flattens the input; it does not affect the batch size. Finally, the `Adam` optimizer is imported. Let's move on to importing the Keras-RL library:

```
from rl.agents.dqn import DQNAgent
from rl.policy import BoltzmannQPolicy
from rl.memory import SequentialMemory
```

The Keras-RL library implements some state-of-the art deep reinforcement-learning algorithms in Python and seamlessly integrates with the deep-learning Keras library. `DQNAgent`, a policy, and a memory model are imported. Now we will define the environment:

```
ENV_NAME = 'CartPole-v0'
```

In this way, we have set the name of the environment. Let's proceed to obtain it:

```
env = gym.make(ENV_NAME)
```

To set the `seed` value, the `numpy` library's `random.seed()` function is used:

```
np.random.seed(123)
```

The `seed` function sets the `seed` of the random number generator, which is useful for creating simulations or random objects that can be reproduced. You have to use this function every time you want to get a reproducible random result. The seed must also be set for the environment:

```
env.seed(123)
```

Now we will extract the actions available to the agent:

```
nb_actions = env.action_space.n
```

The nb_actions variable now contains all the actions available in the selected environment. The Gym will not always tell you what these actions mean, only which ones are available. Now we will build a simple neural network model using the Keras library:

```
model = Sequential()
model.add(Flatten(input_shape=(1,) + env.observation_space.shape))
model.add(Dense(16))
model.add(Activation('relu'))
model.add(Dense(16))
model.add(Activation('relu'))
model.add(Dense(16))
model.add(Activation('relu'))
model.add(Dense(nb_actions))
model.add(Activation('linear'))
print(model.summary())
```

Now that the neural network model is ready to use, let's configure and compile our agent. One problem with using the DQN is that the neural network used in the algorithm tends to forget previous experiences because it overwrites them with new experiences. So we need a list of previous experiences and observations to reform the model with previous experiences. For this reason, a Memory variable is defined that will contain the previous experiences:

```
memory = SequentialMemory(limit=50000, window_length=1)
```

Now we will set the Policy variable:

```
policy = BoltzmannQPolicy()
```

We just have to define the agent:

```
dqn = DQNAgent(model=model, nb_actions=nb_actions, memory=memory,
               nb_steps_warmup=10,target_model_update=1e-2,
               policy=policy)
```

Let's move on to compile the model:

```
dqn.compile(Adam(lr=1e-3), metrics=['mae'])
```

The preceding command compiles an agent and the underlying models to be used for training and testing. Now that the agent is ready, we can train it:

```
dqn.fit(env, nb_steps=1000, visualize=True, verbose=2)
```

The `fit()` function trains the agent on the given environment. At the end of the training, it is necessary to save the obtained weights:

```
dqn.save_weights('dqn_{}_weights.h5f'.format(ENV_NAME), overwrite=True)
```

Saving the weight of a network or an entire structure takes place in an HDF5 file, an efficient and flexible storage system that supports complex multidimensional datasets. Finally, we will evaluate our algorithm for 10 episodes:

```
dqn.test(env, nb_episodes=5, visualize=True)
```

If something has not been sufficiently cleared, there is no need to worry; in Chapter 6, *Continuous Balancing of a Rotating Mechanical System*, we looked more closely at the arguments.

Summary

In this chapter, you learned the basic concepts of Q-learning and Deep Q-learning, and how to use these techniques to control a mechanical system. To start with, an overview of how Segways work was addressed. It is an electric traction-transport vehicle for individual locomotion that can start, stop, and reverse, with simple movements of the passenger-driver body—a slight bend forward or backward, and making curves with the help of a knob on the left-hand side of the handlebar. To show how it works, an inverted pendulum model was implemented.

Then, the OpenAI Gym library was introduced, which helps us to implement algorithms based on reinforcement learning. It includes a growing collection of benchmark issues that expose a common interface, and a website where people can share their results and compare algorithm performance. We explored the different environments available and how to install the library.

Finally, the CartPole system was used to implement Q-learning and Deep Q-learning algorithms. The CartPole system is a classic problem of reinforced learning. The system consists of a pole (which acts like an inverted pendulum) attached to a cart via a joint. The system is controlled by applying a force of +1 or -1 to the cart. The force applied to the cart can be controlled, and the objective is to swing the pole upward and stabilize it.

8
Robot Control System Using Deep Reinforcement Learning

Robots are now an integral part of our living environments. In the industrial field, they represent a valid aid to humankind by replacing people in alienating job. The task of a robot control system is to execute the planned sequence of movements and to identify an alternative path in the presence of obstacles. In this chapter, we address the problem of robot navigation in simple maze-like environments where the robot has to rely on its onboard sensors to perform navigation tasks.

The following topics are covered in this chapter:

- Robot control overview
- Environment to control robot mobility
- Q-learning
- Deep Q-learning

At the end of the chapter, the reader will learn the basis of robot control theory. Discover the evolution of robotics technology, different type of robots. Learn the basic concepts of control architectures. Learn to use the current best policy estimate to generate system behavior through Q-learning and Deep Q-learning algorithms. Understand how to deal robot control mobility through these techniques.

Robot control

A **robot** is a machine that performs certain actions based on the commands that are provided, either on the basis of direct human supervision, or independently based on general guidelines, using the artificial intelligence processes. These tasks typically should be performed at the order to replace or assist humans, such as in the manufacture, construction, or handling of heavy and dangerous materials, in prohibitive or incompatible environments with the human condition, or simply to free a person from commitments. In the following picture is shown an explosive ordnance disposal robot:

A robot should be equipped with guided connections by feedback between perception and action, and not by direct human control. The action can take the form of electromagnetic motors, or actuators, that move a limb, open and close a gripper, or move the robot. Step-by-step control and feedback are provided by a program that runs from an external or internal robot computer, or from a microcontroller. Based on this definition, the robot concept can include almost all automated devices.

Robotics overview

Robotics is a science that studies the behavior of intelligent beings and tries to develop methods that allow a machine, called a robot, equipped with appropriate devices to perceive the surrounding environment and interact with it (sensors and actuators), to perform specific tasks.

It represents the solution to various problems for humans, who can get rid of tasks that are too boring, time-consuming, dangerous, tiring, simple, or precise. The discipline stems from man's desire to create artificial and autonomous devices with artificial intelligence.

The following picture shows an MQ-1 Predator carrying the multi-spectral targeting system with an inherent AGM-114 Hellfire-missile-targeting capability and integrates electro-optical, infrared, a laser designator, and laser illuminator into a single sensor package:

Robotics is not only important to learn how to build and use robots, but also to learn a method of reasoning and experimentation; in fact it collects many interdisciplinary studies, such as mechanics, electronics, information technology, sensors, artificial intelligence, and mathematics.

In 1979, the American Institute of Robots gave a definition of a robot as a programmable and multifunctional tool designed to move materials, components, or tools, through various programmed movements.

Twenty years later, this definition could be considered incomplete, given that nowadays a robot is seen as an instrument used (in science) in science and in industry to take the place of a human being. It could, or could not, resemble a human being and perform, or not perform, that person's duties.

In science fiction, the concern that robots can compete with people, rebel, or even exterminate is a very common topic. Remember that the term comes from a Czech word, robota, meaning forced labor; the word robot was first used to denote a fictional humanoid in a 1920 play, R.U.R., by Karel Čapek, a Czech writer, but it was Karel's brother Josef Čapek who was the word's true inventor.

In the series of stories *I, Robot, Isaac Asimov* enunciated the Three Laws of Robotics in an attempt to control the competition between robots and human beings:

- A robot may not injure a human being or, through inaction, allow a human being to come to harm
- A robot must obey any orders given to it by human beings, except where such orders would conflict with the First Law
- A robot must protect its own existence as long as such protection does not conflict with the First or Second Law

The features of a robot can be summarized as follows:

- **Programmability**: Processing capacity that the designer can combine as they wish
- **Mobility**: Possibility to interact physically with the environment
- **Flexibility**: Ability to exhibit behavior suited to the situation
- **Autonomy**: Possibility of performing one's own duties without interference or conditioning by other members

These features are possible thanks to two essential elements available in every robotic device: a sensor and actuator. A sensor is a device that transforms a physical quantity that one wants to measure, into a signal of a different nature (typically electric) that can be more easily measured or memorized. An actuator is a device that converts energy from one form to another, so that it acts in the physical environment instead of a person. That is, any device used to operate mechanical members or to intervene on hydraulic circuits following commands sent to it by means of an electronic control system.

Robot evolution

The construction of automated devices dates back to ancient times, in fact between 400-350 BC. The Greek Architect of Taranto built a flying dove set in motion by a jet of steam. In 1200 D.C., the first rudimentary automata began to be built: Roger Bacon creates a talking head.

This means that the idea of constructing an artificial individual, endowed with movement and autonomy in their actions, is not therefore of the last few centuries, nor a consequence of the development of information technology and of robotics. In the following picture is shown the dredge of Leonardo da Vinci, exhibited at the L. Da Vinci National Museum of Science and Technology in Milan:

To describe the level of advancement of a robot, the term **generation robots** can be used. This term was coined by Professor Hans Moravec, Principal Research Scientist at the Carnegie Mellon University Robotics Institute in describing the near future evolution of robot technology.

First-generation robots

The robots that characterize the first generation, which began in 1970, are the robotic arms, programmable machines without the possibility of controlling the actual execution modes and without interaction with the external environment.

The robots of the first generation are low-tech devices; in fact they do not operate under servo controls. They are very noisy because of the noise produced by the impact between the arm itself and the mechanical stops used to limit its movement. The use of these types of robots is mainly industrial, in fact in those years they were used for loading and unloading goods or to make simple movements of materials.

Second-generation robots

The assembly line, on the other hand, is part of the second generation of robots. It consists of programmable machines with the possibility of recognizing the external environment. The technology used is of medium quality, and unlike the first generation, robotic arms are equipped with servo controls, and can be programmed for point-to-point displacements. In the following picture is shown an assembly line of a Mercedes factory:

These were controlled by regular programmable logic controllers or minicomputers and were also programmable. They have specific software dedicated to specific applications. Thus, if the robot was intended to perform a certain task, such as loading a machine, it was very difficult to use it for another operation, such as welding. In order to do this, the control system had to be changed. This kind of machine has poor diagnostic capabilities and therefore it is up to the user to go back to the actual causes of a possible failure.

Third-generation robots

These are self-programmable machines and have the ability to interact with the external environment and the external operator in a complex way (vision, voice, and so on) and are able to self-instruct themselves for the execution of an assigned task. The third generation (late 1980s) has now evolved to the point of being able to perform highly sophisticated operations such as space inspections, adaptive arc welding, and assembly operations. In the following picture is shown Sojourner, which is the Mars Pathfinder robotic mars rover that landed on July 4, 1997:

The technology used is of a high standard, and programming can be done online using a prehensile keyboard or offline through a video display. Programming languages do not work at a low level like the second generation ones.

They can be interfaced with a CAD database or with a host computer for data loading/unloading. They are also capable of sending messages to the operator to describe the nature and location of any failures. The simultaneous use of this kind of robot is to perform intelligent tasks.

Fourth-generation robots

Fourth-generation robots are considered the robots of the future. These robots are called androids or humanoids, or automata with human features that mimic human actions and functions. The following picture shows some androids extracted from the movie Automata (directed by Gabe Ibanez with Antonio Banderas as the main actor):

Here, the study was divided into two: on the one hand, the scholars focused on the surprising humanoids, similar to dummies with silicon faces, makeup, and clothes. On the other hand, the so-called bipeds have developed, with human shapes but similar to cartoon robots, also equipped with the ability to learn and move using a wide range of movements. They are no longer just industrial but also social robots, and are sometimes used to investigate the social interaction of humans.

Robot autonomy

An important connotation according to which robots can be classified regards the level of autonomy that these must demonstrate. Autonomy means the ability to function in dynamic and unstructured environments without the need for continuous human intervention. In such environments, many of the specific situations are not known *a priori*, obliging the robot (or any autonomous system) to be able to detect the salient characteristics of the current situation and to behave accordingly, deciding what actions to take. Furthermore, the need to avoid human intervention over long periods of time implies that the full ability of the robot to self-manage and survive (for example, by avoiding to remain physically blocked or to completely deplete energy reserves) must be relied upon. In the following picture is shown a robot vacuum cleaner that recovers its position to recharge its batteries:

Considering industrial robots perform repetitive tasks in the context of a production process, it is obvious that machines of this type require little autonomy. In fact, often these machines simply have to execute a series of predetermined, arbitrarily complex actions, which are defined in the design and programming of the robot.

Usually, these machines perform their tasks inside protected cells (work cells) specially designed to facilitate operations, in which, for security reasons, access is even forbidden while these are in operation. Robots of this type can be developed taking for granted many aspects concerning the working environment, and most of the time it is sufficient to adopt the classic automatic control algorithms, even very complex ones, to provide the robot the ability to operate at its best by exploiting the useful information taken from the environment through the usual feedback loops.

In situations where the environment cannot be artificially modified, and is therefore not known *a priori*, it is clear that the robot must have a certain autonomy in order to cope with the difficulties and dangers that such conditions entail.

Robot mobility

A typical feature of autonomous systems is mobility. A robot that performs the intended task needs to move physically within an environment, and must inevitably incorporate a certain autonomy that allows it to move safely, avoiding obstacles and not posing a threat to any nearby living beings, as shown in the following picture:

Obviously, different levels of autonomy can be identified, from fully autonomous systems that never, or almost never, require human intervention, to remote-controlled systems that can be more or less autonomous depending on whether they rely solely on the commands given to them or whether part of the operations are decided by the robot itself.

Automatic control

Technically speaking, a robot can be seen as a particular type of automatic control, that is, an automaton physically located in an environment of which it can perceive certain characteristics through components called sensors, and on which it can perform actions with the aim of making changes to it. These actions are performed by so-called actuators. All that is interposed between the measurements made by the sensors and the commands given to the actuators can be defined as the control program or the controller of the robot. This is the component in which the intelligence of the robot is encoded and, in a certain sense, it therefore constitutes the brain that must guide its actions in order to obtain the desired behavior. A controller can be implemented in various ways: usually it is software running on one or more microcontrollers physically integrated into the system (onboard), but it can also be obtained through electronic circuits (analog or digital) directly wired into the hardware of the robot. The abstract nature of the software obviously makes it the most flexible solution as this entity is itself easily transferable from one storage medium to another: consequently, to change the controller, and with it the whole behavior assumed by the robot, it is sufficient to change the control software while the hardware remains unchanged, thus allowing us to make changes at virtually no cost.

Control architectures

Being a software, even for the robot control program, it is possible to apply the classical principles of software engineering. First of all, the one concerning the definition of the software architecture of the controller is taken into consideration, that is, the high-level structure and paradigm adopted in the analysis phase to frame the control problem, and in the design phase to model the solution. In the specific case of the control software of a robotic system, the commonly used term is **control architecture**.

The control architecture can be defined as the abstraction that provides the principles according to which to organize the control system, defining its structure, and at the same time imposing constraints on the way in which the problem of control can be solved.

In order for the architecture to be suitable for the development, of a particular control system, it must, as far as possible, reflect the requirements and therefore the desired characteristics. In the case of autonomous systems controllers, the properties that such architectures should enjoy can be summarized as follows:

- **Environment reactivity**: The robot should react to sudden changes in the environment and should be able to take into account external events with timing compatible with the correct and efficient execution of the task it is performing (hard time limits or soft real-time).

- **Intelligent behavior**: This requires the robot to follow common sense rules in order to manifest intelligent behavior and so that reactions to external stimuli are guided by task objectives.
- **Integration of multiple sensors**: Sensors taken singularly often suffer from limited accuracy, reliability, and applicability, which must therefore be compensated for by integrating readings from multiple complementary sensors, possibly of a different nature, which must be exploited to the fullest by the system control (sensor redundancy).
- **Pursuing multiple objectives**: The control system should be able to achieve or maintain a variety of objectives that in certain situations may also be at odds with each other.
- **Robustness**: The robot should have the ability to continue to do its job discreetly (obviously within the limits of the possible) even in the face of imperfect input, unexpected events, and sudden malfunctions. In the following picture is shown a robot equipped with a particular technology that allows it to climb up and down the stairs:

- **Reliability**: The tasks entrusted to the robot should be carried out without failures and without degradation of performance.
- **Programmability**: A very interesting feature is the possibility of subjecting the robot to tasks, described at a certain level of abstraction, even at execution time rather than developing control systems capable of managing only the task envisaged during the design phase.
- **Modularity**: The control system of a robot should be subdivided into simpler subsystems (modules, components) that can be designed, developed, and tested separately, and then incrementally integrated.
- **Flexibility**: The development of a control system generally relies on continuous experiments whose results are used to guide the development and especially the modification, of the current solution, so the more an architecture allows us to create flexible and easily-alterable controllers, the more it is possible to follow this strategy.

- **Extensibility**: A property resulting from the modularity and flexibility of a system that allows an incremental development and prolonged through the integration, verification, and improvement of its components.
- **Scalability**: The system should be able to easily scale in relation to the available computational resources, for example, in the face of the replacement of the processor with a more powerful model or the creation of a parallel infrastructure composed of several interconnected microcontrollers (in this case, the control must be designed as a physically distributed system).
- **Adaptability**: Since the characteristics of the surrounding environment can change unpredictably, a very useful feature for a control system is the ability to adapt to these changes and alter control strategies accordingly (properties such as capacity are desirable of learning at runtime).

In general, each architecture relies on a specific control strategy.

The FrozenLake environment

The FrozenLake environment is a 4 × 4 grid that contains four possible areas: Safe (S), Frozen (F), Hole (H), and Goal (G). The agent controls the movement of a character in a grid world, and moves around the grid until it reaches the goal or the hole. Some tiles of the grid are walkable, and others lead to the agent falling into the water. If it falls into the hole, it has to start from the beginning and is rewarded the value 0. Additionally, the movement direction of the agent is uncertain and only partially depends on the chosen direction. The agent is rewarded for finding a walkable path to a goal tile. The agent has four possible moves: up, down, left, and right. The process continues until it learns from every mistake and reaches the goal eventually.

The surface is described using a grid like the following:

- SFFF (S: starting point, safe)
- FHFH (F: frozen surface, safe)
- FFFH (H: hole, fall to your doom)
- HFFG (G: goal, where the frisbee is located)

In the following is shown the FrozenLake grid (4 × 4):

S	F	F	F
F	H	F	H
F	F	F	H
H	F	F	G

The episode ends when you reach the goal or fall in a hole. You receive a reward of 1 if you reach the goal, and zero otherwise.

The Q-learning solution

Q-learning is one of the most-used reinforcement-learning algorithms. This is due to its ability to compare the expected utility of the available actions without requiring an environment model. Thanks to this technique, it is possible to find an optimal action for every given state in a finished **Markov Decision Process** (**MDP**).

A general solution to the reinforcement learning problem is to estimate, thanks to the learning process, an evaluation function. This function must be able to evaluate, through the sum of the rewards, the convenience or otherwise of a particular policy. In fact, Q-learning tries to maximize the value of the Q function (action-value function), which represents the maximum discounted future reward when we perform actions, a, in the state, s.

Let's face the problem of controlling a robot by offering a first solution based on Q-learning. In the following code, a Q-learning solution for the FrozenLake problem is proposed:

```
import gym
import numpy as np
env = gym.make('FrozenLake-v0') QTable =
np.zeros([env.observation_space.n,env.action_space.n]) alpha = .80 gamma =
.95 NumEpisodes = 2000
RewardsList = [] for i in range(NumEpisodes):
 CState = env.reset()
 SumReward = 0
 d = False
 j = 0
 while j < 99:
 j+=1
 Action = np.argmax(QTable[CState,:] +
np.random.randn(1,env.action_space.n)*(1./(i+1)))
 NState,Rewards,d,_ = env.step(Action)
 QTable[CState,Action] = QTable[CState,Action] + alpha*(Rewards +
```

```
gamma*np.max(QTable[NState,:]) - QTable[CState,Action])
  SumReward += Rewards
  CState = NState
  if d == True:
  break
    RewardsList.append(SumReward)
print ("Score: " + str(sum(RewardsList)/NumEpisodes))
print ("Final Q-Table Values")
print (QTable)
```

As always, we will analyze the code line by line. Let's start by importing the libraries:

```
import gym
import numpy as np
```

Then, we move on to create the environment by calling the `make` method:

```
env = gym.make('FrozenLake-v0')
```

This method creates the environment that our agent will run in. Now, let's initialize the parameters starting with `QTable`:

```
QTable = np.zeros([env.observation_space.n,env.action_space.n])
```

`QTable` has a number of rows equal to the size of the observation space (`env.observation_space.n`), while the columns are equal to the size of the action space (`env.action_space.n`). The FrozenLake environment provides a state for each cell in the 4 x 4 grid, and four actions (up, down, left, and right), returning a 16 x 4 table. This table is initialized with all zeros using the `np.zeros()` function, which returns a new array of a given shape and type, filled with zeros.

Now, we define some parameters:

```
alpha = .8
gamma = .95
```

`alpha` is the learning rate, and `gamma` is the discount factor.

The learning rate determines to what extent newly acquired information overrides old information. A factor of 0 makes the agent learn nothing (exclusively exploiting prior knowledge), while a factor of 1 makes the agent consider only the most recent information (ignoring prior knowledge to explore possibilities). This is the exploration-exploitation dilemma. Ideally, the agent must explore all possible actions for each state, finding the one that is actually most rewarded for exploiting it in achieving its goal.

The discount factor determines the importance of future rewards. A factor of 0 will consider only current rewards, while a factor approaching 1 will make it strive for a long-term high reward.

Now, we set the number of episodes:

```
NumEpisodes = 2000
```

But, what do we mean by the episode? The agent will learn through experience, without a teacher, and this is an unsupervised learning. The agent will explore from state to state until it reaches the goal. We'll call each exploration an episode. Each episode consists of the agent moving from the initial state to the goal state. Each time the agent arrives at the goal state, the program goes to the next episode.

Now, we will create a list to contain total rewards:

```
RewardsList = []
```

At this point, after setting the parameters, it is possible to start the Q-learning cycle:

```
for i in range(NumEpisodes):
```

So, we initialize the system using the `reset()` method:

```
CState = env.reset()
```

Now, we set a control to the episode task:

```
d = False
```

When `d` become `True`, it indicates that the episode has terminated. Then, a cycle-counter is initialized:

```
j = 0
```

It's time to implement the Q-learning table algorithm:

```
while j < 99:
```

We increase the cycle counter at each new step:

```
j += 1
```

Now, we have to choose an action:

```
Action = np.argmax(QTable[CState,:] +
np.random.randn(1,env.action_space.n)*(1./(i+1)))
```

An action is chosen by greedily method-picking from `QTable`. A noise is added because the environment is unknown, so it has to be explored in some way—your agent will do so using the power of randomness. Two functions are used: `np.argmax` and `np.random.randn`. `np.argmax` return the indices of the maximum values along an `axis`. `np.random.randn` return a sample (or samples) from the standard normal distribution.

Now, we use the `step()` method to return the new states in response to the actions with which we call it. Obviously, the action we pass to the method is the one we have just decided:

```
NState,Rewards,d,_ = env.step(Action)
```

As we said, this method returns the following four values:

- `observation`: An environment-specific object representing your observation of the environment.

- `reward`: The amount of reward achieved by the previous action. The scale varies between environments, but the goal is always to increase your total reward. It has `float` as its type.

- `done`: Whether it's time to reset the environment again. Most (but not all) tasks are divided into well-defined episodes, and done being `True` indicates that the episode has terminated. It has `Boolean` as its type.

- `info`: Diagnostic information useful for debugging. It can sometimes be useful for learning. It has `dict` as its type.

We can then update the `QTable` with new knowledge:

```
QTable[CState,Action] = QTable[CState,Action] + alpha*(Rewards +
gamma*np.max(QTable[NState,:]) - QTable[CState,Action])
```

Now, we update the sum of the rewards with the one just obtained. Remember that, for every time step where we keep the pole straight, we get +1 `reward`:

```
SumReward += reward
```

Now, we will set the state for the next learning cycle:

```
CState = Nstate
        if d == True:
            break
```

At the end of each episode, the list of rewards is enriched with a new value:

```
RewardsList.append(SumReward)
```

Finally, we print the results:

```
print ("Score: " +  str(sum(RewardsList)/NumEpisodes))
print ("Final Q-Table Values")
print (QTable)
```

In the following is shown the final `Q-Table`:

```
Score: 0.441
Final Q-Table Values
[[8.09790682e-02 9.69476193e-03 4.11286493e-03 3.72643060e-03]
 [1.28341407e-03 6.03882961e-04 8.06474557e-04 2.68672382e-01]
 [1.91967449e-03 1.92834234e-03 1.35171928e-03 1.44758358e-01]
 [7.17684420e-04 3.66341807e-07 1.37698057e-04 8.63455110e-02]
 [8.34610385e-02 4.22336752e-06 3.86592526e-05 1.25979894e-03]
 [0.00000000e+00 0.00000000e+00 0.00000000e+00 0.00000000e+00]
 [2.97743191e-04 1.84465934e-05 1.15548361e-01 7.03460389e-06]
 [0.00000000e+00 0.00000000e+00 0.00000000e+00 0.00000000e+00]
 [3.05085281e-05 8.22833888e-04 1.18894379e-03 9.85186767e-02]
 [5.88378899e-04 3.46691598e-01 3.80809242e-04 2.51803451e-04]
 [5.10025290e-01 1.83055349e-03 9.49003480e-04 2.15726641e-05]
 [0.00000000e+00 0.00000000e+00 0.00000000e+00 0.00000000e+00]
 [0.00000000e+00 0.00000000e+00 0.00000000e+00 0.00000000e+00]
 [0.00000000e+00 1.13547942e-03 7.02402188e-01 2.29674937e-04]
 [0.00000000e+00 0.00000000e+00 9.45161063e-01 0.00000000e+00]
 [0.00000000e+00 0.00000000e+00 0.00000000e+00 0.00000000e+00]]
```

To improve the result, retuning of the configuration parameters is required.

A Deep Q-learning solution

In the following code, a Deep Q-learning solution for the FrozenLake problem is proposed:

```
import gym
import numpy as np
from keras.models import Sequential
from keras.layers.core import Dense, Reshape
from keras.layers.embeddings import Embedding
from keras.optimizers import Adam
```

```
from rl.agents.dqn import DQNAgent
from rl.policy import BoltzmannQPolicy
from rl.memory import SequentialMemory
ENV_NAME = 'FrozenLake-v0'
env = gym.make(ENV_NAME)
np.random.seed(1)
env.seed(1)
Actions = env.action_space.n
model = Sequential()
model.add(Embedding(16, 4, input_length=1))
model.add(Reshape((4,)))
print(model.summary())
memory = SequentialMemory(limit=10000, window_length=1)
policy = BoltzmannQPolicy()
Dqn = DQNAgent(model=model, nb_actions=Actions,
               memory=memory, nb_steps_warmup=500,
               target_model_update=1e-2, policy=policy,
               enable_double_dqn=False, batch_size=512
               )
Dqn.compile(Adam())
Dqn.fit(env, nb_steps=1e5, visualize=False, verbose=1, log_interval=10000)
Dqn.save_weights('dqn_{}_weights.h5f'.format(ENV_NAME), overwrite=True)
Dqn.test(env, nb_episodes=20, visualize=False)
```

As already done in all the examples proposed so far, we will analyze this code line by line to understand its operating principle. The first part of the code is used to import libraries:

```
import numpy as np
import gym
```

First, we import the numpy library, which will be used to set the seed value. So, we import the gym library, which will help us to define the environment. Having done this, we import some functions of the keras library to build a neural network model:

```
from keras.models import Sequential
from keras.layers.core import Dense, Reshape
from keras.layers.embeddings import Embedding
from keras.optimizers import Adam
```

Keras is a high-level neural network API, written in Python and capable of running on top of TensorFlow, CNTK, or Theano. It was developed with a focus on enabling fast experimentation. With the use of Keras, we will be able to move from idea to result in the shortest possible time so you can spend more time analyzing results. First, the Sequential model is imported; the Sequential model is a linear stack of layers. Then, some keras layers are imported: Dense and Reshape.

A `Dense` model is a fully connected neural network layer. The `Reshape` layer reshapes an output to a certain shape. Then the `Embedding` layer is imported. This layer turns positive integers (indexes) into dense vectors of a fixed size. This layer can only be used as the first layer in a model. Finally, the `Adam` optimizer is imported. Let's move to importing the Keras-RL library:

```
from rl.agents.dqn import DQNAgent
from rl.policy import BoltzmannQPolicy
from rl.memory import SequentialMemory
```

The Keras-RL library implements some state-of-the art deep reinforcement-learning algorithms in Python and seamlessly integrates with the deep learning Keras library. `DQNAgent`, a policy, and a memory model are imported. As policy, `BoltzmannQPolicy` is imported. This policy builds a probability law on q values and returns an action selected randomly according to this law. Now, we will define the environment:

```
ENV_NAME = 'FrozenLake-v0'
```

In this way, we have set the name of the environment, so let's go get it:

```
env = gym.make(ENV_NAME)
```

To set the `seed` value, the `numpy` library's `random.seed()` function is used:

```
np.random.seed(1)
```

The `seed()` function sets the seed of the random-number generator, which is useful for creating simulations or random objects that can be reproduced. You have to use this function every time you want to get a reproducible random result. `seed` must also be set for the environment:

```
env.seed(1)
```

Now, we will extract the actions available to the agent:

```
Actions = env.action_space.n
```

The `Actions` variable now contains all the actions available in the selected environment. Gym will not always tell you what these actions mean, but only which ones are available. Now, we will build a simple neural network model using the Keras library:

```
model = Sequential()
model.add(Embedding(16, 4, input_length=1))
model.add(Reshape((4,)))
print(model.summary())
```

Now the neural network model is ready to use, let's configure and compile our agent. One problem with using the DQN is that the neural network used in the algorithm tends to forget previous experiences because it overwrites them with new experiences. So, we need a list of previous experiences and observations to reform the model with previous experiences. For this reason, a Memory variable is defined that will contain the previous experiences:

```
Memory = SequentialMemory(limit=10000, window_length=1)
```

Now, we will set the policy:

```
Policy = BoltzmannQPolicy()
```

We just have to define the agent:

```
Dqn = DQNAgent(model=model, nb_actions=Actions, memory=memory,
nb_steps_warmup=500, target_model_update=1e-2, policy=policy,
enable_double_dqn=False, batch_size=512)
```

Let's proceed to compile the model:

```
Dqn.compile(Adam())
```

This command compiles an agent and the underlying models to be used for training and testing. Now that the agent is ready, we can train it:

```
Dqn.fit(env, nb_steps=1e5, visualize=False, verbose=1, log_interval=10000)
```

The fit() function trains the agent on the given environment. At the end of the training, it is necessary to save the obtained weights:

```
Dqn.save_weights('dqn_{}_weights.h5f'.format(ENV_NAME), overwrite=True)
```

Saving the weight of a network or an entire structure takes place in an HDF5 file, an efficient and flexible storage system that supports complex multidimensional datasets. Finally, we will evaluate our algorithm for 20 episodes:

```
Dqn.test(env, nb_episodes=20, visualize=False)
```

Our agent is now able to identify the path that allows them to reach the goal.

Summary

In this chapter, you learned the basics of the Theory of Robot Control. A **robot** is a machine that performs certain actions based on the commands that are provided. To describe the level of advancement of a robot, the term **generation robots** can be used. Different generations of robots were addressed to distinguish the correlated features. Robot autonomy and robot mobility topics have been discussed to understand how to handle problems related to the autonomous control of a robot.

Then, we looked at the FrozenLake environment. This is a 4 × 4 grid that contains four possible areas: Safe (S), Frozen (F), Hole (H), and Goal (G). The agent controls the movement of a character in a grid world, and moves around the grid until it reaches the goal or the hole. This environment is particularly suitable for simulating problems related to the mobility of a robot in an environment full of obstacles. After defining the environment, we created an agent that is able to move within the environment and find the goal using an algorithm based on Q-learning. Later, the same problem was addressed through the use of an algorithm based on Deep Q-learning.

Handwritten Digit Recognizer

9

The term **handwriting recognition** (**HWR**) refers to the ability of a computer to receive and interpret intelligible handwritten input from sources such as paper documents, photographs, and touchscreens. Written text can be detected on a piece of paper with optical scanning (**Optical Character Recognition** (**OCR**)) or intelligent word recognition. Alternatively, the movements of a pen tip can be detected, for example from a surface of the computer screen, a task that is generally easier as there are more clues available. These activities involve a wide range of practical applications, including the recognition of online spelling on tablet computers, recognition of the zip code to help sort sent mail, and the verification of signatures in the context of financial transactions.

In this chapter, you will work on building a handwritten digit recognizer in Python. You will be working with an image dataset and will use it to build an image recognition model. Your goal in this chapter is to learn how to apply reinforcement learning concepts to handwritten digit recognition. By the end of this chapter, you will have built a handwritten digit recognition model in Python using an image dataset.

The following topics are covered:

- Image recognition concepts
- Optical Character Recognition
- Autoencoders
- Deep Q-Network
- Handwritten digit recognition

By the end of the chapter, the reader will have learned the basic concepts of image recognition, how OCR works, how to implement an autoencoder to handwritten digit recognition, and how to use an autoencoder and Q-learning to improve the performance of the algorithm.

Handwritten digit recognition

Handwritten digit recognition is a problem widely faced by researchers around the world in recent decades. This is a problem that is difficult to implement, due to the large variation that exists in the available writing styles. The problem has been codified by a handwritten digit recognition method that recognizes and classifies the handwritten digits from 0-9 without any human interaction. In this way, the ability of a computer to interpret handwritten input intelligently from a series of images is verified.

Handwritten digit recognition remains a vital sector because of its enormous practical applications and important financial implications. It involves a wide range of practical applications, including the recognition of online spelling on tablet computers, recognition of the zip code to help sort sent mail, and as the verification of signatures in the context of financial transactions.

The process of recognition of calligraphy presents several problems, such as the fact that handwritten images have various dimensions and therefore must be normalized before the system proceeds with recognition. Therefore, the difficulties do not derive only from the many different ways in which it is possible to write a single digit, but they also derive from the different requirements imposed by the applications used. Furthermore, there are the different degrees of thickness of people's writing and the different positions of writing when it comes to sample margins. As is known, the various writing styles of people depend on characteristics such as age, qualifications, modality, and background. It follows that the recognition of handwritten digits is a relatively complex research task. In fact, even the digits that have been written by the same person at different times may be different. Therefore, it is almost impossible to develop a generic recognizer capable of recognizing an infinite number of writers.

Optical Character Recognition

We have always been particularly sensitive to the problem of the automatic recognition of writing in order to achieve a simpler interaction between humans and machines. Especially in the last few years, this problem has found interesting developments and more and more efficient solutions thanks to a very strong economic interest and an ever-greater capacity to process the data of modern computers. In particular, some countries, such as Japan, and Asian countries in general, are investing heavily in terms of research and financial resources, making state-of-the-art OCR.

It is easy to understand the interest of these countries in this field of research. In fact, we try to create devices able to interpret the ideograms characteristic of those cultures to allow greater comfort in the interaction with the machines. Since there are currently no input devices, such as keyboards, that can represent thousands of characters, we try to acquire this information directly from the script via a digitized scan. However, even in the West, great importance has been given to research into the optical recognition of writing. There are many applications that certainly benefit from an automatic reading; just think, for example, of the automatic interpretation of preprinted models or the recognition of addresses and codes of postal initiation on envelopes.

The approaches to the problem are basically of two types: the approach based on the pattern matching or on the comparison of the model and the one based on the structural analysis. Often, these two techniques are used in combination, managing to obtain remarkable results in terms of recognition and speed.

The first patents obtained on the OCR date back to the 1930s and were registered in Germany by Tausheck (1929—reading machine shown in the following diagram), and in the United States thanks to Hendel (1933). In the following diagram is shown a Tausheck reading-machine scheme:

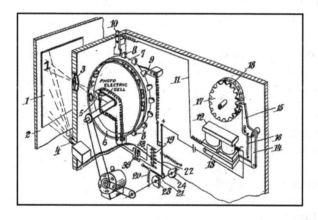

The basic idea is the same and is very simple. Both made use of a simple machine based on a mask overlay approach (template/mask matching). The device used, of course, mirrored the technologies of the time, and was based on an optomechanical approach. A light, which passed through a mechanical mask, was captured by a sensor and then acquired. The recognition of a given character was linked to the greater or lesser correspondence between the sample and the prototype based on the physical overlap of the two elements. In fact, if the light could not reach the sensor, there was a perfect overlap and therefore recognition of the character. This approach is based on the Euclidean axiom of the overlap of the forms.

This methodology, certainly valid, however, has a serious gap in terms of generalization. A small variation of the sample symbol, compared to the prototype, may correspond to a failure to recognize the character. This observation also applies if the sample character is slightly smaller or larger than the prototype or is slightly rotated compared to the prototype. The following diagram shows how digits change during rotation:

These simple alterations lead to errors in recognition. Considerations of this kind show that an approach based only on overlapping does not lead to good results in terms of recognition, even if such a method has the great advantage of being simple, intuitive, and easily applicable both at an algorithmic level and at a mechanical level. From the beginning, therefore, the problem was strongly felt to find a method of comparison between the sample and the prototype that was invariant with respect to scaling and rotation.

Another important consideration must be made on the term of comparison between the sample and prototype. In the overlap-based approach, the characteristic traits and the shape of the two symbols are compared, but this is only one way to proceed. In fact, we could compare some other characteristics (features) that can also be numerical values extracted from appropriate measurements made on the symbols. For example, the moments of inertia of the symbols can be calculated with respect to the orthogonal Cartesian axes or the mass or position of the center of gravity, and so on. Similar symbols will have measurements similar or otherwise included in a certain proximity range.

If the characteristics to be quantified will be n, we can represent each symbol as a point in an n-dimensional hyperspace. In recent years, considerable progress has been made in the state of OCR, but the basic idea of the machines of Tausheck and Hendel continues to be valid. This intuition is based on the principle of overlapping forms, and has given life to a whole series of methods that go by the name of the template-matching method, which together with the structural methods constitute the two strands of development of calligraphic recognition software.

Computer vision

Computer vision is the set of processes that aim to create an approximate model of the real world (3D), starting from **two-dimensional** (**2D**) images. The main purpose of artificial vision is to reproduce human sight. Seeing is understood not only as the acquisition of a 2D photograph of an area, but above all as the interpretation of the content of that area. Information is understood here as something that implies an automatic decision.

A computer vision system is constituted by the integration of optical, electronic, and mechanical components that allow us to acquire, record, and process images both in the visible light spectrum and outside it (infrared, ultraviolet, X-rays, and so on). The result of the elaboration is the recognition of certain characteristics of the image for various purposes of control, classification, selection, and so on.

The artificial vision deals with acquiring, recording, and processing images coming from an electronic medium (for example, a webcam) in order to recognize certain characteristics of the image for various purposes of control, classification, and selection. These operations take place almost immediately in all highly evolved living forms, while for the calculators, it is a complex preliminary procedure to rework and standardize the input data. For this reason, it is very difficult to be able to recreate a visual computer system that is also in a small part similar to that of a human being.

In order to bring the world of computer science, founded on electronics, closer to that of animal vision, based on biology and chemistry, we must ask ourselves how our eyes receive information from outside.

If we find ourselves in front of a red object, we immediately perceive a visual sensation, although neither the object nor a red light beam have reached our optic nerve. What happens is that the object has reflected light of a certain frequency, causing on the retina a series of photochemical changes, which in turn have been translated into appropriate neuronal impulses that the optic nerve has transported to the visual centers of the brain. From a certain point of view, nerve impulses are symbols that represent the red object, which our brain can decode to have a more accurate representation of the external world. The following diagram shows the structure of the eye (source: OpenStax College-Rice University):

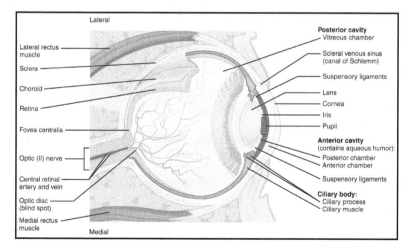

Leaving aside the in-depth treatment of visual functioning in animals, it is easy to see that there are fundamental differences between the biological visual system and the one developed for machines. First of all, nerve cells in the retina and in the cerebral cortex process both chemical and electrical stimuli, while silicone circuits have no possibility of chemical processing. Secondly, the connections between neurons are very numerous and distributed in three dimensions, while the components of a digital computer have fewer connections and these are mainly developed in two dimensions.

In dealing with the subject of vision, we cannot neglect other fundamental aspects, such as the algorithmic question (that is, finding the correct sequence of steps to complete a visual act) and the computational one (that is, what calculation activity is required).

An efficient and elegant algorithm is useless if the hardware (both biological and electronic) is not able to execute it; on the other hand, it is possible that the algorithms that compose a particular visual process—and are singularly effective—cannot then coexist in the same hardware structure.

These three aspects of vision introduce many variables in the development of software that simulates biological vision, and this greatly increases the computational complexity necessary to perform even the simplest perceptual activity.

Handwritten digit recognition using an autoencoder

An autoencoder is a neural network whose purpose is to code its input in small size. The result obtained will then be used to reconstruct the input itself. Autoencoders are made up of the union of the following two subnets:

- Encoder, which calculates the $z = \phi(x)$ function, given an x input, the encoder encodes it in a z variable, also called latent variable. The z variable usually has much smaller dimensions than x.
- Decoder, which calculates the $x' = \psi(z)$ function.

Since z is the code of x produced by the encoder, the decoder must decode it so that x' is similar to x.

The training of autoencoders is intended to minimize the **mean squared error** (**MSE**) between the input and the result.

MSE is the average squared difference between the output and targets. Lower values are indicative of better results. Zero means no error.

For n observations, MSE is given by the following formula:

$$MSE = \sum_{i=0}^{n}(x_i - x_i')^2$$

Finally, we can summarize that the encoder encodes the input in a compressed representation and the decoder returns from it a reconstruction of the input.

Let's define the following terms:

- W: Input—hidden weights
- V: Hidden—output weights

The previous formulas become:

$$z = \Phi(W^*x)$$

And they also become:

$$x' = \Psi(V^*W_1^*x)$$

Finally, the training of autoencoders is intended to minimize the following quantity:

$$\sum_{i=0}^{n}(x_i - V*W*x_i)^2$$

The purpose of autoencoders is not simply to perform a sort of compression of the input or to look for an approximation of the identity function. There are techniques that allow, starting from a hidden layer of reduced dimensions, to direct the model to give greater importance to some data properties, thereby giving rise to different representations based on the same data.

So, an autoencoder is a neural network whose purpose is to code its input into small dimensions and the result obtained to be able to reconstruct the input itself. Autoencoders are made up of the union of the following two subnets: encoder and decoder. To these functions is added another—a loss function calculated as the distance between the amount of information loss between the compressed representation of the data and the decompressed representation. The encoder and the decoder will be differentiable with respect to the distance function, so the parameters of the encoding/decoding functions can be optimized to minimize the loss of reconstruction, using the stochastic gradient.

The following example code solves handwritten digit recognition using an autoencoder in the Keras environment:

```
from keras.layers import Input, Dense
from keras.models import Model
from keras.datasets import mnist
import numpy as np
(x_train, _), (x_test, _) = mnist.load_data()
print (x_train.shape)
print (x_test.shape)
x_train = x_train.astype('float32') / 255
x_test = x_test.astype('float32') / 255
x_train = x_train.reshape((len(x_train), np.prod(x_train.shape[1:])))
x_test = x_test.reshape((len(x_test), np.prod(x_test.shape[1:])))
print (x_train.shape)
print (x_test.shape)

InputModel= Input(shape=(784,))
EncodedLayer = Dense(32, activation='relu')(InputModel)
DecodedLayer = Dense(784, activation='sigmoid')(EncodedLayer)
AutoencoderModel = Model(InputModel, DecodedLayer)
AutoencoderModel.compile(optimizer='adadelta', loss='binary_crossentropy')

history = AutoencoderModel.fit(x_train, x_train,
                epochs=100,
                batch_size=256,
                shuffle=True,
                validation_data=(x_test, x_test))

DecodedDigits = AutoencoderModel.predict(x_test)

import matplotlib.pyplot as plt

plt.plot(history.history['loss'])
plt.plot(history.history['val_loss'])
plt.title('Autoencoder Model loss')
plt.ylabel('loss')
plt.xlabel('epoch')
plt.legend(['train', 'test'], loc='upper left')
plt.show()
n=5
plt.figure(figsize=(20, 4))
for i in range(n):
    ax = plt.subplot(2, n, i + 1)
    plt.imshow(x_test[i].reshape(28, 28))
    plt.gray()
    ax.get_xaxis().set_visible(False)
    ax.get_yaxis().set_visible(False)
```

```
    ax = plt.subplot(2, n, i + 1 + n)
    plt.imshow(DecodedDigits[i].reshape(28, 28))
    plt.gray()
    ax.get_xaxis().set_visible(False)
    ax.get_yaxis().set_visible(False)
plt.show()
```

As always, we will analyze the code line-by-line.

Loading data

This is a database of handwritten digits consisting of 60,000 28 x 28 grayscale images of the 10 digits, along with a test set of 10,000 images. This dataset is already available in the Keras library. The following diagram shows a sample of images of 0-8 from the mnist dataset:

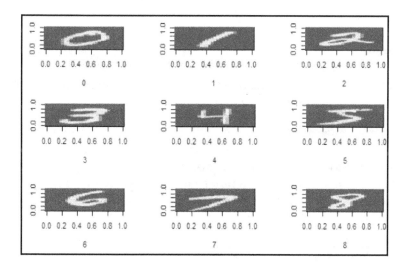

In the first part of the code, we import the libraries we will use later:

```
from keras.layers import Input, Dense
from keras.models import Model
```

This code imports the following functions:

- Input: Used to instantiate a Keras tensor. A Keras tensor is a tensor object from the underlying backend (Theano, TensorFlow, or CNTK). We augment it with certain attributes that allow us to build a Keras model just by knowing the input and output of the model.

- `Dense`: Used to instantiate a regular densely connected *NN* layer.
- `Model`: Used to define the model. The model is the thing that you can summarize, fit, evaluate, and use to make predictions. Keras provides a `Model` class that you can use to create a model from your created layers. It only requires that you specify the input and output layers.

Then the following libraries are imported:

```
import numpy as np
import matplotlib.pyplot as plt
```

First we import the `numpy` library, so we import `matplotlib.pyplot`, which we will use to plot the graph. To import the dataset, simply use the following code:

```
from keras.datasets import mnist
(x_train, y_train), (x_test, y_test) = mnist.load_data()
```

The following tuples are returned:

- `x_train, x_test`: A uint8 array of grayscale image data with the `(num_samples, 28, 28)` shape
- `y_train, y_test`: A uint8 array of digit labels (integers in the range 0-9) with the `(num_samples)` shape

Now we have to normalize all values between 0 and 1. The MNIST images are stored in pixel format, where each pixel (totally 28 x 28) is stored as an 8-bit integer, giving a range of possible values from 0 to 255. Typically, 0 is taken to be black, and 255 is taken to be white. The values in between make up the different shades of gray. Now, to normalize all values between 0 and 1, simply divide each value by 255. So the pixel containing the value 255 will become 1, and the one containing 0 will remain as such; in between lie all the other values:

```
x_train = x_train.astype('float32') / 255
x_test = x_test.astype('float32') / 255
```

By using the `astype()` function, we have converted the input data in `float32` (single-precision float: sign bit, 8-bits exponent, 23-bits mantissa). As we said, each sample image consists of a 28 x 28 matrix. To reduce the dimensionality, we will flatten the 28 x 28 images into vectors of size 784:

```
x_train = x_train.reshape((len(x_train), np.prod(x_train.shape[1:])))
x_test = x_test.reshape((len(x_test), np.prod(x_test.shape[1:])))
```

The `reshape()` function gives a new shape to an array without changing its data. The new shape should be compatible with the original shape. The first dimension of the new shape is the number of observations returned from the `len()`, (`len(x_train)`, and `len(x_test)`) functions. The second dimension represents the product of the last two dimensions of the starting data (28 x 28 = 784). To better understand this transformation, we print the shape of the starting dataset first and then the shape of the transformed dataset:

```
print (x_train.shape)
print (x_test.shape)
```

The following are the results before and after the dataset reshape:

```
(60000, 28, 28)
(10000, 28, 28)
(60000, 784)
(10000, 784)
```

Model architecture

Now we will build the model using the Keras functional API. As we saw before, first we have to define the input:

```
InputModel = Input(shape=(784,))
```

This returns a tensor that represents our input placeholder. Later, we will use this placeholder to define a model. At this point, we can add layers to the architecture of our model:

```
EncodedLayer = Dense(32, activation='relu')(InputModel)
```

The `Dense` class is used to define a fully connected layer. We have specified the number of neurons in the layer as the first argument (32), the `activation` function using the `activation` argument (`relu`), and finally the input tensor (`InputModel`) of the layer.

Remember that given an *x* input, the encoder encodes it in a *z* variable, also called a latent variable. The *z* variable usually has much smaller dimensions than *x*; in our case, we have passed from 784 to 32 with a compression factor of 24.5.

Now let's add the decoding layer:

```
DecodedLayer = Dense(784, activation='sigmoid')(EncodedLayer)
```

This layer is the lossy reconstruction of the input. For another time, we have used the `Dense` class with `784` neurons (dimensionality of the output space), the `sigmoid` `activation` function, and `EncodedLayer` output as input. Now we have to instantiate a model as follows:

```
AutoencoderModel = Model(InputModel, DecodedLayer)
```

This model will include all layers required in the computation of `DecodedLayer` (output) given `InputModel` (input). In the following list are some useful attributes of the `Model` class:

- `model.layers`: A flattened list of layers comprising the model graph
- `model.inputs`: The list of input tensors
- `model.outputs`: The list of output tensors

So, we have to configure the model for training. To do this, we will use the `compile` method, as follows:

```
AutoencoderModel.compile(optimizer='adadelta', loss='binary_crossentropy')
```

This method configures the model for training. Only two arguments are used:

- `optimizer`: String (name of optimizer) or optimizer instance.
- `loss`: String (name of objective function) or objective function. If the model has multiple outputs, you can use a different loss on each output by passing a dictionary or a list of losses. The loss value that will be minimized by the model will then be the sum of all individual losses.

We have used the `adadelta` optimizer. This method dynamically adapts over time, using only first-order information, and has minimal computational overhead beyond vanilla stochastic gradient descent. The method requires no manual tuning of the learning rate and appears robust to noisy gradient information, different model architecture choices, various data modalities, and selection of hyperparameters.

Furthermore, we have used `binary_crossentropy` as a `loss` function. The `loss` functions are computationally feasible functions representing the price paid for inaccuracy of predictions in classification problems.

At this point, we can train the model:

```
history = AutoencoderModel.fit(x_train, x_train,
                    batch_size=256,
                    epochs=100,
                    shuffle=True,
                    validation_data=(x_test, x_test))
```

The `fit` method trains the model for a fixed number of `epochs` (iterations on a dataset). Here, the arguments passed are explained to better understand their meaning:

- x: A Numpy array of training data (if the model has a single input), or list of Numpy arrays (if the model has multiple inputs). If the input layers in the model are named, you can also pass a dictionary mapping input names to Numpy arrays. x can be `None` (default) if feeding from framework-native tensors (for example, TensorFlow data tensors).
- y: A Numpy array of target (label) data if the model has a single output, or a list of Numpy arrays if the model has multiple outputs. If the output layers in the model are named, you can also pass a dictionary mapping output names to Numpy arrays. y can be `None` (default) if feeding from framework-native tensors (for example, TensorFlow data tensors).
- `batch_size`: Integer or `None`. This is the number of samples per gradient update. If unspecified, `batch_size` will default to `32`.
- `epochs`: An integer. It is the number of epochs to train the model. An epoch is an iteration over the entire x and y data provided. Note that in conjunction with `initial_epoch`, epochs is to be understood as the final number of epochs. The model is not trained for a number of iterations given by epochs, but merely until the epoch of index epochs is reached.
- `shuffle`: A Boolean to decide whether to shuffle the training data before each epoch or `str` (for `batch`). `batch` is a special option for dealing with the limitations of HDF5 data; it shuffles in batch-sized chunks. It has no effect when `steps_per_epoch` is anything other than `None`.
- `validation_data`: A tuple (x_val and y_val) or tuple (x_val, y_val, and `val_sample_weights`) on which to evaluate the loss and any model metrics at the end of each epoch. The model will not be trained on this data. `validation_data` will override `validation_split`.

A `History` object is returned. Its `history.history` attribute is a record of training loss values and metrics values at successive epochs, as well as validation loss values and validation metrics values (if applicable).

Our model is now ready, so we can use it to automatically rebuild the handwritten digits. To do this, we will use the `predict()` method:

```
DecodedDigits = AutoencoderModel.predict(x_test)
```

This method generates output predictions for the input samples (`x_test`). Running this example, you should see a message for each of the `100` epochs, printing the loss, and accuracy for each, followed by a final evaluation of the trained model on the training dataset. This is shown in the following screenshot:

```
Prompt dei comandi
Epoch 88/100
60000/60000 [==============================] - 6s 100us/step - loss: 0.0979 - val_loss: 0.0963
Epoch 89/100
60000/60000 [==============================] - 6s 98us/step - loss: 0.0979 - val_loss: 0.0962
Epoch 90/100
60000/60000 [==============================] - 6s 101us/step - loss: 0.0978 - val_loss: 0.0962
Epoch 91/100
60000/60000 [==============================] - 6s 102us/step - loss: 0.0977 - val_loss: 0.0961
Epoch 92/100
60000/60000 [==============================] - 6s 103us/step - loss: 0.0976 - val_loss: 0.0960
Epoch 93/100
60000/60000 [==============================] - 6s 108us/step - loss: 0.0976 - val_loss: 0.0960
Epoch 94/100
60000/60000 [==============================] - 7s 118us/step - loss: 0.0975 - val_loss: 0.0959
Epoch 95/100
60000/60000 [==============================] - 6s 106us/step - loss: 0.0974 - val_loss: 0.0959
Epoch 96/100
60000/60000 [==============================] - 7s 113us/step - loss: 0.0974 - val_loss: 0.0958
Epoch 97/100
60000/60000 [==============================] - 7s 121us/step - loss: 0.0973 - val_loss: 0.0957
Epoch 98/100
60000/60000 [==============================] - 8s 141us/step - loss: 0.0973 - val_loss: 0.0957
Epoch 99/100
60000/60000 [==============================] - 8s 125us/step - loss: 0.0972 - val_loss: 0.0956
Epoch 100/100
60000/60000 [==============================] - 7s 120us/step - loss: 0.0971 - val_loss: 0.0956

C:\pythonscript\GEN>
```

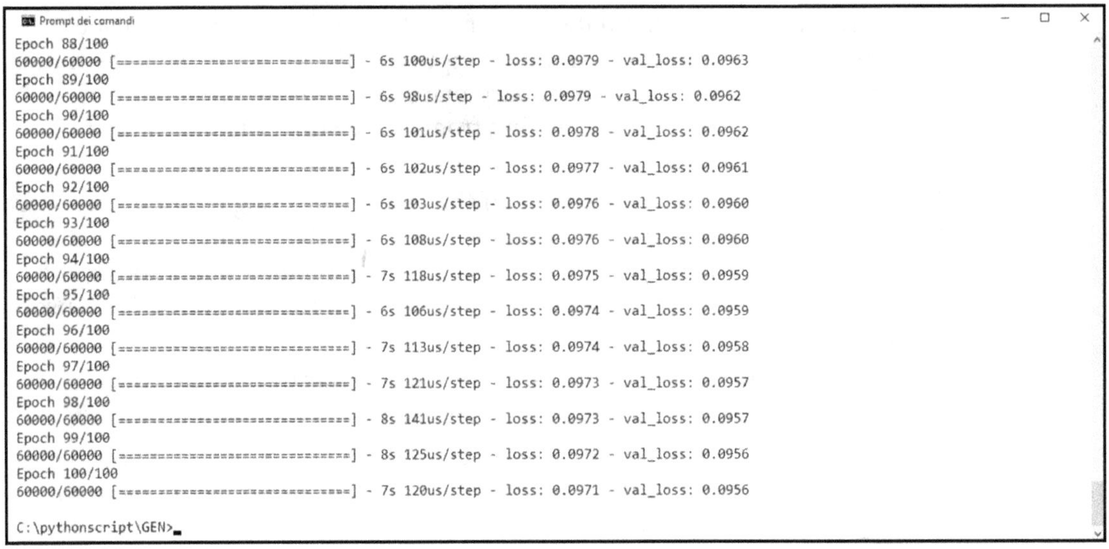

To get an idea of how the `loss` function varies during the epochs, it can be useful to create a plot of `loss` on the training and validation datasets over training epochs. To do this, we will use the Matplotlib library as follows:

```
plt.plot(history.history['loss'])
plt.plot(history.history['val_loss'])
plt.title('Autoencoder Model loss')
plt.ylabel('loss')
plt.xlabel('epoch')
plt.legend(['train', 'test'], loc='upper left')
plt.show()
```

A plot of loss on the training and validation datasets over training epochs is shown in the following graph:

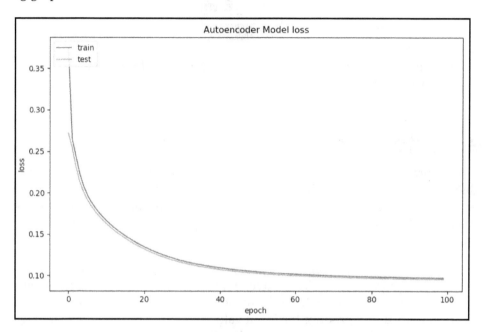

Our work is done; we just have to verify the results obtained. We can print to the screen the starting handwriting digits and those reconstructed from our model. Of course, we will do it only for some of the 60,000 digits contained in the dataset; in fact, we will limit ourselves to displaying the first five. We will also use the Matplotlib library in this case:

```
n=5
plt.figure(figsize=(20, 4))
for i in range(n):
    ax = plt.subplot(2, n, i + 1)
    plt.imshow(x_test[i].reshape(28, 28))
    plt.gray()
    ax.get_xaxis().set_visible(False)
    ax.get_yaxis().set_visible(False)
    ax = plt.subplot(2, n, i + 1 + n)
    plt.imshow(DecodedDigits[i].reshape(28, 28))
    plt.gray()
    ax.get_xaxis().set_visible(False)
    ax.get_yaxis().set_visible(False)
plt.show()
```

The results are shown in the following screenshot:

As you can see in the preceding screenshot, the result is very close to the original, meaning that the model works well.

Deep autoencoder Q-learning

As we saw in previous chapters, reinforcement learning demonstrates insufficient adaptability to high-dimensional input data. This problem is overcome by using low-dimensional characteristics vectors to represent high-dimensional input. However, finding useful vectors of features can be complicated, as it requires a good understanding of the problem.

One way to change the dimensionality of data is the autoencoder. Autoencoders are artificial neural networks with a hidden layer, which has the desired dimensionality of the input data; both input and output levels have the same amount of units. In these models, the network is trained to reproduce the input values in the output level. As we saw in the previous section, the autoencoder learns two functions: an encoder function and a decoder function.

During reinforcement learning, the amount of data available is constantly increasing. This data can be used to find a better low-dimensional representation. However, reapplying new features every time new data is collected requires the training of a new autoencoder on all the data, which usually takes a long time.

After each iteration of the training, the reconstruction error is evaluated and the amount of hidden units is modified appropriately. If the error is very large, new features are added. If the error is decreasing, similar features are merged to reduce the complexity of the model.

The following snippet shows pseudocode for the Q-learning algorithm, as reported in Chapter 1, *Overview of Keras Reinforcement Learning*:

```
set parameters α,γ, ε
Initialize arbitrary action-value function
Repeat (for each episode)
   observe current state s
   choose a from s using policy from action-value function
   Repeat (for each step in episode)
      take action a
      observe r, s'
      update action-value function
      update s
```

As already mentioned in the preceding code, it is necessary to use low-dimensional characteristics vectors to represent high-dimensional input data. One method to learn the functions for this task is to use autoencoders. However, this requires gathering enough input data to find a useful representation. In general, the process of teaching an agent with Q-learning from large input data is similar to the following pseudocode:

```
collect initial input data
train autoencoder on available input data
set parameters α,γ, ε
Initialize arbitrary action-value function
Repeat (for each episode)
   observe current state H
   transform observation into low dimensional representation s
   choose a from s using policy from action-value function
   Repeat (for each step in episode)
      take action a
      observe r, s'
      update action-value function
      update s
```

In this way, the autoencoder is trained only on the input data initially given. Then the parameters and action-value functions are initialized. Then the Q-learning cycle is inserted, in which the observed current state is transformed into its representation of a low-dimensional feature using the autoencoder. Using this feature vector, Q-learning is performed as usual. To gather the data needed to find a useful feature vector, we need to do a lot of experiments before actually starting to form the agent.

Summary

In this chapter, you learned how to solve a handwritten digit-recognition problem. Starting from the basis of the OCR and computer vision concepts, we learned how to elaborate simple images.

Then, an autoencoder was used for handwritten digit recognition. An autoencoder is a neural network whose purpose is to code its input into small dimensions and the result obtained to be able to reconstruct the input itself. The purpose of autoencoders is not simply to perform a sort of compression of the input or look for an approximation of the identity function; but there are techniques that allow us to direct the model (starting from a hidden layer of reduced dimensions) to give greater importance to some data properties. Thus they give rise to different representations based on the same data.

Finally, autoencoders and reinforcement learning concepts were joined to improve the performance of the model.

10
Playing the Board Game Go

Games have always been a phenomenon of human culture, where people manifest intelligence, interaction, and competition. But games are also an important theoretical paradigm in logic, artificial intelligence, computer science, linguistics, biology, and lately more and more in the social sciences and in psychology. Games, especially strategy games, offer reinforcement-learning algorithms an ideal and privileged environment for testing, as they can act as models for real problems. In this chapter, will learn how to use reinforcement-learning algorithms to address a problem in game theory.

The following are the topics covered:

- Basic concepts of game theory
- Game theory practical applications
- AlphaGo DeepMind project
- Monte Carlo Tree Search
- Convolutional networks

At the end of the chapter, the reader will have learned basic concepts of game theory, how the AlphaGo DeepMind project works, how the **Monte Carlo Tree Search** (**MCTS**) performs a deep search—until it reaches a final state—and how convolutional networks guide the tree-search procedure.

Game theory

Game theory is the mathematical science that studies and analyzes the individual decisions of a subject in situations of conflict or strategic interaction with other rival subjects aimed at the maximum profit of each subject. In such situations, the decisions of one can influence the results achieved by the other(s), and vice versa, according to a feedback mechanism, by seeking competitive and/or cooperative solutions through models.

The theory of games has its distant origins in 1654 from a correspondence between Blaise Pascal and Pierre de Fermat, on the calculation of probabilities for gambling.

The expression **game theory** was first used by Émile Borel in the 1920s. Borel took care of the *théorie des jeux*, of zero-sum games with two players and tried to find a solution known as John von Neumann's concept of solving a zero-sum game.

The birth of modern game theory can be made to coincide with the release of the book *Theory of Games and Economic Behavior* by John von Neumann and Oskar Morgenstern in 1944 (in the following picture is shown the book cover), although other authors (such as Ernst Zermelo, Armand Borel, and John von Neumann himself) had written of game theory:

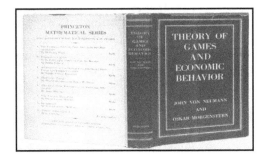

The idea of these two scholars can be described informally as the attempt to describe human behavior mathematically in those cases in which the interaction between people involves the winning, or dividing, of some kind of resource.

The most famous scholar to have subsequently dealt with the theory of games, in particular with regard to non-cooperative games, is the mathematician John Forbes Nash Jr., to whom Ron Howard's "A Beautiful Mind" is dedicated (in the following picture is shown a movie poster):

Eight Nobel Prizes in Economics were awarded to scholars who dealt with game theory. A Crafoord Prize has also been awarded to John Maynard Smith, a distinguished biologist and geneticist, and a professor at the University of Sussex for a long time, for his contribution in this field.

Basic concepts

Game theory has as its main objective the victory: everyone must be aware of the rules of the game, and be aware of the consequences of every single move. The set of moves that an individual intends to perform is called a strategy. Depending on the strategies adopted by all the players, each one receives a payoff according to an adequate unit of measurement. The reward can be positive, negative, or null. A game is called a constant sum if for each player's payout there is a corresponding loss for others. In particular, a zero-sum game between two players represents the situation in which the reward is paid from one player to another. The strategy to follow is satisfactory for all players; otherwise it is necessary to calculate and maximize the player's mathematical hope or expected value, which is the weighted average of the possible rewards, each weighed for the respective probabilities of the event.

In a game, there are one or more contenders who try to win the game, that is, to maximize their winnings. The winnings are defined by a rule that establishes quantitatively what is the reward of the contenders according to their behavior; this function is called a function of payments. Each player can undertake a finite-infinite number of actions or decisions that determine a strategy. Each strategy is characterized by a consequence for the player who has adopted it and which can be a reward (positive/negative). The result of the game is completely determined by the sequence of their strategies and the strategies adopted by the other players.

How do we characterize the result of the game for each player? If you measure the consequence of a strategy in terms of reward, each strategy can be matched with a value: a negative value will indicate a payment to the opponent, that is, a penalty; a positive value will indicate winnings, that is, the collection of a prize. The gain or loss due to the generic player associated with his strategy and the strategies taken at a given moment by all the remaining players is expressed by the monetary value indicated by the payment function.

 The decisions taken by a player naturally collide or are in accordance with the decisions made by the other players and from such situations derive various types of games.

A useful tool to represent the interactions between two players, two companies, or two individuals is a double-entry decision matrix or table. This decision table serves to show the strategies and winnings of a game conducted by two players.

The decision matrix is therefore a representation through which we catalog all the possible results of the interactions between players and we assign the value of the reward that in each situation competes to each player. Another form of representation concerns the sequence with which each decision is taken or the actions are conducted. This characteristic of each game can be described by means of a tree graph, representing every possible combination of the contenders' play from an initial state to the final states where the winnings are distributed, as shown in the following diagram:

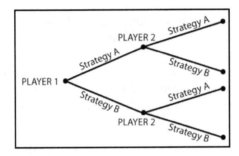

To describe a strategic situation, four basic elements are needed:

- **Players**: The decision-makers in the game (who is involved?)
- **Actions**: The possible actions, or moves, that players can choose from (what can they do?)
- **Strategies**: The action plans of the players (what are they going to do?)
- **Winnings**: The possible gains that players get (what do they earn?)

 A strategy is therefore a complete and contingent plan, or a decision-making decision, that specifies how the player must act in any possible circumstances in which they may be called upon to decide.

Being a complete contingent plan, a strategy often defines what action a player must choose in circumstances that may not be achieved during the game.

Game types

Games can be classified according to different paradigms:

- Cooperation
- Symmetry
- Sum
- Sequencing

Cooperative games

A cooperative game is presented when the interests of the players are not in direct opposition to each other, but there is a commonality of interests. Players pursue a common goal, at least for the duration of the game; some of them may tend to associate to improve their payoff. The guarantee is given by the binding agreements. What is the mathematical representation of a shared interest? The concept of the union of individual interests in a coalition or alliance is expressed by the definition of essential play, while the value of a generic coalition is measured by a function called a characteristic function.

In contrast, in non-cooperative games, also called competitive games, players cannot enter into binding agreements (even by regulation), regardless of their objectives. This category answers the solution given by John Nash with his Nash Equilibrium, probably the most famous notion for the whole theory, thanks to its vast field of applicability. The criterion of rational behavior adopted in non-cooperative games is individual and is called the maximum strategy.

Symmetrical games

In a symmetrical game, the profits deriving from the adoption of a particular strategy depend only on the other strategies employed, not by those who are playing them. If players' identities can be changed without changing the payoff, then a game is symmetrical.

In contrast, in asymmetrical games, there are no identical series of strategies for both players. It is possible, however, that a game has identical strategies for both players, but that it is asymmetric.

Zero-sum games

The zero-sum games are a special case of constant-sum games in which the constant is zero. The zero-sum games model all the conflicting situations in which the contrast of the two players is total: the winning of a player coincides exactly with the loss of the other. In other words, the sum of the winnings of the two contenders according to the strategies used is always zero. In chess, for example, it means that the only three possible results are victory, defeat, and draw (reward: +1, -1, and 0).

Sequential games

In sequential games, subsequent players retain some knowledge of previous actions. This does not mean that they know every action of the previous players. For example, a player may know that a previous player has not performed a certain action, while they do not know which of the other available actions the first player actually performed.

Game theory applications

Game theory has always interested scholars because of its usefulness in the practical field and in all fields of human work:

- **Philosophy**: Analyzed game theory because it provides a way to clarify the logical difficulty of some philosophers, such as Kant, Rousseau, Hobbes, and other social and political theorists.
- **Economy**: Many of the speculations in the business world can be modeled using the methodology of game theory. A famous example is that of the similarity between the setting of oligopolies' prices and the prisoner's dilemma.
- **Biology**: Although nature is often considered brutal, there is cooperation between many different species. The reason for this coexistence can be modeled using game theory.
- **Artificial intelligence**: A human being is able to make decisions based on the environmental stimuli they receive. Instead, machines can make a decision only if programmed with decision lists based on a number of conditions. This limit can be overcome by artificial intelligence, which can give the machine the ability to make new unplanned decisions from their creators. This would require that programs be able to generate new payoff matrices based on observed stimuli and experience.

In the following subsection, we will examine some practical cases of application of the rules deriving from game theory.

Prisoner's dilemma

The prisoner's dilemma is a complete information game proposed in the 1950s by Albert Tucker as a game theory problem. The dilemma can be described as follows. Two people are accused of committing a crime. The investigators arrest them both and put them in two different cells, preventing them from communicating with each other. Each of them is given two choices: to collaborate, or not to collaborate. The following are also explained to them:

- If only one of the two collaborators accuses the other, the collaborator avoids the penalty, but the other is sentenced to three years in prison
- If both accuse each other, they are both sentenced to two years
- If neither of them collaborates, both are sentenced to one year, because they're already guilty of illegal port of arms

The dilemma can equally describe the arms race in the 1950s by the US and the USSR (the two prisoners) during the Cold War.

This game can be described with the following decision matrix:

A / B	Confess	Stay silent
Confess	(2,2)	(0,3)
Stay silent	(3,0)	(1,1)

The best strategy of this non-cooperative game is (stay silent, stay silent) because we do not know what the other will choose to do. For each of the two, the aim is to minimize their own conviction.

The stay silent strategy is strictly dominated by the confess strategy. By eliminating the strictly dominated strategies, one arrives at the Nash Equilibrium, where the two prisoners collaborate and have two years in prison. The best result for the two is of course not to collaborate (one year of prison instead of two), but this is not a balance.

Suppose the two promised not to cooperate in case of arrest. They are now locked up in two different cells and wonder if the promise will be kept on the other; if a prisoner does not respect the promise and the other does, the first is then released. There is therefore a dilemma: to collaborate or not to collaborate. Game theory tells us that there is only one balance (stay silent, stay silent).

If we think of the US and the USSR as the two prisoners, and confession as the atomic armament (on the contrary, denial would be equivalent to unilateral disarmament), the dilemma describes as for the two nations it was inevitable at the time of the cold war, slow down the arms race, although this final result was not optimal for either of the two superpowers (and for the whole world).

Stag hunt

Stag hunt is a game, proposed for the first time by Jean-Jacques Rousseau, whose scenario presents two men who can choose in a hunting trip whether to try to catch a stag or a hare. Their decision must be made without knowing the decision of the other, and taking into account that to capture a deer, it is necessary that both decide to choose the latter as an objective, while the hare only requires the commitment of one man. The game also specifies that the hare is a less satisfying reward than the deer, which is a better meal, even if it is divided between the two hunters who cooperated. Because each hunter ignores what the other's decision will be, it is a non-cooperative game.

This game can be described with the following decision matrix:

A \ B	Stag	Hare
Stag	(3,3)	(0,2)
Hare	(2,0)	(1,1)

Using pure strategies, the only solution of Nash's Equilibrium is found by shooting at the hare. In this way, you avoid the risk of not getting anything, which would be the result if you shoot at the stag and the other player at the hare. With a mixed strategy approach, Nash's Equilibrium consists of shooting at the stag with a 75% chance, and a 25% for the hare.

Chicken game

The chicken game is a game of game theory with zero sum. The information is complete and there are two players participating at the same time. The classic example is based on the challenge of the movie *Rebel Without a Cause* with James Dean from 1955, in which two guys make a car race by launching the cars simultaneously toward a cliff. If both swerve before arriving, they will both will make a bad impression with their peers; if one swerves and the other continues for a longer stretch of road, the first will make the figure of the chicken, while the second will gain the respect of their peers. If both continue on the road, they will die.

As in the prisoner's dilemma, the cooperation of both is an unstable equilibrium, which does not hold up even in the short term, that is, in the case of a one-off game. Look at the payoff matrix:

A \ B	Swerve	Straight
Swerve	(0,0)	(-1,1)
Straight	(1,-1)	(-10,-10)

In this game, neither player has a dominant strategy and there are two potential balances: (Swerve, Straight) and (Straight, Swerve). The game is said to be non-coordination, since it is better for both to adopt the opposite strategy than that of the other player. Of course, each of the two players has a predilection for a particular balance. The solution of the game comes from the credible declaration of one of the two players of the intention of not wanting to swerve at any cost. The other player will be forced to turn first to avoid driving off the cliff.

The Go game

Go is a strategic board game for two players. Go originated in China, where it has been played for at least 2,500 years; it is very popular in East Asia, but has spread to the rest of the world in recent years. It is a very complex game strategically despite its simple rules; a Korean proverb says that no game of Go has ever been played twice, which is likely if you think that there are 2.08×10^{170} different possible positions on a 19 × 19 goban.

Go is played by two players who alternately place black and white pieces (called stones) on the empty intersections of a grid of black lines (called goban) within a 19 × 19 grid. The aim of the game is to control a zone of the goban greater than that controlled by the adversary; for this purpose the players try to arrange their stones so that they cannot be captured, carving out at the same time the territories that the opponent cannot invade without being captured. In the following picture is shown a 19 x 19 goban:

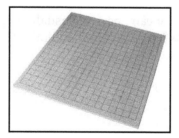

Apart from the size of the goban and the starting positions, the rules have been maintained over the centuries, so that it can be considered the oldest game still played.

Basic rules of the game

Two players, black and white, alternately place a stone of their color in an empty (intersecting) point of the grid drawn on the goban. Normally Nero moves first; in case of a handicap game, when one of the two players is much stronger than the other, the weaker takes black and has two or more handicap stones on the goban, and Bianco moves first. The official grid consists of 19 × 19 lines, but the rules apply to all grids; once played, a stone cannot be moved to a different place.

Stones of the same color that are adjacent horizontally or vertically form a group, whose liberties are the sum of the liberties of the stones from which it is composed and which cannot be divided subsequently, form to all effects a single larger stone. Only the stones that are connected to one another by lines drawn on the goban form a group; the diagonally adjacent stones are not connected. Groups can be enlarged by playing other stones on intersections close to them or connected together by playing a stone on an intersection that is adjacent to two or more groups of the same color.

Most rules do not allow a player to play a stone so that one of his groups remains without freedom, a sort of suicide, with one exception: if the new stone captures one or more opposing stones, these are removed first, leaving the stone just played with at least one freedom. It is said that this rule prohibits suicide.

Players cannot make a move that returns the game to the position immediately preceding that of the opponent; this rule, called the ko rule, serves to prevent infinite repetitions of the same moves.

Instead of playing a stone, a player can pass; this usually happens when the player thinks they have no other useful moves left to play. When both players pass consecutively, the game ends and the score is calculated.

Scoring rules

There are two methods of scoring to determine the winner of a game; only occasionally these two methods lead to different results and each of these counting methods has advantages and disadvantages. The first method (called the Japanese count) calculates the controlled territory, and is the one used in Japan and Korea, and probably the one originally used in China; the second method (called Chinese count), calculates the occupied area, and is the one used in China starting, it is believed, from the 15th century.

With area-based counting, a player's score is the number of stones in their color on the goban plus the empty intersections surrounded by them. The area-based score requires players to keep the captured stones, called prisoners, to which they add the dead stones at the end of the game. The score is equal to the number of empty intersections surrounded by the player's stones plus the number of captive stones.

The AlphaGo project

AlphaGo is a software for the game of Go developed by Google DeepMind. It was the first software able to defeat a human champion in the game without a handicap and on a standard-sized goban (19 × 19).

 DeepMind is a British company of artificial intelligence controlled by Alphabet. It was founded in 2011 as DeepMind Technologies and was acquired by Google in 2014.

According to David Silver, a researcher at DeepMind, the AlphaGo project was launched in 2014 to study how deep neural networks could be applied to the game of Go.

AlphaGo represented a significant advancement over pre-existing go-to game programs. Over 500 games played against other software, including Crazy Stone and Zen—AlphaGo (running on a single computer) has won all but one game—and running a series of similar matches, but turning on an AlphaGo cluster has won all 500 games and won 77% of the games against itself performed on a single machine.

The distributed version employed 1,202 CPUs and 176 GPUs, about 25 times more than the single computer hardware. In the following screenshot is shown the project site:

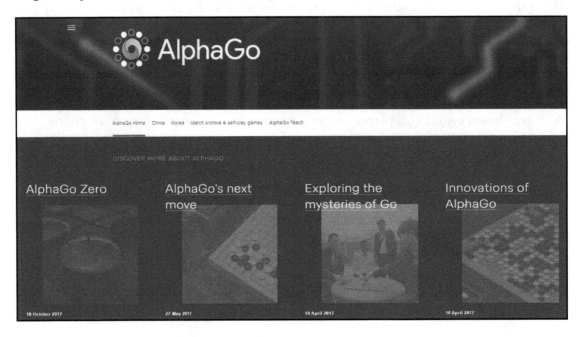

In October 2015, AlphaGo defeated the European champion Fan Hui for 5 to 0, becoming the first software able to defeat a human master in the game without a handicap and on a standard-sized goban. The public announcement was made only on 27th January, 2016, coinciding with the publication of an article in Nature that describes the algorithm used by the software.

Between the March 9th and 15th, 2016, AlphaGo held a meeting with South Korean player Lee Sedol, one of the strongest Go players in the world. The match in five games, played respectively on the 9th, 10th, 12th, 13th, and 15th of March, was held at the Four Seasons Hotel in Seoul and was broadcast on a live stream. AlphaGo ran on the cloud platform of Google, whose servers are located in the United States, and the moves made by the software were reported on the goban by Aja Huang, a member of the DeepMind team and amateur player of Go. The meeting adopted the Chinese rules, with a komi of 7.5 points, a reflection time of 2 hours, and a 60-second byoyomi. The computing power used was similar to that used in the meeting with Fan Hui.

At the time of the meeting, Lee Sedol held the second-highest number of victories in the world in the international Go championships. Although there was no official international ranking, some sources considered Lee Sedol to be the fourth-best player in the world at the time. AlphaGo had not been specifically configured to address Lee's style of play.

AlphaGo won Lee Sedol's first three games for abandonment. He won the fourth game, in which AlphaGo left the one hundred and eighty move. The software finally won the last game for abandonment.

It is not the first time that a computer has beaten a human at a game. On February 10th, 1996, IBM's supercomputer Deep Blue was the first to beat the current world chess champion in a single game; the legendary Garry Kasparov won three matches, drawing two, and the final result of four to two was his historical way because that was the last victory of a world champion of chess against a computer.

The year after, Deep Blue returned to the table of the challenge and this time for Kasparov there was nothing to do. Kasparov was furious, but in that anger there was the frustration that humanity had been seen to be surpassed by a machine, no longer only on the level of physical force, but on that of intelligence.

Years later, thinking back to that defeat, Kasparov says that since then the computers have evolved to the point that even the last chess application we have in the mobile phone today would beat the current chess champion. It's a matter of memory and computing power; after all, it is enough to load tens of thousands of games and all the possible variants onto the computer and it wins. Now you do not need that anymore either.

The difference with AlphaGo is that Deep Blue had been trained by humans who had set all possible strategies. In the case of AlphaGo, the robot has learned by itself without any human intervention. Its secret lies in its "humanity"; this system of artificial intelligence has taken as a model the neural networks of the human brain. Thanks to this characteristic, AlphaGo plays in a similar way to humans and presented itself to the historic well-trained challenge, after playing millions of games against itself.

The AlphaGo algorithm

The algorithm behind AlphaGo consists of two parts:

- A tree-search procedure
- Convolutional networks that guide the tree-search procedure

In total, three convolutional networks of two different kinds are trained: two policy networks and one value network.

AlphaGo's algorithm uses a combination of machine learning and tree-search techniques, along with an extensive gaming and human learning phase. It uses the MCTS for the selection of moves, guided by two deep neural networks (value network and policy network). Before being sent to neural networks, the input is analyzed in a preprocessing phase to extract some features (for example, the adherence of the moves to a series of common patterns).

In the first phase of the training, the neural networks carry out supervised learning based on the human game, trying to imitate it using a database of about 30,000,000 moves from historical games. Once a certain amount of play is reached, learning continues by reinforcing it by playing against other instances of itself.

The software is programmed to abandon the game if the probability of victory falls below a certain threshold, which, for example, in the meeting of March, 2016, with Lee Sedol was set at 20%.

Monte Carlo Tree Search

MCTS is a heuristic search algorithm for some types of decision-making processes, particularly those used in game theory. Traditional artificial-intelligence algorithms are very powerful, yet they require a lot of memory in their execution. In 2006, Kocsis and Szepesvari, with the aim of improving the classic algorithms, introduced the MCTS. Compared to the Minimax, the main difference of the MCTS method is that the expansion of the state tree does not take place completely.

The minimax, in decision theory, is a method to minimize the maximum (minimax) possible loss; alternatively, to maximize the minimum gain (maximin). It was discovered in the theory of games in the case of a zero-sum game with two players, both in the case of alternative moves (shifts) and simultaneous moves, being subsequently extended to more complex games and decisions supported in the presence of uncertainty.

While the minimax expands the whole tree and then chooses the best move, the MCTS performs a deep search until it reaches a final state. At this point, it evaluates the current state, assigns a value to that node, and propagates it to all those paths up to the root. This procedure is repeated several times by constructing a tree incrementally and asymmetrically, choosing to each iteration the most urgent node to be expanded.

This choice is made on the basis of a policy aimed at balancing the exploration of the parts not yet visited and the exploitation of the nodes that seem promising. The construction of the tree stops arbitrarily depending on the time or memory available. A further advantage is that it does not have to calculate the values of the intermediate states. Considering only the situation in the final states requires less knowledge of the domain. Kocsis and Szepesvari have shown that Monte Carlo Tree Search, having enough time and memory, converges to the optimal result of minimax.

The basic algorithm of the MCTS method consists in constructing a search tree iteratively until the pre-established amount of time or memory is reached. Each node represents a state in the domain and each of its children is a possible next state. The process can be divided into four phases:

- **Selection**: Starting from the root-node R, we recursively choose an optimal child-node until an L-node is reached
- **Expansion**: If L is not a terminal node (that is, the game does not end), one or more child nodes are generated and one C is chosen
- **Simulation**: It simulates an execution on the new C node to produce a result
- **Back propagation**: The result of the simulation is propagated backward (up to the root) through the selected nodes, updating their statistics

In the following diagram are shown the MCTS steps:

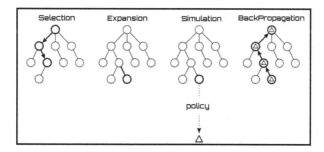

For selection and expansion, the tree policy is used, which decides which node to consider. Instead, for the simulation, the default policy is used, which implements the knowledge of the domain and produces an estimate of the state value corresponding to the final leaf.

The procedure we have seen can be applied to any game whose positions have a finite number of moves and a finite length. For each position, all possible moves are determined; k random games are played to the end and scores are recorded. The move that leads to the best score is chosen.

In applying this procedure, the main problems arise from the selection of child nodes. In order to maintain a certain balance between the exploitation of the deep variants after the moves with a high average winning rate and the exploration of the moves with few simulations, some measures are necessary. The **Upper Confidence Bound for Trees** (**UCT**) is applied to balance exploitation and exploration in games. The following formula is applied to choose the next node to be expanded:

$$UCT = X_j + C\sqrt{log\frac{N}{n_j}}$$

In this formula:

- N is the number of times the current node (that is, the parent) has been chosen
- n_j is the number of times the child was chosen
- C is a positive parameter to set
- X_j is the average of the value totalized by the j node

This algorithm balances the use of collected rewards (exploitation) with the exploration of seldom-visited nodes. Given that, in the initial sampling, the random component weighs heavily, the nodes must be visited a certain number of times before these values are effectively estimated.

Convolutional networks

Essentially, the **convolutional neural networks** (**CNNs**) are artificial neural networks. In fact, just like the latter, CNNs are made up of neurons connected to each other by weighted branches (weight); the training parameters of the nets are once again the weight and the bias.

In CNNs, the connection pattern between neurons is inspired by the structure of the visual cortex in the animal world. The individual neurons present in this part of the brain (visual cortex) respond to certain stimuli in a narrow region of the observation, called the receptive field. The receptive fields of different neurons are partially overlapped so that they cover the entire field of view altogether. The response of a single neuron to stimuli taking place in its receptive field can be mathematically approximated by a convolutional operation.

Everything related to the training of a neural network, that is, forward/backward propagation and updating the weight, also applies in this context; moreover, a whole CNN always uses a single function of differentiable cost. However, CNNs make the specific assumption that their input has a precise data structure, such as an image, and this allows them to take specific properties in their architecture in order to better process such data.

The normal neural networks stratified with a fully connected architecture, where every neuron of each layer is connected to all the neurons of the previous layer (excluding bias neurons), in general do not scale well with the increase in the size of the input data.

Let's take a practical example: suppose we want to analyze an image to detect objects. To start, let's see how the image is processed. As we know, in the coding of an image, it is divided into a grid of small squares, each of which represents a pixel. At this point, to encode the color images, it will be enough to identify for each square a certain number of shades, different color gradations, and to code each one by means of an appropriate sequence of bits. In the following diagram is shown a simple image encoding:

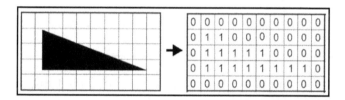

The number of squares in the grid defines the resolution of the image. For example, an image that is 1,600 pixels wide and 800 pixels high (1600 x 800) contains (multiply) 1,280,000 pixels (or 1.2 megapixels). To this, we must add the three color channels, finally obtaining *1600 x 800 x 3 = 3,840,000*. So each neuron completely connected in the first hidden layer would have 3,840,000 weights. This is only for a single neuron, but then considering the whole network, the thing would certainly become unmanageable.

CNNs are designed to recognize visual patterns directly in images represented by pixels, and require an amount of zero or very limited preprocessing. They are able to recognize extremely variable patterns, such as freehand writing and images representing the real world.

Typically, a CNN consists of several alternate convolutional and subsampling levels (pooling) followed by one or more fully connected final levels in the case of classification. In the following diagram is shown a classic image-processing pipeline:

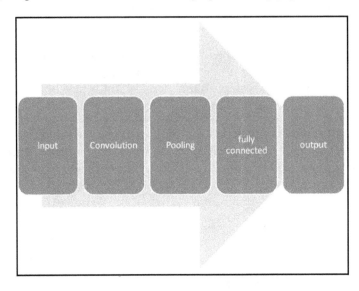

To solve problems in the real world, these steps can be combined and stacked as often as necessary. You can have two, three, or more layers of convolution. You can enter all the pooling you want to reduce the size of the data.

To explore the structure of a CNN, we will use a practical example: starting from the images as input layers, there will be a certain series of convolutional layers, interspersed with the **rectified linear unit** (**ReLU**) layer and, when necessary, from standardization and pooling layers, and finally there will be a last series of FC layers, before the output layer. In the following diagram is an example of the CNN architecture:

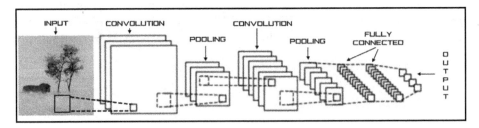

The basic idea is to start with a large image and continuously reduce data, step by step, until you get a single result. The more convolutional passages you have, the more the neural network will be able to understand and process complex functions.

In the AlphaGo architecture, two neural networks are implemented:

- **Policy network**: Decides which next move/action to take
- **Value network**: Provides the winner of the game from the current position

AlphaGo uses the two preceding networks to reduce the enormous complexity of the search tree to a small, manageable search space. In this way, the hundreds of different moves at every step necessary in a brute-force algorithm are replaced with some of the best-possible moves suggested by the policy network.

Furthermore, the value network reduces the depth of the search. In each position, the value network tries to predict which player will win instead of traversing the bottom tree to evaluate it. Thus it returns a value that quantifies how good the moves suggested by the possible network are.

Summary

In this chapter, you learned the general concepts of game theory. Game theory is the mathematical science that studies and analyzes the individual decisions of a subject in situations of conflict or strategic interaction with other rival subjects aimed at the maximum profit of each subject. Game theory's main objective is the victory; everyone must be aware of the rules of the game, and be aware of the consequences of every single move. The set of moves that an individual intends to perform is called a strategy. We have analyzed the different types of games predicted by the theory and various practical applications in real time: the prisoner's dilemma, stag hunt, and chicken game.

Then we explored the AlphaGo DeepMind project. Go is a strategic board game for two players. AlphaGo is a software for the game of Go developed by Google DeepMind. It was the first software able to defeat a human champion in the game without a handicap and on a standard-sized goban (19 × 19). AlphaGo's algorithm uses a combination of machine learning and tree-search techniques, along with an extensive gaming and human-learning phase.

Then we looked at MCTS. MCTS is a heuristic search algorithm for some types of decision-making processes, particularly those used in game theory. It performs a deep search until it reaches a final state.

Finally, we covered convolutional networks. CNNs are artificial neural networks that are made up of neurons connected to each other by weighted branches (weight); the training parameters of the nets are the weight and the bias. These networks are used to guide the tree-search procedure.

11
What's Next?

Reinforcement learning is an automatic learning technique that aims to implement systems able to learn and adapt to the changes in the environment in which they are immersed, through the distribution of a reward called reinforcement, which consists of evaluating their performance. It can be implemented by means of different algorithms, such as Q-learning, to be inserted into the system in which learning is to be carried out. This technology is increasingly widespread, thanks to its ability to interact with the environment.

In this chapter, we will summarize what has been covered so far in this book, and what the next steps are from this point on. You will learn how to apply the skills you have gained to other projects and real-life challenges in building and deploying reinforcement learning models, and other common technologies that data scientists often use. By the end of this chapter, you will have a better understanding of real-life challenges in building and deploying machine learning models, and additional resources and technologies to learn to sharpen your machine learning skills.

The following topics are covered:

- DeepMind AlphaZero
- IBM Watson
- The Unity Machine Learning Agents toolkit
- Inverse reinforcement learning
- Deep Deterministic Policy Gradients
- Hindsight Experience Replay

At the end of the chapter, the reader will have explored some practical examples of application of technologies based on reinforcement learning, and will understand the future challenges in the use of reinforcement-learning algorithms.

Reinforcement-learning applications in real life

As we have already said, reinforcement learning is a programming philosophy that aims to create algorithms able to learn and adapt to changes in the environment. This programming technique is based on the assumption of being able to receive stimuli from the outside according to the choices of the algorithm. So, a correct choice will result in a prize, while an incorrect choice will lead to a penalization of the system. The goal of the system is to achieve the highest-possible prize and consequently the best-possible result.

With such a model, the computer learns, for example, to beat an opponent in a game (or to drive a vehicle) concentrating its efforts on performing a given task, aiming to achieve the maximum reward value; in other words, the system learns by playing (or driving) and by the mistakes made improving performance precisely according to the results achieved previously.

The applications of reinforcement learning are already numerous, some of which entered our daily life without us actually realizing it. As mentioned, systems based on learning with reinforcement are the basis of the development of self-driving cars that, through machine learning, learn to recognize the surrounding environment (with data collected by sensors, GPS, and so on) and adapt their behavior according to the specific situations they face/overcome.

The programs that deal with web-user profiling also take advantage of machine learning, learning from the behavior and preferences of the users who surf on websites, platforms, or mobile applications; an example is those that we are commonly used to seeing and using on eCommerce platforms, such as Amazon, or entertainment and access to content such as Netflix or Spotify.

In the following sections, we will see some practical examples of the application of technologies based on reinforcement learning.

DeepMind AlphaZero

AlphaZero is an artificial-intelligence algorithm based on machine-learning techniques developed by Google DeepMind. It is a generalization of AlphaGo Zero, a predecessor developed specifically for the game of Go, and in turn an evolution of AlphaGo, the first software capable of achieving superhuman performances in the game of Go. Like AlphaGo Zero, it uses the **Monte Carlo Tree Search** (**MCTS**), guided by a deep convolutional neural network trained for reinforcement.

On December 5th 2017, the DeepMind team published a preprint on arXiv in which some of the results obtained by AlphaZero were presented in several classic table games, reaching a superhuman level in the game of chess, shogi, and Go with only a few hours of training, overcoming world champion programs in their respective disciplines: Stockfish for chess, Elmo for shogi, and AlphaGo Zero for Go.

Stockfish is a multi-platform open source UCI chess engine, originally developed by Tord Romstad and Marco Costalba as a fork of Glaurung, another open source engine previously developed by Romstad himself, and is currently maintained by an open source programmer community.

Elmo is a software that implements an evaluation function and a joseki for the game of shogi, created by Makoto Takizawa.

AlphaGo Zero is a version of DeepMind's Go software, AlphaGo. AlphaGo's team published an article in the journal *Nature* on October 19, 2017, introducing AlphaGo Zero, a version created without using data from human games, and stronger than any previous version [1]. By playing games against itself, AlphaGo Zero surpassed the strength of AlphaGo Lee in three days by winning 100 games to 0, reached the level of AlphaGo Master in 21 days, and exceeded all the old versions in 40 days.

In particular, an instance of AlphaZero won a match of 100 games against Stockfish, earning 25 wins with white, 3 with black, and a draw for the rest of the games. The authors estimate that AlphaZero surpassed Stockfish's game strength after the first four hours of training (about 300,000 mini-batches).

The main differences between AlphaZero and its predecessor are as follows:

- AlphaGo Zero uses Bayesian optimization techniques to tune the search parameters in every single game, while AlphaZero uses constant parameters during all the games.
- In training, the games of AlphaGo Zero are generated by the best instance (best player) obtained during the previous iterations, and after each iteration the performance of the new instance is measured against the best player, replacing that if it can beat that with a margin of at least 55%. Instead, AlphaZero uses a single neural network that is continuously updated, without waiting for the end of each iteration.

- Go (unlike chess and shogi) is symmetrical for certain reflections and rotations; AlphaGo Zero uses the symmetries both in training (performing data augmentation through eight possible rotations and reflections for each position), and in the evaluation phase (applying a random symmetry to the input before submitting it to the neural network, to delete the average bias due to rotation or reflection). AlphaZero cannot take advantage of these technical solutions.
- A chess game (unlike Go) can end in a draw; while AlphaGo estimates and optimizes the probability of victory, AlphaZero estimates and optimizes the expected result of the match (expressed in numerical form).

DeepMind explained that AlphaGo had been shown around 100,000 matches to start improving, while AlphaGo Zero was only taught the rules of the game. The computer has begun to play against itself, making mistakes and correcting itself in millions of games, becoming more and more able to beat its predecessor quite easily.

David Silver, the AlphaGo Zero programmers' manager, explained that by not using human data, they could remove the limits of human knowledge, thus allowing this supercomputer to search and find its strategies, unpublished even for the most aggressive players of Go. All this, using fewer processors than before: 4 instead of the 48 **Tensor Processor Unit** (**TPU**) of AlphaGo. Machines built by Google for the development of artificial intelligence, are already using TPU to understand and translate the different languages with its Translate software, or to recognize faces in the photos in our Google Photos. In the following picture is shown a Google TPU:

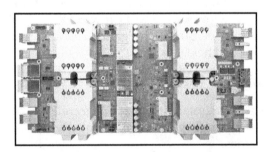

At the moment, Google has announced that it is able to connect up to 64 of these TPUs together, reaching a computational power of 11.5 petaFLOPS, equal to about 1,000,000,000,000,000,000 operations per second; to get an idea of the computing capacity, a normal computer, such as the one on which this text was written, comes to about 10,000,000,000.

Similar to its predecessors, AlphaGo Zero relied on a deep neural network to learn the abstract concepts behind the game. It then used learning by reinforcement to beat new opponents, but forgetting how to defeat previous versions of themselves. There is a fundamental difference compared to the past. Previous software used two separate neural networks, one to predict the best probable moves and one to decide which of them would guarantee victory. In the second case, they relied on a process called rollout, a series of game simulations to test the possible consequences. AlphaGo Zero has merged the functions into a single neural network which it asks directly to predict the move that will win. It's like asking it to make a prediction to a single expert instead of relying on 100 hypotheses of ordinary people. The new software could find applications in robotics, in the manufacture of new materials, and in chemistry. In fact, it could be used in complex research, such as those on all the possible configurations of protein-folding.

IBM Watson

Watson is a system of artificial intelligence, able to answer questions expressed in a natural language, developed within the DeepQA project of IBM by the research team directed by David Ferrucci. The name was chosen in honor of the first president of IBM, Thomas J. Watson.

In February 2013, IBM released the first commercial application of the Watson software system for managing lung cancer treatment decisions at the Memorial Sloan-Kettering Cancer Center, in collaboration with the WellPoint health insurance company.

IBM describes it as an advanced application of natural language processing, information retrieval, knowledge representation, automatic reasoning, and machine learning technologies in the field of open-domain question-answering built on the basis of DeepQA, IBM's formulation of technology hypotheses, massive collection of counter-tests, analyses, and scoring (ability to achieve a goal). In the following picture, an IBM Watson hardware is shown:

Watson uses the IBM DeepQA software, and the Apache UIMA framework. The system has been programmed in several languages, such as Java, C ++, and Prolog, and runs on the SUSE Linux Enterprise Server 11 system using Apache Hadoop as a framework for distributed computing.

The system is optimized to manage the workload required to generate hypotheses, to recognize maximum evidence, and analyze data, integrating extremely parallelized POWER7 processors. Watson consists of a grid of 90 IBM Power 750 servers, each of which is equipped with a 3.5 GHz eight-core POWER7 processor, with 4 threads per core. In total, the system has 2,880 threads of POWER7 processors, and 16 terabytes of RAM.

According to John Rennie, Watson can analyze 500 GB, equivalent to 1,000,000 books, every second. IBM designer and consultant Tony Pearson estimated Watson's hardware costs at $3,000,000. However, its performance of 80 teraFLOPS is not enough to make it onto the list of Top 500 Supercomputers.

The project's story comes after Deep Blue's chess victory against champion Garry Kasparov in 1997.

Deep Blue was a computer produced by IBM, expressly designed to play chess.

In 2004, IBM's research manager, Charles Lickel, after a dinner with colleagues, noted that there was a profound silence in the restaurant where they had dined. He immediately discovered the cause: Ken Jennings was in the middle of his 74th game of Jeopardy!, and practically the entire audience of the restaurant was stuck in front of the television, in the middle of the dinner, to follow the show.

Jeopardy! is a US television quiz that consists of a general competition between the various competitors, broadcast on NBC since 1964.

Thrilled by the idea of the TV quiz as a possible challenge for IBM, Lickel spoke about the idea, and in 2005, IBM's chief executive officer, Paul Horn, bet on the idea of Lickel, launching the idea of playing in his department at Jeopardy! with an IBM system. At the beginning, Horn found it difficult to find staff members who wanted to embark on a much more complicated challenge than the chess game without words, and then David Ferrucci accepted the offer. In a challenge organized by the US government, Watson's predecessor, a system called Piquant, was able to correctly answer only 35% of the questions, and spent several minutes on each.

To win the challenge, Watson would have to answer in no more than a few seconds, and at the same time, the questions posed by the gameshow would no longer have to be considered impossible to solve. In the initial tests carried out in 2006 by David Ferrucci, Watson was given 500 questions from previous editions of the quiz show. While the best human competitor had given the answers in half the time and had correctly answered 95% of the questions, the first version of Watson could only give 15% correct answers. During 2007, a team of 15 people was formed with the aim of solving the problem in 3 to 5 years' time. In 2008, researchers said Watson could compete with Jeopardy!'s human champions.

In February 2010, Watson could already beat Jeopardy!'s competitors. Although the system was primarily a work of IBM, several universities around the world have collaborated: Rensselaer Polytechnic Institute, Carnegie Mellon University, University of Massachusetts Amherst, University of Southern California Information Sciences Institute, University of Texas at Austin, Massachusetts Institute of Technology, and University of Trento, New York Medical College.

Watson, in February 2011, has participated in three episodes of the Jeopardy!, defeating its human opponents, in the only human-machine confrontation in the show's history. In the three episodes, broadcast from February 14th to 16th, Watson defeated Brad Rutter, known as the champion who won the most money by participating in Jeopardy!, and Ken Jennings, the record holder of the show. The following picture shows the challenge between the three contenders:

Watson has consistently outclassed its human opponents as to how quickly the response is booked, but it has had some difficulty with some categories of questions, especially those with short clues that contained few words. For each clue, the three most likely Watson responses were shown on the television screen. Watson had access to 200,000,000 pages of structured and unstructured content, including the full text of Wikipedia, with an occupancy of 4 terabytes of disk space. During the game, Watson was not connected to the internet. Watson received the first prize of $1,000,000.

According to IBM, the goal is to have computers able to interact in natural language with people through a wide range of applications and processes, understanding the questions posed by human beings and providing answers in a language understandable by them. IBM's general consultant, Robert C. Weber, proposed using Watson in legal research. The company intends to use Watson in other fields with a large amount of information, such as telecommunications, financial services, and government choices.

Watson is based on IBM Power 750 servers available on the market since February 2010. IBM is also thinking about launching the $ 1,000,000,000 DeepQA application on the market, reflecting the $ 1,000,000 price needed to buy a server that meets the minimum requirements for running Watson. IBM expects the price to fall substantially within a decade thanks to technological improvements.

In 2013, it was announced that three companies were working with IBM to create programs that integrated Watson technology. Fluid is developing a vendor application called The North Face, designed to provide advice to customers on the network. Welltok is developing an application to advise people on how to improve their health. MD Buyline is developing an application to advise medical institutions in decisions regarding the purchase of equipment. But, these are just some of the many IBM Watson applications.

There are four processes through which Watson's thoughts take shape:

- Parsing of the application, so that it is well-formed and interpretable
- The text is linked to existing knowledge, disambiguating its meaning from the context identified
- Relationships are extracted from the text to deepen the understanding of it
- Acquisition of information from the text, thus increasing the knowledge base on which the subsequent understanding process will be formed; the machine is able to learn

The interest many companies have in Watson is related to its ability to efficiently manage the multitude of data collected during the analysis prior to the excavations for extractions, as well as to better manage the enormous amount of communications and internal data of a company.

The complexity and the heterogeneity of data, many of which are unstructured and not corporate, are the most difficult obstacles and, despite the improvement of classical analytical methods, the construction of useful information from disaggregated data remains only partially realized. If we consider that the data is generated seamlessly by people, information systems, devices of all kinds for more than a trillion objects connected to each other, and that every day it produces a quantity equal to 2.5 billion gigabytes, it is clear that the volume effect contributes to the increase in complexity in a relevant way.

Therefore, it is essential to consider data as a new natural resource, from which competitive strength can be derived. This is provided that you use tools and processes to have real-time analytical skills and ability to extract knowledge.

Let's see in detail some of the IBM Watson applications that are already a reality. One example is Watson for Cyber Security, the industry's first augmented intelligence technology, designed to help analysts examine thousands of natural language search reports, previously inaccessible to even the most modern security tools. A recent IBM study found that only 7% of security professionals currently use cognitive tools, but this use is expected to triple over the next 2-3 years. Over the past year, Watson has been trained in the language of cyber security, powered by over 1,000,000 documents on the subject, and is now able to help analysts examine thousands of natural language research reports. Over the past 5 years, IBM has created over 300 security operations centers for customers in dozens of industries, including consumer goods distribution, retail sales, banking, and education.

In the health field, Watson Health, launched by IBM in April 2015, employs 2,000 specialists, and analyzes large quantities of medical reports and case studies. In a few seconds, Watson helps to formulate the diagnosis and find the best care by comparing the case under examination with all those in the archive, operations that would take a doctor 10,000 weeks, explains the American group of IBM Watson Health. In March 2017, IBM announced the launch of Watson Health's first European center for excellence in Milan, on the Expo area for the Human Technopole Italy 2040 research center, with which the Italian government aims to establish an international hub in the field of genomics, big data, population aging, and nutrition. IBM plans to invest up to $150,000,000 over the next few years.

Watson's abilities include being able to read the flows of all Facebook posts and all the tweets that are published, used by companies to anticipate trends. The company has access only to published content, but does not know who the author is. For example, this potential was applied to the Sanremo Italian Festival, when IBM during the 5 days of the festival, made available some Watson Analytic's skills, the cognitive tool that includes human language allowing simulation and prediction of results, analyzing over 290,000 comments on the web.

The Unity Machine Learning Agents toolkit

In September 2017, the Unity Machine Learning team introduced the Machine Learning Agents Toolkit. As the most popular creation engine in the world, Unity is at the crossroads between machine learning and gaming. In creating this toolkit, Unity researchers used reinforcement-learning algorithms. In this way, the gaming community will be able to use the latest machine learning technologies.

Since Unity's purpose is to democratize the development of the game, this new feature is already available to all those who want to immerse themselves in it, in a simple and immediate way. For this, the machine learning team has created some small demos to show how it works from the bottom up. For example, you can analyze the machine learning Roguelike demo, which is a 2D action game in which the player has to fight fierce, intelligent slimes. These enemies controlled by machine learning will attack without giving a break to our hero, and they will escape when they feel that their life is in danger. In the following screenshot is shown a machine learning Roguelike screen:

Unity's **Machine Learning Agents (ML-Agents)** toolkit was released as a beta version. The ML-Agents SDK allows researchers and developers to transform games and simulations created using the Unity Editor into environments where intelligent agents can be trained using deep reinforcement-learning, evolutionary strategies, or other machine learning methods through a simple-to-use Python API. This beta version of Unity ML-Agents toolkit has been released as open source software, with a set of example projects and baseline algorithms to get you started.

Essential elements of the toolkit are as follows:

- **Agent**: Each agent can have a unique set of states and observations, take unique actions within the environment, and receive unique rewards for events within the environment. An agent's actions are decided by the brain it is linked to.
- **Brain**: Each brain defines a specific state and action space, and is responsible for deciding which actions each of its linked agents will take.
- **Academy**: The academy object within a scene also contains as children all brains within the environment. Each environment contains a single academy that defines the scope of the environment.

A variety of training scenarios are possible, depending on how agents, brains, and rewards are connected. Here are a few examples:

- **Single-Agent**: A single agent linked to a single brain. The traditional way of training an agent.
- **Simultaneous Single-Agent**: Multiple independent agents with an independent reward functions linked to a single brain.
- **Adversarial Self-Play**: Two interacting agents with an inverse reward functions linked to a single brain.
- **Cooperative Multi-Agent**: Multiple interacting agents with a shared reward function linked to either a single brain or multiple different brains.
- **Competitive Multi-Agent**: Multiple interacting agents with an inverse reward function linked to either a single brain or multiple different brains.
- **Ecosystem**: Multiple interacting agents with an independent reward function linked to either a single brain or multiple different brains.

Unity's ML-Agents toolkit is only at the beginning of development, and the Unity team plans to iterate quickly and provide additional features for both those of you who are interested in Unity as a platform for machine learning research, and those of you who are focused on the potential of machine learning in game development.

FANUC industrial robots

FANUC is one of the largest makers of industrial robots. In recent years, the Japanese company has concentrated its efforts on the use of artificial intelligence in the field of robotics. In particular, they are developing robots that use reinforcement learning to understand how to perform complex tasks.

Just give the robot a task, such as how to move objects from one container to another, and spend the night understanding how to perform this task to the fullest. In the morning, the machine will be able to perform the job as if it had been programmed by an expert. FANUC presented a robot trained through reinforcement learning during the Tokyo International Robot Exhibition in December 2017. In the following picture are shown FANUC robots:

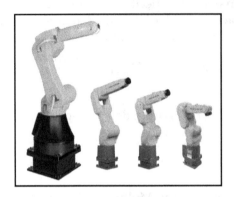

Industrial robots are equipped with extreme precision and speed, but they must normally be programmed very carefully to perform seemingly easy tasks such as grasping an object. Actually, it takes a long time to train a robot to do this, and eventually these robots work only in tightly controlled environments.

FANUC's robot uses a technique based on deep reinforcement learning. In its training, the robot tries to collect objects during the acquisition of video footage of the process. Whenever it succeeds or fails, remember how the object appeared: this knowledge is then used to perfect a deep learning model or a large neural network, which controls its action. In-depth learning has proven to be a powerful approach in model recognition in recent years.

In practice, after about eight hours, it reaches up to 90% accuracy or greater, which is almost the same as if an expert programmed it. It works during the night, and the next morning is ready for use.

One of the great potential benefits of the learning approach is that it can be accelerated if several robots work in parallel and share what they have learned. So, eight robots working together for an hour can do the same thing as an eight-hour machine. This form of distributed learning, called cloud robotics, is becoming a big trend in both research and industry.

The ability to recognize objects is essential for training robots. This is why FANUC started a collaboration with NVIDIA to add the company's graphics-processing units to its machines. This collaboration has the goal to implement artificial intelligence on the **FANUC Intelligent Edge Link and Drive (FIELD)** system to increase robotics productivity and bring new capabilities to automated factories worldwide.

The FIELD system is a platform to improve factory production and efficiency with advanced artificial intelligence. By combining artificial intelligence and edge-computing technology, the FIELD system processes the edge-heavy sensor data collected from various machines to make the machines intelligently and flexibly collaborate to achieve advanced manufacturing capabilities.

NVIDIA's graphics-processing units and deep-learning technology will be used to help FANUC robots recognize, process, and respond to their surroundings. It is particularly important for learning reinforcement, the way machines use artificial intelligence to adopt new skills through practice.

A robot can capture video of itself to see how it worked, then analyze and develop information as it improves over time. Industrial robots are big and dangerous, and they are really good at performing a single task over and over again with precision. As we said, the idea is that when FANUC's robots learn together, they learn faster. And, NVIDIA's technology is particularly suitable for parallel processing, which means it can handle thousands of computational tasks simultaneously. In the following picture is shown an NVIDIA GPU:

Essential features of the collaboration are as follows:

- Deep learning robot training with NVIDIA GPUs
- GPU-accelerated AI inference in FANUC Fog units used to drive robots and machines
- Embedded systems for robots to do inference locally

It is clear that FANUC will not be the only company to invest in a project of this type. The use of reinforcement learning for the management of robots representing a sector that offers many prospects for development.

Automated trading systems using reinforcement learning

Foreign exchange (**Forex**) is the international market where exchange takes the place of currencies. In this market, there are different entities, including international banks, central banks, commercial companies, intermediaries, and small investors.

The Forex market is the most liquid in the world; the daily contractual volumes of the Forex market exceeds $1.9 trillion and is made up of a huge one amount of participants. Unlike the stock market, there is no clearing house or stock exchange where transactions are physically conducted, but the latter are conducted by the huge amount of geographically distributed market participants.

The foreign exchange market was initially not open to small investors because, in order to participate, it was necessary to have a large amount of capital. Today, however, thanks to leverage, even small investors can interact in this market.

Thanks to the rapid development of information technology in recent decades, the possibility of trading automatically was born in the financial markets. This novelty makes it possible to operate on the market in a totally automated way, thanks to the programming of special software.

This evolution has allowed the implementation of trading strategies, allowing it to operate on the market without having to necessarily be present in front of the computer.

A trading strategy indicates the decision-making process that a trader uses to decide what actions to take on the market. It includes a number of factors that take into account different aspects of the market and capital management.

The advantages of using an automatic system are numerous:

- The decision-making process is autonomous, in such a way as to eliminate any interpretative component
- The risk is limited because it is always calculated systematically
- Nothing is left to discretion, because the indications provided by the system are always followed

- You have the opportunity to analyze and operate simultaneously on a large number of financial instruments, 24 hours a day
- Using an automated trading system speeds up the strategy-testing process

In addition, the trader can choose whether to use a trading system as a decision support or as a system for immediate operation on any signal generated by the program.

To interact with the Forex market, the MetaTrader software platform is available, which allows direct and simple transactions to be carried out. The same platform also allows us to use software called **Expert Advisors** (**EA**), written in a particular programming language (MQL), to perform trading automatically. In the following screenshot is shown the software:

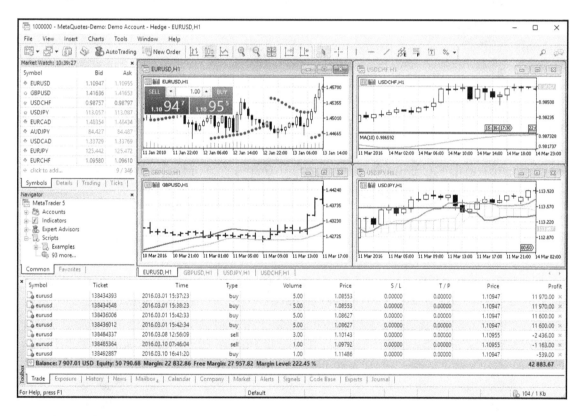

A trading software platform is a program that allows you to perform online trading operations. Over the years, many have been developed, each with different characteristics, to better adapt to the needs of investors. However, one of the most popular is MetaTrader. This is due to the fact that this platform, besides being free and easy to use, is also the most-used program by brokers to provide their own trading services.

MetaTrader offers numerous features, all reachable through the menu bar, in particular the following:

- Opening a new chart for each available financial instrument
- Inserting a wide range of technical indicators used by traders, as further information to be able to predict price movements
- Viewing the Strategy Tester
- Opening the Editor for the creation of EA

The Editor includes a series of functions that allow the programmer to create the EA. This is a common software-development platform, which includes the text editor used to write the source code of the program, and the compiler for compiling this code.

The programming language used to develop our EA is called MQL5. It is a programming language similar to C, which has a series of special functions already implemented that allow us to manage interactions with the market.

As a rule, the EA execute their algorithm at each change of the market (tick). To implement this type of behavior, a special function, called Ontick, is used, which is called at each tick in the market.

Another feature offered by MetaTrader is the Strategy Tester. This tool offers us the possibility to test its EA, simulating its execution on the data of the past. In this section, it is possible to choose the EA to be tested, the financial instrument on which to run the user, the initial budget from which to start, the period, and the precision with which to perform the test (based on the frequency with which the price changes). After choosing the desired settings, it is possible to determine the input parameters of the AE in the relevant board and start the simulation.

With this software, it is possible to create an EA able to completely replace the decision-making process of the trader. The decisions that a trader has to make cover several aspects:

- At what price level to enter and exit the market
- Which risk to assume (in terms of capital), in the single trade, in such a way that the capital suffers a loss that does not exceed a certain percentage value
- Calculating the entry size appropriate to the risk determined previously
- Opening the desired position, using the appropriate commands offered by the platform
- Managing the trade open to the market

Therefore, the EA determines the price levels to enter, automatically calculates the quantity of lots to buy according to the risk assessed by the trader, executes the buy and sell operations according to what strategy it suggests, and finally manages the open trade.

In the creation of an EA, we can implement all the technologies to find the optimal values of the parameters that are used within an automatic trading strategy, in order to maximize performance.

To achieve this, it is possible to identify the parameters that most influence the performance of the strategy, interfacing the automatic trading program with the learning algorithms for reinforcement.

Next steps for reinforcement learning

Nowadays, seeing machines that perform tasks in place of humans has become a normal thing. From the automation of production processes, to the assembly line, to quick and precise calculations, to the execution of instructions with a margin of error that is very minimal if not inexistent. But, when the problems become much more complex, we resort to techniques of artificial intelligence that consist of creating algorithms that can help the software to learn from experience—this is called machine learning.

The machines learn autonomously, starting not from a list of predefined rules, but from a model and instructions through which to learn the right rules to solve the problem in question. These technologies are already widely used—for example, to combat spam and credit card fraud, to make economic and financial forecasts, for voice recognition and manual writing, for automatic image classification, to understand our tastes and give suggestions, and to improve our newsfeeds and search results.

At this point, it is legitimate to ask, "What will this technology offer us in the future?" Google has announced that it will go from a **Mobile first** to **AI first** approach. This transition will take place through the products that it has so far offered to the public. Services such as Google Maps will automatically recognize signals from the external environment through machine learning. In this new approach, the intention to use artificial intelligence and machine learning as a basis for all their products and services is clear. Let's see what the future challenges are in the use of reinforcement-learning algorithms.

Inverse reinforcement learning

In **reverse reinforcement learning** (**IRL**), the reward function is derived from the observed behavior. As we have learned, in reinforcement learning, we use rewards to learn the behavior of a particular system. In IRL, this function is reversed; in fact, the agent observes the behavior of the system to understand what goal it is trying to achieve.

In an IRL, problem we start from the following:

- Measurements of an agent's behavior over time
- Measurements of the sensory input to that agent
- A model of the physical environment

Based on this data, we determine the reward function that the agent is optimizing. An example of Inverse reinforcement learning applied in simple domains such as Atari games was released from OpenAI and DeepMind in 2017. The DeepMind researchers have shown that these techniques may be economically scalable to modern systems.

Learning by demonstration

Learning by demonstration can be seen as a special case of supervised learning; the teacher or supervisor provides both input and the desired output, which is the fundamental concept of the supervised learning paradigm. The difference from a classical problem of supervised learning consists, however, is the fact that, through the demonstration, the strategy for solving the problem is also supplied to the robot. In practice, the robot mimics the behavior of the supervisor, which is why learning by demonstration is also called learning by imitation.

Once the general problem has been analyzed and formalized, in particular after carefully choosing the main aspects of the demonstration, it is necessary, considering the problem in its entirety, to choose which imitation process is more efficient for solving the problem.

This learning paradigm can be particularly useful for training a robot. Suppose the robot control system is working and a human operator is using it. If the operator takes the arm of the robot, they makes a move with it, then the robot will play the same action at a later time. In the reproduction phase, the robot mimics this behavior.

Deep Deterministic Policy Gradients

Deep Deterministic Policy Gradients (**DDPG**) is a policy-gradient algorithm that adopts a stochastic behavior policy for exploration. This algorithm estimates a deterministic target policy, which is much easier to learn. Policy-gradient algorithms use the following policy iteration:

- Evaluate the policy
- Then, follow the policy gradient to maximize performance

DDPG is out of policy and uses a deterministic target policy, and for these reasons the use of the Deterministic Policy Gradient theorem is allowed. DDPG is also a critical algorithm-actor; it mainly uses two neural networks: one for the actor and one for the critic. These networks calculate the action forecasts for the current state and generate a **time difference** (**TD**) error signal each time. As input of the actor's network, the current state is adopted, while as output a single real value is chosen that represents an action chosen by a continuous action space. The output of the critic is simply the estimated Q value of the current state and of the action given by the actor. The deterministic policy-gradient theorem provides the update rule for the actor's network weights. The critical network is updated by the gradients obtained from the error signal TD.

Reinforcement learning from human preferences

Often in everyday problems, it is not possible to define a well-specified reward function. In fact, many tasks involve complex, poorly-defined, or difficult-to-specify goals. For example, suppose you want to use reinforcement learning to train a robot to clean a house. It is not easy to define an adequate reward function, which will have to depend on the data coming from the robot sensors. If we could successfully communicate our real goals to our agents, it would be a significant step toward resolving these issues.

If we have demonstrations of the desired task, we can extract a reward function using the inverse reinforcement learning. Furthermore, we can use the imitation of learning to clone the proven behavior. However, these approaches are not directly applicable to behaviors that are difficult to demonstrate to humans (such as controlling a robot with many degrees of freedom but an inhuman-like morphology). A solution to the problem could be to allow a human being to provide feedback on the current behavior of our system and to use this feedback to define the activity. In principle, this is part of the reinforced learning paradigm, although using human feedback directly as a reward function is prohibitive for RL systems that require hundreds or thousands of hours of experience.

In deep reinforcement learning from human preferences, the agent learns a reward function from human feedback and then optimizes that reward function. It therefore represents a solution to sequential decision problems without a well-specified reward function.

The algorithm has the following characteristics:

- Allows you to solve tasks for which we can only recognize the desired behavior, but not necessarily demonstrate it
- Allows agents to be taught by non-expert users
- Scales to big problems
- It's cheap with user feedback

This algorithm fits a reward function to the human's preferences while simultaneously training a policy to optimize the current predicted reward function.

Hindsight Experience Replay

One of the abilities humans have is to learn from our mistakes and adapt next time to avoid making the same mistake. This is the basis of reinforcement-learning algorithms. The greatest difficulties in implementing these algorithms are encountered when dealing with scattered prizes. Consider the following scenario: a learning agent must control a robot arm to open a box and place an object inside it. While defining the reward for this task is simple and straightforward, the underlying learning problem is difficult. The agent must uncover a long sequence of correct actions to find a configuration of the environment that produces the sparse reward—the object placed inside the box. Discovering this poor reward signal is a difficult exploration problem for which success through random exploration is highly unlikely.

A new technique, called Hindsight Experience Replay, promises to help solve this problem. This technique allows efficient learning based on poor and binary rewards, thus avoiding the need for complicated rewarding techniques. It can be combined with an arbitrary reinforcement learning off-policy algorithm.

This approach is particularly suitable in cases of the manipulation of objects with a robotic arm, in particular, in the tasks of push, sliding, and pick-and-place.

In any case, only binary rewards are used that indicate whether the activity is completed. Ablation studies show that Hindsight Experience Replay is a crucial ingredient that makes training in these difficult environments possible. Other studies show that policies trained on a physical simulation can be implemented on a physical robot and successfully complete the activity.

Summary

In this chapter, we explored some practical examples of the application of technologies based on reinforcement learning.

First, we addressed the DeepMind AlphaZero project. AlphaZero is an artificial-intelligence algorithm based on machine learning techniques developed by Google DeepMind. It is a generalization of AlphaGo Zero, the predecessor developed specifically for the game of Go and in turn the evolution of AlphaGo, the first software capable of achieving superhuman performances in the game of Go.

Then, we explored the IBM Watson project. This is a system of artificial intelligence, able to answer questions expressed in natural language, developed within the DeepQA project of IBM by the research team directed by David Ferrucci. We looked at Unity's ML-Agents toolkit, FANUC industrial robots, and an automated trading system.

Finally, we discussed some future challenges in the use of reinforcement-learning algorithms. We learned about inverse reinforcement learning, learning by demonstration, reinforcement learning from human preferences, DDPG, and Hindsight Experience Replay.

Other Books You May Enjoy

If you enjoyed this book, you may be interested in these other books by Packt:

Hands-On Reinforcement Learning with Python

Sudharsan Ravichandiran

ISBN: 978-1-78883-652-4

- Understand the basics of reinforcement learning methods, algorithms, and elements
- Train an agent to walk using OpenAI Gym and Tensorflow
- Understand the Markov Decision Process, Bellman's optimality, and TD learning
- Solve multi-armed-bandit problems using various algorithms
- Master deep learning algorithms, such as RNN, LSTM, and CNN with applications
- Build intelligent agents using the DRQN algorithm to play the Doom game
- Teach agents to play the Lunar Lander game using DDPG
- Train an agent to win a car racing game using dueling DQN

Hands-On Transfer Learning with Python
Dipanjan Sarkar, Raghav Bali, Tamoghna Ghosh

ISBN: 978-1-78883-130-7

- Set up your own DL environment with graphics processing unit (GPU) and Cloud support
- Delve into transfer learning principles with ML and DL models
- Explore various DL architectures, including CNN, LSTM, and capsule networks
- Learn about data and network representation and loss functions
- Get to grips with models and strategies in transfer learning
- Walk through potential challenges in building complex transfer learning models from scratch
- Explore real-world research problems related to computer vision and audio analysis
- Understand how transfer learning can be leveraged in NLP

Leave a review - let other readers know what you think

Please share your thoughts on this book with others by leaving a review on the site that you bought it from. If you purchased the book from Amazon, please leave us an honest review on this book's Amazon page. This is vital so that other potential readers can see and use your unbiased opinion to make purchasing decisions, we can understand what our customers think about our products, and our authors can see your feedback on the title that they have worked with Packt to create. It will only take a few minutes of your time, but is valuable to other potential customers, our authors, and Packt. Thank you!

Index